What's Wrong
With My
Fruit Garden?

What's Wrong With My Fruit Garden?

100% ORGANIC SOLUTIONS FOR BERRIES, TREES, NUTS, VINES, AND TROPICALS

David Deardorff and Kathryn Wadsworth

TIMBER PRESS
Portland • London

Published in 2013 by Timber Press, Inc.
The Haseltine Building
133 S.W. Second Avenue, Suite 450
Portland, Oregon 97204-3527
timberpress.com

6a Lonsdale Road
London NW6 6RD
timberpress.co.uk

Printed in China
Book design: Laura Lovett | By Design

Library of Congress Cataloging-in-Publication Data

Deardorff, David C.
  What's wrong with my fruit garden? : 100% organic
solutions for berries, trees, nuts, vines, and
tropicals/David Deardorff and Kathryn Wadsworth.
      p. cm.
  Includes index.
  ISBN 978-1-60469-488-8 (hardcover)
  ISBN 978-1-60469-358-4 (pbk.)
  1. Fruit-culture. 2. Fruit—Diseases and pests—
Control. 3. Fruit trees—Wounds and injuries—
Diagnosis. 4. Organic gardening. I. Wadsworth,
Kathryn B.
II. Title.
  SB357.24.D43 2014
  634'.049774—dc23   2013009257

A catalog record for this book is also available from
the British Library.

For Ana Marguerite
and Eleanor Rose
with love and admiration

Contents

Prepare for Success

THE QUEST FOR THE MOST DELECTABLE, WHOLESOME fruits and nuts has taken humankind to every part of the globe. When our ancestors traversed the savannah and spread outward, we initiated a long and successful survival strategy: hunting and gathering the incredible bounty of the natural world. Thousands of years later, we learned to save the seeds of our most precious plants, replanting them, and then returning to the same locations each season. Eventually we settled in one place and began to tend the plants that had become our benefactors.

The plants that feed us best are the ones we continue to tend with great care. In turn our care has become their most successful survival strategy. Apples from the mountains of Central Asia now grow worldwide, tended by their human caretakers throughout North America, New Zealand, Chile, and elsewhere. Oranges, walnuts, grapes, and blueberries thrive with an enormous entourage of people caring for their every need, because they have made themselves especially mouthwatering and sustaining for us.

Have you ever thought about the apparent intelligence of these resourceful plants on which we depend? We propagate them and ensure their pollination. We feed and water them, and tend them when they are ill. We have become tribes of caregivers, devoted to meeting all their requirements. Our service to our plant partners is a privilege and a gift. What better way to repay the kindness of nature, and to connect with the abundance of the natural world?

The reward for tending your own fruit garden goes beyond stewardship of the green world. It helps us too. There is an expanding body of evidence that indicates homegrown fruit has higher nutrient values and better flavor. The more we learn about the importance of a diet rich in antioxidants, the more we know it just makes sense to grow our own fruits and nuts. As anyone who has shopped for organic produce knows, it's expensive, but over time cultivating it yourself will save you money. Even if you have only a small yard or balcony, given enough sunlight, you can raise fruit at home.

There are a few key factors to take into account while preparing for that bountiful harvest. Right from the start you need to know about temperature, soil, light, and water needs for plants you want to grow. With few exceptions, fruits and nuts are perennials. You commit to these plants for years, so choosing the right plant, putting it in the right place, and selecting the best cultivar for your situation and taste is really important. For instance, if you live in the subtropics, the right type of plant might be a banana and a good cultivar would be 'Dwarf Cavendish', the easiest to grow in a small home garden.

Take some time to research pest- and disease-resistant plants that are available in your region. Some heirloom varieties and modern hybrids carry resistance in their genes. For example, both 'Liberty' and 'Chehalis' apple cultivars are resistant to apple scab, a common and serious fungal disease of apples worldwide. To find pest- or disease-resistant cultivars, look at plant labels and catalog descriptions. If they do not mention resistance, assume the plant is susceptible. Experienced neighbors, nearby fruit growers, extension agents, or master gardeners can give you local knowledge about who's succeeding with which cultivars. This allows you to choose cultivars that are best suited to your location and likely to remain healthy.

When choosing a cultivar, local knowledge is invaluable. Talk to experienced neighbors, your county extension agent or master gardener organization, or local fruit clubs to determine which cultivars do best in your climate.

[opposite, top] Citrus fruits from the jungles of Southeast Asia now inhabit huge tracts of land in Southern California, Florida, and Central and South America.

[opposite, bottom] Right plant, right place. Apple trees thrive in temperate zones, such as in this mountainous West Virginia orchard. This particular cultivar performs well in this specific location, where it gets the right number of days of winter chill. Besides, the grower loves the way 'Honeycrisp' tastes.

TEMPERATURE

The fruits and nuts in this book have a wide range of temperatures in which they thrive, or in which they die. Learn about your climate. How cold is your winter and how long does it last? Just how long and dry is your long, dry summer? When do you expect first frosts? How many days a year, on average, do temperatures top 86°F where you live? Look up climate data for your location: in the United States, go to ncdc.noaa.gov/cdo-web/; in Canada, visit climate.weatheroffice.gc.ca/climateData/canada_e.html. If you do not have Internet access, the reference librarian at your local library should be able to help you get information on your growing season. Your county extension agent or master gardener organization is another excellent source for this.

In each plant portrait we'll cover this important information about temperature: a plant's hardiness, that is, how low the temperature can go before it croaks, as expressed in USDA Hardiness Zones (see the chart in backmatter for specific temperature ranges); its chilling requirement (the average number of winter hours below 45°F needed to break dormancy in the spring, produce flowers, and set fruit); and its yearly tolerance of or need for heat (temperatures above 86°F). It's important to remember that the hours of winter cold need not be consecutive, and that the recommended days of heat are annual (not seasonal) totals. Once you know about your local climate and the plant species' particular needs, you are ready to choose a cultivar. Remember that each cultivar of each species is different, and its needs will vary.

During your conversations with local experts, take into account that "hardiness" refers only to a plant's ability to tolerate freezing temperatures. It does not mean a plant is tough when it faces other adverse conditions such as drought, disease, or pests. "Tenderness" does not mean that your plant is soft-hearted, but rather that it might freeze if planted where it is too cold.

Plant labels and catalog descriptions help you discover a cultivar's tolerance of or need for cold or heat. Read them carefully. Another aid to guide you in your choice is the USDA Hardiness Zone number that all U.S. nurseries put on plant labels. This number tells you only the plant's ability to withstand cold. It does not tell you whether the plant needs a certain amount of cold or heat to set fruit, or any other factor. You will find this information in each plant portrait.

❊ See chart on page 14.

SOIL

The living ecosystem in which all plants grow needs our care and protection to stay healthy. This starts with healthy, biologically active soil. The tiny community beneath our feet consists of bacterial and fungal decomposers that break down organic plant matter. Larger multicellular organisms like beneficial nematodes feed on the decomposers. And these, in turn, become food for still larger creatures like insects and worms. All these organisms ultimately utilize the energy captured by plants from the sun, which is stored in dead plant material. In other words, to create healthy, biologically active soil, feed this dynamic community dead plant material: compost, organic fertilizer, manure, and mulch.

The healthier your soil is, the more likely your plants will be stress-free. Stress renders plants susceptible to disease infection and pest infestations. By maintaining healthy soil you also reduce moisture- and nutrient-stress for your plants. Also, nurturing a species-rich, ecologically diverse community of organisms in your soil allows the good fungi and bacteria to outcompete the bad guys: pests and diseases. Here's the kicker: the more you feed your soil, the less you need to feed your plants with supplementary fertilizers.

If your plants are already in the ground, rake mulch away and sprinkle organic fertilizer around the base of the plant at the beginning of each growing season. Read the label on the fertilizer to calculate the correct amount. Scuffle the fertilizer into the soil lightly to a depth of a ½ inch or so, then spread 1 inch of compost over the soil. Replace the mulch and add more until you have a depth of 3 inches. To discourage disease and other moisture-related issues, keep the mulch 2 inches away from the plant's trunk or stem. If you are adding a new plant, whether to a pot or in the ground, keep reading to hear all about the soil mix you should use in "How to Plant" (page 25).

❊ **See chart on page 16.**

LIGHT

All fruits and nuts need full sun. That's six to eight hours a day. There are almost no exceptions to this rule; nevertheless the "rule" is very confusing for lots of people and requires interpretation. If it's cloudy all day, do you still have sun? Good question; and the answer is yes. Cloud cover is not shade. Have you read all the studies or been reminded by your mom that you can get sunburned on a cloudy day? Well, it's true. Clouds diffuse light, but they do not block the light plants need for metabolism and growth. Shade from a building or the dense canopy of a tree does block the light plants need.

Six to eight hours of sun in Phoenix is very different from the same number of hours in Seattle. In general the more cloud cover you have and the cooler the temperatures are, the more hours of light you need. If you live where the light is intense and the temperatures are high, then plants appreciate dappled shade. If your yard, balcony, or patio is in deep shade and you still want to grow some fruit, look to native, fruit-producing plants that grow well in the forests of your region. For instance, we in the Pacific Northwest are blessed with native berry bushes, like evergreen huckleberry (*Vaccinium ovatum*), that thrive in deep shade.

❊ **See chart on page 18.**

WATER

All fruit needs regular water and consistent moisture. That means they want about 1 inch a week. How can you tell whether your plant is getting that much? Put an empty tuna can in your yard where both rain and water from your watering system will reach it. Place the can in the shade to minimize evaporation. If you use a sprinkler, place the can where the spray reaches it. If you use a drip-trickle system, place it under one of the emitters. If you use a soaker hose, bury the can under a section of the hose. If you hand-water, be sure you deliver the same amount of water to the plants and the tuna can. At the end of one week, measure the depth of water in the can. If there is less than 1 inch of water in it, you need more supplemental water each week.

We've done a little calculating to make your watering tasks easier. One gallon of water equals 231 cubic inches. Assuming no rainfall in a week, you will use 62 gallons of water that week to water a 100 square foot area with 1 inch of water. Do your best to water the ground, not the foliage, so that moisture-loving pathogenic fungi and bacteria on leaves and stems dry out before they can infect your plant. The best way to deliver water is with a soaker hose or drip-trickle system.

❊ **See chart on page 20.**

How to Recognize Temperature-Related Problems

Symptom	Diagnosis	Solution
Sections of bark crack open and fall off the tree. Branches fail to leaf out in spring and appear to be dead. Whole trees may be killed in severe winter weather.	**Freeze damage**	Modify the effects of cold, page 247
Foliage of broadleaf evergreens turns brown at the tips and edges during winter. Damage is especially severe on the windward side of the plant.	**Winter desiccation**	Modify the effects of cold, page 247
The bark on trunks and branches cracks open in winter. These cracks tend to disappear during the growing season.	**Frost cracks**	Modify the effects of cold, page 247
Plants break dormancy normally and begin to flower. Overnight, the flowers on fruit trees and berry bushes turn to brown mush.	**Frost damage**	Select late-blooming cultivars

Symptom	Diagnosis	Solution
 The leaves of your plants turn black on a hot summer day after you have sprayed sulfur to control fungal diseases.	**Sulfur phytotoxicity**	Modify the effects of heat, page 247
 An otherwise healthy deciduous plant fails to leaf out and flower in spring.	**Lack of winter chill**	Modify the effects of heat, page 247
 Leaf tips and edges turn brown and die during the summer growing season.	**Leaf scorch**	Modify the effects of heat, page 247 Light solutions, page 253 Manage water, page 253
 Leaves are small, turn yellow, and drop earlier than normal. Much less fruit than you expected matures. Fruit size is too small. Plants are stunted.	**Too hot**	Modify the effects of heat, page 247 Light solutions, page 253 Manage water, page 253

How to Recognize Soil-Related Problems

Symptom	Diagnosis	Solution
 Tips and edges of leaves turn brown and die. It looks like the plant is suffering from drought but the soil is moist.	Fertilizer overdose	Soil solutions, page 248 Make and use compost, page 248 Make raised beds, page 250 Use organic fertilizer, page 250 Check and improve drainage, page 256
 Young leaves at the tips of branches turn yellow but the main veins stay green.	Iron or manganese deficiency	Soil solutions, page 248 Make and use compost, page 248 Use organic fertilizer, page 250 Nutrition guidelines, page 251 Measure and modify pH, page 252
 Older leaves at the base of branches turn yellow. The main veins may or may not stay green.	Nitrogen or magnesium deficiency	Soil solutions, page 248 Make and use compost, page 248 Use organic fertilizer, page 250 Nutrition guidelines, page 251 Measure and modify pH, page 252
 Plants produce excessive soft succulent vegetative growth, and few flowers or fruits. Plants are easily damaged by winter freezes.	Excess nitrogen	Soil solutions, page 248 Make and use compost, page 248 Make raised beds, page 250 Use organic fertilizer, page 250

Symptom	Diagnosis	Solution
 Plants are stunted, leaves are small, and growth is poor. Fruit production, if any, is undersized and of poor quality.	**Insufficient nutrients**	Soil solutions, page 248 Mulch, page 262
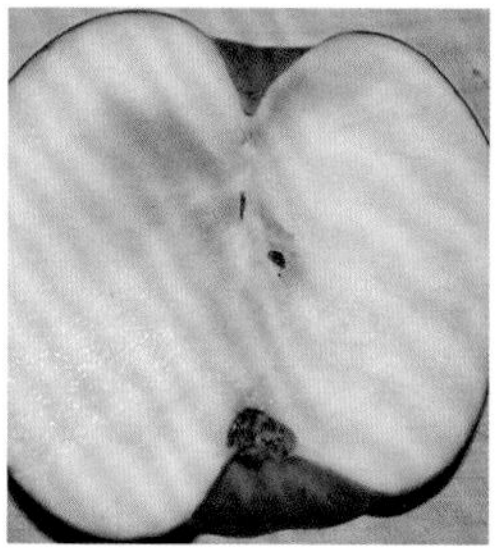 The flesh of an apple contains clear, glassy, water-soaked areas that are much sweeter than normal. The fruit is edible.	**Water core, caused by irregular watering**	Soil solutions, page 248 Manage water, page 253 Use effective watering techniques, page 255
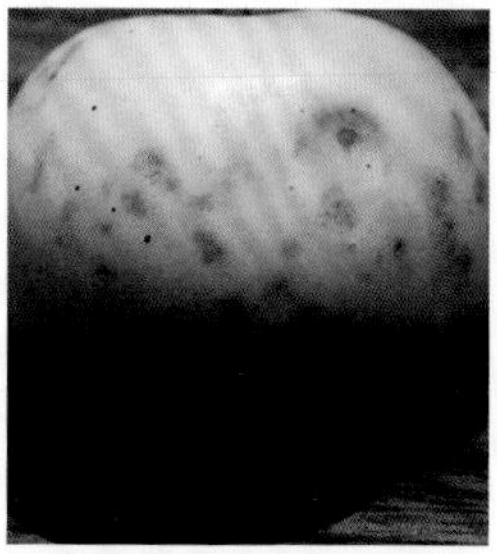 Small water-soaked spots dot the surface of the lower half of maturing apples. These become brown, sunken spots. The flesh below the spots is brown and corky and the fruit is inedible.	**Bitter pit, caused by irregular watering**	Soil solutions, page 248 Manage water, page 253 Use effective watering techniques, page 255
 Blueberries grow poorly and produce little fruit. New leaves are yellowish bronze and growth is stunted.	**Soil is too alkaline**	Soil solutions, page 248 Measure and modify pH, page 252

How to Recognize Light-Related Problems

Symptom	Diagnosis	Solution
 Recent transplants wilt, leaves turn brown at tips and edges, and/or turn yellow.	**Transplant shock**	Light solutions, page 253 Water solutions, page 253
 Fruit develops large brown to black patches on the side exposed to direct sun.	**Sunburn**	Light solutions, page 253
 Trunks and main branches, especially of young trees, turn brown, become sunken, and crack open on the side exposed to direct sun.	**Sunburn**	Light solutions, page 253
 Leaves turn brown at the tips and edges in bright light, high temperatures, and wind.	**Leaf scorch**	Modify the effects of heat, page 247 Light solutions, page 253 Manage water, page 253

Symptom	Diagnosis	Solution
Plants have pale green leaves and spindly stems. Undersized fruit tastes insipid.	**Insufficient light**	Light solutions, page 253

Evergreen huckleberry (*Vaccinium ovatum*) growing wild, in the shade, Kala Point, Washington.

How to Recognize Water-Related Problems

Symptom	Diagnosis	Solution
 Leaves wilt in dry soil and turn yellow. They turn brown at tips and edges as the tissue dies. Plants may shed their leaves.	**Not enough water**	Water solutions, page 253
 Stunted plants bear undersized fruit and small yields.	**Not enough water**	Water solutions, page 253
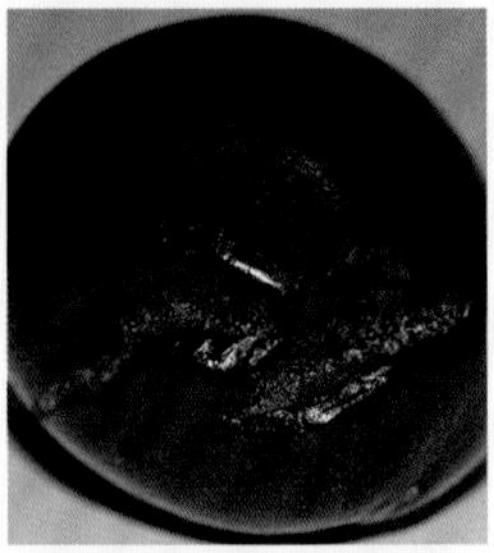 Fruit cracks open just as it's getting fully ripe. Cherries are especially prone to this problem.	**Irregular watering cycling from very dry to very wet**	Water solutions, page 253
 Plants in pots wilt in dry soil. Plant recovers when watered but quickly wilts again.	**Rootbound**	Water solutions, page 253 Rootbound, page 258

Symptom	Diagnosis	Solution
 Plants in pots wilt in wet soil. Plant does not recover when watered.	**Too much water**	Watering the container plant, page 256
 Plant drops its leaves in wet soil. Leaves wilt and turn yellow. Check roots for root rot fungi.	**Poor drainage**	Check and improve drainage, page 256
 Leaves wilt in bright light, hot temperature, and high wind. Leaves turn brown at tips and edges if plant is not given some water.	**Too hot**	Modify the effects of heat, page 247 Water solutions, page 253
 Patches of rough corky tissue mar the fruit. Fruit is edible.	**Russeting, caused by fruit staying wet for too long**	Water soil, not foliage, page 255 Prune properly, page 264

How to Recognize Other Environmental Disorders

Symptom	Diagnosis	Solution
 Plant sets abundant but undersized fruit. Plant lacks symptoms of pests or disease.	**Too much fruit**	Too much fruit, page 257 Prune properly, page 264
 Limbs break just as fruit matures.	**Lack of thinning**	Too much fruit, page 257 Prune properly, page 264
 No fruit forms. Plant is old enough to produce a crop and flowered well in spring.	**Poor pollination**	Pollination, page 28 Poor pollination, page 257 Encourage beneficial organisms, page 260
 The trunk or main stem has bark missing near the soil level. You do not see evidence of rodent damage.	**Mechanical damage**	Mechanical damage, page 257

Symptom	Diagnosis	Solution
 You see deformed, discolored foliage and twisted stems but no evidence of pests or diseases.	**Chemical damage**	Chemical damage, page 257
 Plants in pots fail to flower and fruit satisfactorily, grow slowly, and wilt frequently.	**Rootbound**	Rootbound, page 258

PLANTING

Just as it affects which plants you can successfully cultivate, your specific situation determines how and in what form you will acquire your new plant. Nursery plants come in three different states: bare-root, containerized, or balled and burlapped (B&B).

Bare-root. This is the least expensive and most common choice for purchasing deciduous fruit and nut plants. Just as the name implies, the roots of bare-root plants have no soil or growing media of any kind around them. Bare-root plants are often available in the widest variety of cultivars. Having more choices maximizes your opportunity to select the best cultivars for your climate. The biggest drawback of this choice is that you must plant in early spring when bare-root plants are available in nurseries. In many regions this means you'll have to provide supplemental irrigation all summer. Another limitation is that only temperate zone deciduous fruits and nuts are available as bare-root plants. Subtropical evergreens like avocado, banana, citrus, guava, loquat, and olive are never available as bare-roots because they lose too much water through their leaves.

In late winter or very early spring, commercial growers dig up deciduous fruit and nut trees, berry bushes, and vines while they are still leafless and dormant. Workers remove all the soil from the root system and trim the roots to shorten them. The plants are trucked to your local garden center. Mail-order nurseries pack the root systems with moisture-retentive material, wrap them in plastic, and ship them directly to your door.

However you obtain your bare-root plants, it is imperative that the root systems stay moist. If the roots dry out the plants will die. Put plants in the ground or container where you plan to grow

them before they break dormancy and leaf out. This means you have a very short time frame, only a few weeks a year in very early spring, to purchase and plant bare-root plants.

Containerized. Plants grown in pots are more expensive than bare-root plants but the additional expense is often outweighed by the flexibility you have in choosing the planting time that works for you. They are available year-round and you can plant them any time the soil is not frozen, at your convenience, whether they are dormant or in active growth. The best planting time depends on your climate. Put plants in the ground at the time of year when you expect rainfall. This gives plants a huge boost toward getting established in their new location.

Because container-grown trees take up a lot of space at nurseries and garden centers, the number of different cultivars of deciduous fruits and nuts available in containers can be limited. Subtropical evergreen fruits, on the other hand, are always available as container-grown material. Most garden centers will have a small quantity of evergreen species and selected deciduous fruit and nut trees, berry bushes, and vines available year-round. Mail order nurseries have a wider selection and will ship containerized fruit plants, but the bigger the plants, the heavier the pots; shipping costs can be substantial.

Balled and burlapped. Often called B&B, these plants have had their root systems dug up with a ball of soil around the roots kept intact. This root ball is then wrapped tightly with burlap and tied with rope or wire to keep the soil from cracking or falling off. Balled and burlapped is generally the most expensive way to obtain your deciduous fruits and nuts. You will have the fewest number of cultivars to choose from. You can almost always find evergreen fruits, like avocado, banana, citrus, loquat, guava, or olive, as B&B

plants any time of year. However, you will rarely find deciduous fruit or nuts, such as apples, peaches, walnuts, berry bushes, or vines, as B&B plants. Sometimes you can purchase larger, more mature plants as B&Bs, but a word to the wise: get help; these large trees are extremely heavy and difficult to maneuver.

Balled and burlapped plants, whether evergreen or deciduous, can be planted any time of year, as long as the soil is not frozen. You can plant them when they are dormant or in active growth. As with any plant, put them in the ground or container when you expect good rainfall, so that they get plenty of moisture in their new home.

How to plant. Now you've got the plants, with their roots in various formats, where and how do you plant them? You will have to decide if you want to put them directly in the ground, including in raised beds, or into containers.

How to plant in the ground

1. The first thing you have to do is select a site that provides the temperature, soil, light, and water your plant needs to do its best. Find this information in each plant portrait. Also look at the quality of the soil, drainage, and pH. Review the earlier introductory section on soil, and read more in "Soil Solutions" (page 248) and "Check and Improve Drainage" (page 256). Use this knowledge to select an alternate planting site if you see potential problems.

2. Dig a hole. Yep, even though we advocate disturbing the soil as little as possible, there is no getting around this task. The hole should be two to three times wider than the roots, pot, or root ball of the plant you're putting in the ground. It should be no deeper than the roots. Basically you want a wide, shallow hole, 2 to 3 feet across and 12 to 18 inches deep. As you remove soil from the hole, pile it up close to the edge; you're going to need it later.

If you're digging into lawn grass, an aggressive competitor for water and nutrients, remove it in a wide circle about 3 feet across. Use a flat shovel for this purpose and cut the grass about 1 inch below the soil level. Put the grass and the soil that comes with it in your compost pile or use it to patch holes in your lawn.

3. Examine the soil in the bottom and sides of your hole and decide whether or not you need to amend it. If you have healthy, biologically active soil you may not need to add anything. But in certain places in North America, you may face problem soils, like high pH alkaline soil in the Desert Southwest, or heavy clay or sandy soils in the Pacific Northwest. And on the Big Island of Hawaii you may have no soil at all, just lava. All these problem soils need nutritional amendments for plants to thrive.

If you decide to amend the soil, mix one part compost to three parts soil you removed from the planting hole. Use this mix when you refill the hole. We have three reasons for this recommendation. The small amount of compost added to heavy clay soil will improve the structure of the soil and allow it to drain better. By the same token, a little compost will help a sandy soil to retain moisture. On the other hand, if the soil in your planting hole is too rich the hole will act like a container, and roots will not grow out into the native soil beyond the hole. In other words, in this situation, 75 percent of the backfilled soil is native garden soil, while 25 percent is rich compost.

4. If you were not able to relocate a plant that needs special soil, then you should also add amendments to address soil pH. Blueberries, for example, require acid soil, and if native soil is neutral or alkaline you'll need to acidify the soil by adding sulfur to it. Follow the package directions.

5. Set your plant in the hole so that its original soil line is on the same plane as the surrounding soil. Do not plant too deep or too shallow. Position your containerized or B&B plant just deep enough to make the top of the soil surrounding the root system match the soil level of your garden. To gauge how deep to set your bare-root plant, look for the change of color on the bark that shows you where the original soil line was. Refill the planting hole with just enough soil to reach this line.

6. Prop or hold your plant at the correct level and start to backfill by refilling the hole with the soil you removed.

7. If your plant is bare-root, spread the roots out and away from the trunk in all directions. Poke the soil under and around the roots with your fingers and jiggle the plant to make sure the soil has no air pockets around the roots. If your plant is in a container, slide it out of the pot and loosen the sides of the root ball with your fingers to get the roots spreading out to the sides, then backfill. If your plant is B&B, remove the burlap and all the rope or wire that held it in place, then plant as you would a container-grown plant.

8. After the hole is properly filled, make a 2- to 3-inch-tall earthen dam surrounding the hole to create a reservoir for water.

9. Fill the reservoir with water.

10. When the water has drained away, fill the reservoir with a thick layer of mulch, keeping the mulch 2 inches away from the trunks or stems.

11. Provide support. If you are planting a tree you may need to stake it to help stabilize it. Rocking back and forth in the wind can loosen roots and prevent the tree from becoming established in its new home. Pound a sturdy stake into the ground a few inches away from your tree then loosely tie your tree to the stake. Vines like grapes, kiwi, or passionfruit will need a trellis or fence to climb on, as will trailing blackberries. Blueberries and raspberries generally do not need support.

How to plant in containers

1. Choose the pot. Many dwarf and semi-dwarf fruit and nut plants grow well in large pots. The pot should be wider than the root system of your plant by several inches. Also, avoid any pot with a neck that is narrower than the body of the pot because, sooner or later, you're going to have to pull your plant out of the pot. If the neck is too narrow you'll either destroy your pot or ruin your plant to get it out. Make sure there are drainage holes in the bottom of the pot and do not put a layer of gravel in the bottom of the pot.

2. Select potting soil, not topsoil or native soil from the garden. Soil for containers has to be light and well drained, with plenty of air spaces; potting soil is designed to do just that. In a container, garden soil becomes way too dense and airless for successful plant growth. Add a good balanced organic fertilizer, following the directions on the package. If your plant has special pH needs, you'll also need to adjust the pH by adding sulfur or dolomite lime. Again, follow label directions.

3. Place small pieces of window screen over the drain holes, and then put a handful of potting soil over the screen to hold it in place.

4. Set a bare-root fruit or nut plant in the container and spread the roots out to the sides and away from the center. For plants from a container, slide the plant out of its original pot and set it into its new pot. Use your fingers to loosen the soil of the root ball and spread out the roots. For B&B plants, remove the burlap and all the rope or wire from the root ball, and then set the plant into the pot. Again, loosen the roots and spread them out.

5. Check the height of the original soil line. Look for the change in color at the base of the stems or trunk to tell you where that is.

6. Fill the pot with the amended potting soil up to within 2 inches from the top. Make sure the plant's original soil line is also 2 inches below the top of the pot, but no deeper. For bare-root plants, jiggle the plant up and down to get potting soil under and around the roots. Poke potting soil between the roots with your fingers to eliminate air pockets.

7. Water the plant by filling the pot up to the rim with water and letting it drain away.

8. Top-dress your pot with attractive mulch such as shredded bark. Do not use "Beauty Bark"—it may be loaded with herbicides.

9. Provide support. Tall fruit and nut trees will need to be staked in order to stabilize them in the wind, so pound a stake into the potting soil and tie your tree loosely to the stake. Fruiting vines should be placed near a support structure for them to climb on.

10. Do not put your pot into a saucer to catch the water coming out of the drainage holes unless the pot has feet or you prop the pot up on pebbles. Avoid leaving the pot to sit in water. Waterlogged soil is the number one killer of potted plants.

11. When your tree has been in its container for a couple of years, pull it out of its pot in winter when it is dormant. Cut off 1 inch of roots and soil all around the root ball. Put a layer of fresh potting soil in the bottom of your pot and put your plant on top of it. Then pack fresh potting soil all around the sides and top of the root ball. Top-dress with mulch, and you're done.

Strawberries grow so well in containers, you may just decide to keep them in basic "nursery black." Just make sure drainage is adequate so that they never become waterlogged.

POLLINATION

In order for a plant to bear fruit it has to have sex. As you may have learned in Biology 101, a sperm, contained in the pollen, must fertilize an egg, contained in the ovary of a flower, in order to create offspring. With plants, the next generation is a seed. The developing seed triggers the plant's ovary to mature and ripen into what we call a fruit. A peach is a mature, ripened ovary that contains a seed that has resulted from sexual reproduction. As is so often the case, when we're talking about sex, and pollination, things get complicated. The terminology alone is enough to make your head swim. Be sure to read the plant portraits to learn any pollination requirements specific to the species you want to grow. Peruse plant tags and catalog descriptions to learn the fertility characteristics of the various cultivars. The definitions that follow will help you understand the terms you will encounter.

Self-fertile. Most flowers contain both male and female sex parts. However, only a few plants can pollinate themselves. These plants are self-fertile; they do not need another plant to make seeds, and, therefore, to bear fruit. About half the plants featured in this book are self-fertile. You should be aware, however, that many self-fertile fruit and nut plants produce a bigger and better crop if they have access to pollen from cultivars that are different from themselves.

Self-incompatible. Many fruit and nut plants are completely unable to pollinate themselves even though they have male and female sex parts inside the same flower. Their own sperm will not fertilize their own eggs. They make viable sperm in the pollen and viable eggs in the ovary, but a built-in genetic incompatibility prevents self-fertilization from taking place. These plants are self-incompatible. They need a different cultivar to ensure that their flowers get pollinated.

There is another complicating factor to consider when discussing self-incompatibility. All named cultivars are clones; they are identical to each other, with identical genetic characteristics. So, if you plant two fruit or nut trees with the same cultivar name, and that cultivar is self-incompatible, you will still get no fruit because they cannot pollinate each other. Most apple varieties are self-incompatible, and 'Red Delicious' is no exception. One 'Red Delicious' tree is absolutely unable to pollinate another 'Red Delicious' tree.

All peaches are self-fertile. You need to plant only one cultivar to get a crop. If you have room, though, plant two different cultivars, because they will make more fruit.

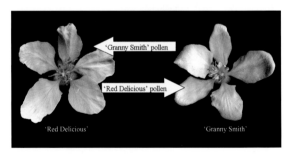

The self-incompatible 'Red Delicious' apple flower will produce no fruit unless a different apple cultivar, like 'Granny Smith', is nearby to act as a pollenizer. Since 'Granny Smith' is also self-incompatible, it too must have an effective pollenizer nearby.

Pollen sterile. Some cultivars of fruit and nut plants are unable to make viable sperm within the pollen. They are pollen sterile. A pollen sterile tree can never pollinate any plant. Only its egg and ovary are viable. So, a pollen sterile tree can bear fruit only if there is a different cultivar nearby that has pollen to provide sperm. If you plant a 'Red Delicious' (self-incompatible) apple tree and a 'Jonagold' (pollen sterile) apple tree, this is what will happen: 'Red Delicious' produces viable pollen to pollinate 'Jonagold' so you will get a crop of 'Jonagold' apples. But since 'Jonagold' is pollen sterile you will get no 'Red Delicious' apples.

Dioecious. Some fruit plants, like kiwi, persimmon, and a number of mulberries, have male flowers and female flowers on different plants. The word *dioecious* ("two houses") refers to a plant that has separate sexes on different plants. You have to have a male plant and a female plant in order to get fruit. Male flowers do not have ovaries and so male plants bear no fruit at all. Even though they take up valuable garden real estate, you have to have a male because your female cannot bear fruit unless she gets pollinated by the male.

Monoecious. All melons and watermelons, and all nut trees, except almond, bear male flowers and female flowers on the same plant. Male flowers do not have female sex parts, and female flowers do not have male sex parts. *Monoecious* ("one house") signifies that flowers of both sexes are separate, but borne on the same plant. Most monoecious plants in this book are self-fertile, so theoretically you need plant only one individual. However, plants will produce larger crops if you plant two different cultivars so they can cross-pollinate.

❀ ❀ ❀

Now that you've made your preparations, you are ready to take the next step. Move on to the plant portraits to learn which plants you can grow and how to do it.

Our first yummy blueberries of the year; and we grow them in containers on the back deck under forest giants.

Plant Portraits

Almond

Stone Fruit Problem-Solving Guide, page 217

DESCRIPTION. The almond (*Prunus dulcis*) has an edible seed enclosed inside a stony shell that looks like a peach pit. The seed is commonly referred to as a "nut" although, botanically, the fruit is a drupe just like a peach. Closely related to peaches, nectarines, apricots, cherries, and plums, the almond lacks the sweet juicy flesh that surrounds the pit in its cousins. Oddly enough, all the stone fruits, except sweet almonds, contain bitter-tasting, and poisonous, cyanide in their seeds.

Almonds originated in Asia Minor, but, in antiquity, humans carried them to the Mediterranean and beyond. The ornamental trees sold as flowering almond in nurseries are not the same species, and do not produce edible nuts.

Trees burst into bloom with white to pale pink blossoms in late winter or very early spring. The fruits, which look like fuzzy, green, young peaches, develop through the summer and ripen in late summer or early autumn. When ripe the leathery outer covering splits open to reveal the pit which contains the edible seed.

The trees grow 20 to 30 feet tall and wide, becoming dome-shaped with age. They drop their gray-green leaves in autumn but don't bother dressing up in colorful fall foliage. Each leaf is 3 to 5 inches long with a serrated margin.

TEMPERATURE. Almond trees are hardy in zones 7 to 9 but do their best in zone 9. The trees will tolerate temperatures below 0°F, but their very early bloom season means the flowers are subject to frost damage, which can destroy the nut crop. For most cultivars, 500 to 600 hours below 45°F meets the winter chilling requirement. Low-chill cultivars need only 200 to 300 hours. Ninety to 150 days per year above 86°F results in a good nut crop.

Almonds do not fare well in rainy summer climates because summer rainfall promotes fungal and bacterial diseases of the developing fruit. Regions with hot, dry summers and cool, wet winters—a Mediterranean climate like Central California—are best.

SOIL, LIGHT, AND WATER. All fruit needs healthy, biologically active soil, full sun, and regular water. Review the Introduction for guidance on how to provide these three essential elements.

GARDEN USES. Almond trees are an attractive addition to the landscape. They serve as beautiful flowering trees in spring, shade trees in summer, and a source of healthful nutritious nuts in autumn. Combine them with berry bushes, ornamental shrubs, and herbaceous perennials to create a garden that functions like a natural plant community. Such a polyculture garden offers complex structure, high species diversity, and biologically active soil. Currants, gooseberries, raspberries, and ornamental shrubs like caryopteris combine well with almond trees. Perennials that work well planted under and around them include Russian sage, fava beans, shallots, garlic, daffodils, yarrow, strawberries, mizuna, borage, and comfrey.

Almond trees can be grown in large containers but will require root trimming (page 26). When your tree has been in its container for two to three years, pull it out of its pot in winter when it is dormant. Trim 1 inch of the roots off all sides of the root ball. Add a layer of fresh potting soil to the bottom and sides of your pot and put the root-trimmed tree back in the same container. Top it off with fresh potting soil and finish with a layer of mulch.

POLLINATION. Some almond cultivars are self-fertile. Others are self-incompatible. See the Introduction for an overview of pollination and its terminology.

PRUNING. Prune almond trees when they are dormant, in autumn or winter. Have a look at "Prune Properly" (page 264) for tips.

PROBLEM-SOLVING. Almonds, apricots, cherries, peaches, plums, and nectarines are species in the genus *Prunus,* commonly called stone fruits, and all have the same issues. As you will see when you turn to the Stone Fruit Problem-Solving Guide on page 217, there are a lot of pests and diseases to contend with, but following the guidelines in this plant portrait, reviewing the Introduction, and reading the recommendations in "Change the Growing Conditions" (page 247) will help you keep your almonds healthy.

Apple

Pome Fruit Problem-Solving Guide, page 198

DESCRIPTION. Long-lived, strong, and sturdy, the apple tree develops great character with age. It is a deciduous tree which, in standard-size trees that have not been grafted to dwarfing rootstocks, will grow 20 feet tall and 25 feet wide. Most cultivars are available as semi-dwarf trees which grow 8 to 12 feet tall and 10 to 15 feet wide. Dwarf trees grow 5 to 8 feet tall and wide. Most semi-dwarf and dwarf trees are obtained by grafting to specific dwarfing rootstocks, but a few true genetic dwarfs also occur.

The apple tree has been cherished by humans for untold millennia and we have carried this tree with us to every corner of the globe. As a result there are approximately 7,500 different named cultivars of this beloved fruit tree. The domestic apple, *Malus domestica*, is an ancient hybrid that originated by natural cross-pollination between *M. sieversii*, *M. sylvestris*, and other wild apple species in Asia Minor. With genes from so many species in its background it's no wonder the domestic apple comes in so many different colors, textures, and flavors.

The apple has lovely white flowers that often have a pink blush when they first open. Flowers are 1 to 1½ inches across and have five petals. The flowers have both male and female sex parts and are borne in clusters on specialized short shoots called spurs.

Different qualities of the fruit—color, texture, taste, and season—determine whether a cultivar is best used as a dessert apple for eating fresh, for cooking, for preserving as apple sauce or apple butter, or for making juice and cider. Color varies by cultivar. Apples may be green, yellow, red, or have multicolored stripes and blushes. Most cultivars have white flesh but there are a few with pink to red flesh. The texture of the flesh varies from crisp and juicy to dry and mealy. Merely sweet in some cultivars, the fruit may be both sweet and tart in others. Early apples ripen in summer, midseason apples in early autumn, and late apples in autumn.

TEMPERATURE. Most apple cultivars grow very well in zones 5 to 9. Some will survive even the very cold winters of zone 3. For most cultivars, winter chilling requirement is 500 to 1,000 hours below 45°F, but a few low-chill varieties flower and fruit successfully with only 300 to 500 hours. If your region experiences more than 120 days annually above 86°F, you'll need to search out cultivars adapted to high heat in order for your trees to produce high-quality fruit.

SOIL, LIGHT, AND WATER. All fruit needs healthy, biologically active soil, full sun, and regular water. Review the Introduction for guidance on how to provide these three essential elements. Adequate water is especially important when the fruit is developing. Avoid allowing the soil to dry out completely or become waterlogged. Be sure to water the soil, not the foliage.

GARDEN USES. The apple tree has distinctive character through all seasons and deserves a place of honor in any landscape. Its profuse spring blossoms rival those of any flowering ornamental. We like to surround apple trees with a mix of flowers, vegetables, and herbs that attract beneficial insects, including pollinators, predators, and parasitoids, to help keep pests at bay. Space standard trees 16 feet apart. Plant semi-dwarf trees 10 to 12 feet apart. Plant dwarf trees 8 feet apart. Dwarf trees also do well in very large pots or half whiskey barrels.

POLLINATION. Most apple cultivars are self-incompatible. A few, such as 'Golden Delicious', 'Mollie's Delicious', and 'Chehalis', are self-fertile. Others, such as 'Jonagold', 'Mutsu', and 'Stayman', are pollen sterile, unable to pollinate themselves or any other apple tree. Pollen sterile cultivars still bear perfectly good apples as long as they get cross-pollinated by a different cultivar. See the Introduction for an overview of pollination and its terminology.

PRUNING. Apple trees need to be pruned every year in winter while they're dormant. As your trees grow and mature, open their center to light and air. Prune them to a central leader, modified central leader, or open vase style. Do not head back or thin more than a third of the branches in any given year. Pruning more than that can stimulate the growth of water sprouts. Have a look at "Prune Properly" (page 264) for more tips.

PROBLEM-SOLVING. Apple trees are fairly easy and very satisfying to grow, but sometimes despite your best efforts, problems crop up. Following the guidelines in this plant portrait, reviewing the Introduction, and reading the recommendations in "Change the Growing Conditions" (page 247) will help you keep your apple trees healthy. See the Pome Fruit Problem-Solving Guide, page 198, for specific information on pests and diseases of apples and other pome fruits.

Apricot

Stone Fruit Problem-Solving Guide, page 217

DESCRIPTION. The apricot, *Prunus armeniaca*, is a stone fruit, with a bony pit that encloses and protects the seed. Close relatives include cherries, peaches, nectarines, almonds, and plums. Hybrids between apricots and plums are common. Plumcots, aka apriplums, are half plum and half apricot. The pluot, at three-quarters plum and one-quarter apricot, resembles the plum more than the apricot. The aprium, at three-quarters apricot and one-quarter plum, most closely resembles the apricot.

Apricots have been grown from antiquity in the Middle East and for at least 3,000 years in India and probably longer in China, where they originated. The species was originally thought to have come from Armenia, thus the epithet "armeniaca."

Apricots have white or pink, five-petaled flowers and are among the first fruit trees to flower in early spring. Consequently, their flowers are often damaged by frost. They flower and fruit best in regions where late spring frosts are rare. Fruiting time varies among cultivars, with some ripening in late spring and others ripening in summer.

The fruit is soft, easily bruised, and covered with very short, velvety fuzz. The fruit is also very pretty, orange to amber in color, often with a reddish blush. Not nearly as juicy as peaches, plums, or cherries, apricots dry beautifully and make superb aromatic and flavorful preserves. Eaten fresh the fruit is sweet with a delicate and more subtle taste than its stronger flavored cousins. Our favorite cultivars are somewhat tart as well as sweet.

The apricot is a smallish deciduous tree to 20 feet tall and wide with attractive foliage. The rounded heart-shaped leaves are reddish bronze when new, passing through shades of yellow-green to darker green as they mature.

TEMPERATURE. Apricots are generally hardy to zone 4, but hardiness varies by cultivar. Most have a winter chilling requirement of about 700 hours below 45°F. Several low-chill cultivars, with a chilling requirement of only 300 to 400 hours, do well in zones 8 and 9.

Apricots are one of the most drought-tolerant fruit trees you can grow. However, their maximum heat tolerance for good fruit production is 120 days per year above 86°F. Apricot production will be unreliable in climates that are hotter than this.

SOIL, LIGHT, AND WATER. All fruit needs healthy, biologically active soil, full sun, and regular water. Review the Introduction for guidance on how to provide these three essential elements.

GARDEN USES. The apricot tree serves double duty, for fruit production and as an ornamental shade tree, because its foliage is attractive and so are the flowers. In the polyculture garden, apricots and other fruit trees provide the complex, three-dimensional structure that emulates natural plant communities. This creates habitat for wild partners such as pollinators, predators, and parasitoids, all beneficial organisms that contribute to your success in growing organic fruit. Garden favorites to plant around your apricot trees include flowers like yarrow, daylilies, and echinacea, vegetables like garlic, chives, and onion, and herbs like sage, dill, and fennel.

Apricot trees can be grown in large containers. Treat them as you would a bonsai and trim the roots each year (page 26).

POLLINATION. Most apricot cultivars are self-fertile, but even with these, crossing between two different cultivars will increase the number of fruits you get. A few require cross-pollination with another apricot variety. See the Introduction for an overview of pollination and its terminology.

PRUNING. Prune apricot trees in summer, right after you harvest the fruit. Summer pruning helps to avoid eutypa dieback, a fungal disease, and also generates the new wood in the current season's growth which will bear flower buds next year. Have a look at "Prune Properly" (page 264) for more tips.

PROBLEM-SOLVING. Apricots, almonds, cherries, peaches, plums, and nectarines are species in the genus *Prunus*, commonly called stone fruits, and all have the same issues. As you will see when you turn to the Stone Fruit Problem-Solving Guide on page 217, there are a lot of pests and diseases to contend with, but following the guidelines in this plant portrait, reviewing the Introduction, and reading the recommendations in "Change the Growing Conditions" (page 247) will help you keep your apricot trees healthy.

Avocado

Avocado Problem-Solving Guide, page 102

DESCRIPTION. The avocado, *Persea americana*, is a large, tropical, evergreen tree that grows up to 60 feet tall. It hails originally from south-central Mexico. Peoples of the New World from Peru to the Rio Grande have cultivated it for centuries, and it remains highly prized for its savory fruit. Like olives it contains valuable oil, which makes it a heart-healthy addition to your diet. The avocado contains cholesterol-lowering monounsaturated fatty acids, omega-3 oil, and cancer-fighting antioxidants. Who knew guacamole was so good for you?

Botanists recognize three varieties of the species. The Mexican avocado (var. *drymifolia*) tolerates more cold than the other types, and has flavorful fruit rich in healthful oil. The West Indian avocado (var. *americana*) is the least cold-tolerant of the three and has milder tasting fruit with less oil than the Mexican variety. The third variety (var. *guatemalensis*) is intermediate between these two in terms of both cold tolerance and fruit characteristics.

Avocados generally bloom January through March. Although each tree covers itself with thousands of flowers, only 100 to 200 flowers will develop into fruit. Mexican-type fruits mature six to eight months after bloom, and Guatemalan types mature 12 to 18 months after blooming. The fruits mature on the tree and can remain there, where they stay in good condition for quite a while. Oddly they do not ripen on the tree; they ripen three to eight days after they've been harvested or have fallen to the ground.

The large, heavy, pear-shaped or round fruits dangle from the tree on long stalks. Botanically speaking, the fruit is a berry, like a tomato. But this berry contains only one large, inedible seed. Creamy soft, light green and yellow flesh surrounds the seed. The fruits have either warty-pebbly skin, or smooth and shiny skin; the skin color may be green, purple and green, or nearly black.

Although wild avocado trees grow quite large, most cultivars are much smaller and easier to manage in the home landscape. Many cultivars mature at around 20 to 24 feet; some are taller, to 40 feet; some are smaller, to 12 feet. Pay attention to catalog descriptions and plant labels to select a tree of an appropriate size for your garden.

TEMPERATURE. Avocados are hardy in zone 9 and higher. As tropical evergreens, avocado trees do not have a winter chilling requirement. They prefer less than 120 days per year above 86°F.

SOIL, LIGHT, AND WATER. All fruit needs healthy, biologically active soil, full sun, and regular water. Review the Introduction for guidance on how to provide these three essential elements.

GARDEN USES. Avocado trees develop great character with age, and the trees have high value as ornamentals. Their evergreen foliage casts dense shade all year long, offering cool, shady microclimates in which to expand your garden palette. In the polyculture garden, the tree's crown provides complex structure and good habitat for a number of beneficial wild partners. If you choose a polyculture approach, site shade-tolerant plants beneath this tree's generous canopy. Good shrubs to try: strawberry guava, pineapple guava, *Aucuba japonica*, or camellia. Flowers, herbs, and ground covers: impatiens, ajuga, hosta, mint, or *Vinca minor*.

Smaller cultivars are easily grown in large pots or half whiskey barrels on your patio or deck. In cold-winter climates, put avocado trees in pots—with wheeled pot caddies to simplify the task of moving them outdoors for the summer and indoors for the winter. Be sure to give them as much light as possible year-round. Many people start their own trees by planting a seed, pointy side up, in a pot and keeping it on a sunny windowsill. These home-germinated trees function as houseplants during the winter, and make attractive ornamentals. Container-grown avocados that must go inside for the winter will usually not bear fruit. They will need annual root trimming (page 26).

POLLINATION. Like most flowers, avocado flowers contain both male and female sex parts. And, like most flowers, the blossoms last for several days. Which is a lucky thing because these flowers have a most unusual feature: they change gender in the middle of the day. Truly, we are not making this stuff up. Type-A flowers grow on one tree, and type-B flowers grow on another. Type-A trees are functionally female in the morning, but become functionally male in the afternoon. Type-B trees have flowers that are functionally female in the afternoon and become functionally male on the morning of the second day. In the morning then, a type-B tree can pollinate a type-A tree, and the type-A tree will bear fruit. In the afternoon, a type-A tree can pollinate a type-B tree, and the type-B tree will bear fruit. What a complicated sex life!

Even though an avocado is technically self-fertile, you really need two trees—one type A and one type B—to get fruit. If you have space for only one tree, ask a neighbor who has an avocado what type it is—A or B—and choose the other type for your garden. Then rely on the bees to carry pollen back and forth. You and your neighbor can share the fruit crop. See the Introduction for an overview of pollination and its terminology.

PRUNING. Avocados need very little pruning other than shaping for ease of harvest and to open the center to light and air. Have a look at "Prune Properly" (page 264) for tips.

PROBLEM-SOLVING. Avocado trees can have a number of pest and disease problems, but following the guidelines in this plant portrait, reviewing the Introduction, and reading the recommendations in "Change the Growing Conditions" (page 247) will help you keep them healthy. See the Avocado Problem-Solving Guide, page 102, for specific information on pests and diseases.

Banana

Banana Problem-Solving Guide, page 109

DESCRIPTION. Bananas and plantains (*Musa acuminata*, *M. balbisiana*) are large-leaved, tropical, evergreen plants grown in the humid tropics and subtropics throughout the world. The banana's original home was the Indo-Malaysian region. Banana fruits are sweet and eaten fresh, while plantains are starchy and need to be cooked before eating. Delicious and extremely popular, bananas are the fourth-largest fruit crop in the world after tomatoes, grapes, and oranges.

A banana plant is a giant herb that has no woody tissue in its trunk at all. In fact, the "trunk" itself isn't even a stem. It's a pseudostem made up of tightly wrapped leaf petioles—the part of the leaf that attaches it to the base of the banana plant. These pseudostems are firm enough to act like stems and hold the leaves, flowers, and fruit high in the air, as if the plant were a tree. Each pseudostem bears one gigantic flower cluster, and when the fruit matures from these flowers, the pseudostem dies to the ground. Underground, the perennial rhizome continuously generates new pseudostems, or pups, as the old ones fruit and die.

Flowering and fruiting time in the banana is triggered by the age of each pseudostem, not by temperature or day length. Every pseudostem flowers and sets fruit when it has been growing for 10 to 15 frost-free months. An inflorescence emerges from the center of the foliage as a long stalk with large, football-shaped, purple bracts at the tip that cover the flowers like a hood. The first flowers to form are all female; these appear in clusters, and many clusters form on each inflorescence. Male flowers appear later, and these bear pollen, but will not bear fruit. The female flowers develop into clusters of banana fruits, which are called hands.

The fruit of a banana is, botanically speaking, a berry. It's a fleshy fruit that doesn't split open at maturity. They start out bright green but gradually turn yellow or red as they mature. You can harvest all the bananas while they are still green; they ripen very well after harvesting. Alternatively you can harvest the fruit one hand at a time as they ripen on the plant.

Wild bananas contain large, hard seeds. Cultivated bananas are seedless because the plants are all parthenocarpic, which means they can set fruit without pollination. Many are also triploid, which means they have three sets of chromosomes, and any plant with three sets of chromosomes cannot make seeds.

You may see the letters aaa, aab, abb, or bbb on banana plant labels. These designate that the plants are triploids; it also gives you information on the plant's parentage. The letter A tells you that the plant was bred from *Musa acuminata*; the letter B tells you that the plant was bred from *M. balbisiana*. Clearly three As means the banana is all acuminata, whereas three Bs means it's all balbisiana. Any combination of As and Bs tells you that the plant is a hybrid between the two species.

TEMPERATURE. Bananas survive winter temperatures in frost-free areas that remain above 32°F—zone 10a and higher. Banana plants like it warm, and stop growing whenever the temperature drops below 53°F. But they don't like it too warm; they also stop growing whenever the temperature exceeds 100°F. They're best adapted to areas with more than 60 days per year above 86°F. Because bananas are tropical evergreen plants, they have no chilling requirement. Temperatures that are too low, below 53°F, or too high, above 100°F, will increase the time it takes for the plant to flower and bear fruit. If you live in a climate where winter temperatures drop to 10°F, you can grow bananas as ornamental perennials. The tops die to the ground, but the rhizome will resprout in spring. You will, however, never get fruit.

SOIL, LIGHT, AND WATER. All fruit needs healthy, biologically active soil, full sun, and regular water. Review the Introduction for guidance on how to provide these three essential elements. Bananas are heavy feeders and require annual applications of organic fertilizer to keep up with their rapid growth rate. They also lose large quantities of water through those huge leaves, so provide plenty of water to be sure they are adequately hydrated. Be careful when you water; they also demand good drainage to avoid root rot, the number one killer of banana plants.

GARDEN USES. Banana plants are extremely handsome ornamentals, imparting a lush tropical ambiance to your landscape. Wind will tatter the foliage, so provide them with wind protection to maintain their beautiful leaves in good shape. Combining fruit trees with berry bushes, ornamental shrubs, and herbaceous perennials creates a garden that functions like a natural plant community. Such a garden becomes a polyculture with complex structure, high species diversity, and biologically active soil. Plants that do well with bananas include figs, passionfruit, citrus trees, hibiscus, gingers, and cannas.

Many banana cultivars, especially the dwarf varieties, are easily grown in large containers like half whiskey barrels. Periodically you will need to pull the plants out of the container, trim the roots, and repot with fresh soil (page 26).

POLLINATION. Banana cultivars do not need to be pollinated in order to bear fruit. In the wild bananas are pollinated by bats, birds, and bees.

PRUNING. Each pseudostem needs to be cut to the ground after you have harvested all the fruit.

PROBLEM-SOLVING. Following the guidelines in this plant portrait, reviewing the Introduction, and reading the recommendations in "Change the Growing Conditions" (page 247) will help you keep your bananas healthy. If you run into trouble, turn to the Banana Problem-Solving Guide, page 109, for specific information on pests and diseases.

Blackberry

Bramble Problem-Solving Guide, page 123

DESCRIPTION. Blackberry plants—*Rubus fruticosus*, *R. ursinus*, and hybrids (boysenberry, loganberry, marionberry, and tayberry)—are brambles, a type of perennial shrub. Humans have been harvesting and eating wild blackberries for millennia and have been hybridizing them to create new cultivars for at least a century. There are hundreds, perhaps thousands, of blackberry cultivars from which to choose. You can easily find a delicious one that perfectly suits your home garden.

These rambling plants produce large, white to pale pink flowers in early summer. The fruit ripens from mid-summer into autumn depending on the cultivar. A gentle tug will pull fully ripe blackberry fruit from the plant. If it doesn't come away from the plant easily, it isn't ripe yet. Ripe fruit is soft and will stain your fingers purple.

Blackberries grow new stems, also called canes, from the crown of the plant each year, and each cane lives for only two years. The first-year canes are called primocanes. In its second summer that primocane is called a floricane because it now flowers, sets fruit, and then dies as the fruit matures. Keep in mind that the canes die, not the plant. These are perennials.

There are two types of cultivars: summer-bearing and ever-bearing. Primocanes of summer-bearing cultivars begin growth in spring, mature through the summer without flowering, and survive through the winter. The canes are leafless through the winter in most climates. In their second summer the primocanes flower, set fruit, and die. Primocanes of ever-bearing cultivars flower and set fruit in the autumn of their first year. The leafless canes live through the winter, then flower and set fruit again in the summer of their second year. Then those canes die.

Blackberry plants come in three forms: erect free-standing bushes with self-supporting upright canes and branches; trailing, low-growing, vine-like plants that need the support of a trellis to keep them off the ground; and semi-erect or semi-trailing brambles with canes that arch away from the center of the plant. Most cultivars bear stout murderous prickles all along their canes, but a few varieties are unarmed. During the growing season, all blackberry canes will take root and sprout new plants wherever their tips touch the ground, so they can be invasive. Keeping the canes up off the ground on a trellis will mitigate this problem.

Trailing blackberry cultivars produce several 20-foot-long primocanes every summer, but erect varieties are generally less than half that size. You need to know what kind of blackberry you have and how big it will grow before you can determine how far apart to plant them and how large a trellis you'll need.

TEMPERATURE. Hardiness varies by cultivar, zones 5 to 8. The most cold-tolerant blackberries are the erect types, the least are the trailing types. Some low-chill cultivars need as little as 200 hours below 45°F annually in order to break dormancy and flower. Typical varieties, however, need from 500 to 1,000 hours of cold. Heat tolerance also varies by cultivar, with the erect types, again, being more heat tolerant than trailing ones. All blackberries appreciate hot summers, and their optimum temperature is around 80°F. However, they languish in areas that average more than 150 days above 86°F annually.

SOIL, LIGHT, AND WATER. All fruit needs healthy, biologically active soil, full sun, and regular water. Review the Introduction for guidance on how to provide these three essential elements.

GARDEN USES. Combine bramble bushes with trees, ornamental shrubs, and herbaceous perennials. In the polyculture garden, blackberries do well on the south side of fruit trees, at the edges of the trees' canopies, where the berries will get full sun. Garlic and strawberries play well with them, along with herbs and flowers in the mint, carrot, and daisy families that attract beneficial insects.

POLLINATION. All blackberries are self-fertile. See the Introduction for an overview of pollination and its terminology.

PRUNING. In summer-bearing cultivars, prune away the growing tip of first-year canes in summer when they get to be 4 to 5 feet tall. This causes lateral branches to grow and produce abundant fruit within easy reach in the second year. When second-year canes have finished fruiting, prune them at ground level in the fall, or anytime it's convenient through the winter.

Ever-bearing cultivars should have the top third of the cane pruned away when first-year fruiting is finished in the autumn. In its second year that same cane will produce an abundant summer crop on the bottom two-thirds, and then die. Have a look at "Prune Properly" (page 264) for tips on pruning brambles.

PROBLEM-SOLVING. Birds sneaking in to steal your crop will likely be your biggest headache. Following the guidelines in this plant portrait, reviewing the Introduction, and reading the recommendations in "Change the Growing Conditions" (page 247) will help you keep your blackberries healthy and productive. See the Bramble Problem-Solving Guide, page 123, for specific information on pests and diseases of blackberries and raspberries.

Blueberry

Blueberry Problem-Solving Guide, page 115

DESCRIPTION. All the commonly grown blueberry species and their hybrids are long-lived deciduous shrubs with attractive foliage, pretty little bell-shaped flowers, and brilliant red-orange to yellow fall color. They're native to North America. All grow new stems from under the ground every year, which means they sucker freely. Everybody should have a few blueberry bushes. They're easy to grow and loaded with healthful antioxidants, and we find that our homegrown organic ones taste way better than store-bought ones.

Blueberry bushes flower in the spring on stems and side branches that grew the previous season. Each bud produces as many as six small, bell-shaped, pinkish white flowers. After the bees do their work pollinating the flowers, you'll get clusters of delicious blue berries from July into September.

Blueberry fruits are indeed technically berries. As the name implies, the berries are blue when ripe—very dark blue beneath a powdery light blue coating. Fully ripe berries are sweeter than almost ripe ones, but we like to harvest both because the almost ripe berries add a delicious degree of tartness.

The most commonly grown blueberry is the northern highbush, *Vaccinium corymbosum*, a shrub that grows to 7 feet tall. Its native range is Nova Scotia south to Alabama and west to Wisconsin. Most blueberry bushes you'll find in the nursery will be named cultivars of this species. *Vaccinium angustifolium*, the lowbush blueberry, is a shrub that grows to 18 inches tall, spreading to 2 feet wide. It's native from eastern and central Canada south to West Virginia and west to Minnesota. Half-high blueberries are hybrids between the two species. As you might guess, they are taller than the lowbush and shorter than the highbush, thus "half-high."

Rabbiteye blueberries, shrubs to 15 feet tall, are native from North Carolina south to Florida and west to Texas. Formerly classified as *Vaccinium ashei* or *V. virgatum*, botanists have reclassified these plants as another form of *V. corymbosum*. Nurseries and plant catalogs will most likely continue to carry rabbiteyes under their old scientific names for years to come. You might also see southern highbush blueberry listed; it's a hybrid between *V. darrowii* and *V. corymbosum*.

TEMPERATURE. Northern highbush blueberries are hardy in zones 4 to 7. Most need 800 to 1,000 hours of winter chilling below 45°F. They prefer less than 90 days per year above 86°F.

Lowbush blueberries are hardy in zones 3 to 7. Most need 1,000 to 1,200 hours of winter chilling below 45°F. They tolerate up to 120 days per year above 86°F.

Half-high blueberries are hardy in zones 3 to 7. Like their lowbush parents they require 1,000 to 1,200 hours of winter chilling below 45°F. Like their highbush parents they prefer less than 90 days above 86°F annually.

Rabbiteye and southern highbush blueberries are hardy in zones 7 to 9. Their winter chilling requirement is as little as 150 hours at 45°F. Rabbiteye blueberries tolerate heat very well, as much as 150 days per year above 86°F.

SOIL, LIGHT, AND WATER. All fruit needs healthy, biologically active soil, full sun, and regular water; review the Introduction for guidance on these three essentials. In addition, all blueberry types need acidic soils with a pH of 4 to 5. We give our plants coffee grounds every day and that works well for us. You can read about measuring and modifying the pH of your soil in "Soil Solutions" on page 252.

GARDEN USES. Blueberry bushes are lovely ornamental shrubs for your landscape. Their spring floral display is not very showy because the flowers are small, but their fall color is spectacular. Grow them with plants that share their need for acid soil. We grow them with camellia, rhododendron, gardenia, azalea, and strawberry tree. They're also easy to grow in containers. We've had several of the highbush types in large pots for more than five years, and they're very happy, as long as we keep them well fed and watered. They'll need root trimming after five years (page 26).

POLLINATION. Blueberries are self-fertile but you'll get bigger crops of larger berries if you have at least two different cultivars for cross-pollination. See the Introduction for an overview of pollination and its terminology.

PRUNING. Blueberries produce their best fruit on stems that are younger than six years old. All stems at the plant's base that are 1 inch or more thick should be removed down to the soil line each year, but never prune away more than one-third of the stems. Each plant produces new stems from underground every year so always keep the young stems to replace the old stems you remove. Have a look at "Prune Properly" (page 264) for tips on pruning blueberries.

PROBLEM-SOLVING. We have found our blueberries to be completely trouble-free. Following the guidelines in this plant portrait, reviewing the Introduction, and reading the recommendations in "Change the Growing Conditions" (page 247) will help you keep your blueberries just as healthy. See the Blueberry Problem-Solving Guide, page 115, for specific information on pests and diseases.

Cherry

Stone Fruit Problem-Solving Guide, page 217

DESCRIPTION. Desirable fruit trees for the home garden include sweet cherry (*Prunus avium*), pie cherry (*P. cerasus*), Nanking cherry (*P. tomentosa*), and their hybrids. Cherries, along with their cousins apricot, almond, plum, peach, and nectarine, are stone fruits.

Native to Europe, North Africa, and Asia Minor, sweet and pie cherries have been consumed by humans for more than 4,000 years. Both species are cultivated worldwide wherever the climate is appropriate. The shrubby Nanking cherry, native to Asia, is less well known outside of Asia.

Cherries flower in spring and fruit ripens in summer. Flowers are white with five petals. They do not flower as early in spring as plums or almonds, but the flowers may still sometimes be damaged by frost. Best climates for fruit production have dry summers, because cherries tend to split open if rain falls while they are ripening.

Plump, glossy cherries may be nearly black, dark red, red, yellow with a red blush, or yellow. Flavor varies by cultivar. Usually not very tart, sweet cherries are generally eaten fresh. Pie cherries are tart, even sour, and are baked into pies and cobblers. Nanking cherries are both sweet and tart.

Standard-sized sweet cherry trees, the largest of the three species, easily reach 35 feet tall and wide. Dwarf and semi-dwarf sweet cherry trees fit modern lot sizes better than the standards. Pie cherry trees grow to 20 feet tall and wide. Nanking cherries only get 8 feet tall and 10 feet wide. All three species are deciduous and some cultivars have attractive yellow/orange/red fall color.

TEMPERATURE. Sweet cherries are hardy to zone 5. Pie cherries and Nanking cherries are much hardier, to zone 3. However, once trees break dormancy and begin to flower they are very sensitive to frosts. It is harder to get a good crop of cherries in regions with unpredictable spring frosts and unsettled weather. Cherry trees are adaptable to the mild-winter climates of zones 8 and 9, but they require cold weather in order to break dormancy. The chilling requirement for sweet cherries is 700 to 800 hours below 45°F, but low-chill cultivars which need only 200 to 300 hours are available. Pie cherries need around 500 hours below 45°F. The winter chilling requirement of Nanking cherry is unknown. Cherry trees prefer less than 90 days annually above 86°F.

SOIL, LIGHT, AND WATER. All fruit needs healthy, biologically active soil, full sun, and regular water. Review the Introduction for guidance on how to provide these three essential elements.

GARDEN USES. All cherries have ornamental value, because their flowers are very showy and generously produced. Some cultivars also have lovely fall color. Include Nanking cherry in the shrub layer of your garden along with currants, gooseberries, and raspberries. Sweet cherries and pie cherries both serve as an overstory layer in the polyculture garden. Plants to include under and around your cherries are fava beans, fennel, dill, garlic, shallots, lettuce, and yarrow. Cherries can be grown in large containers but will require regular root pruning (page 26).

POLLINATION. Most sweet cherry cultivars are self-incompatible. Some are self-fertile. It's actually even more complicated than that, because while sweet cherry A can pollinate B and C, it cannot pollinate D. So there are many combinations to learn about. This is why reading labels and catalog descriptions is so important. Pie cherries are self-fertile, and they do not pollinate sweet cherries. Nanking cherries are self-incompatible. See the Introduction for an overview of pollination and its terminology.

PRUNING. Prune cherry trees in summer, right after you harvest the fruit. Summer pruning helps to avoid eutypa dieback, a fungal disease. Have a look at "Prune Properly" (page 264) for more tips.

PROBLEM-SOLVING. Almonds, apricots, cherries, peaches, plums, and nectarines are species in the genus *Prunus*, and all these stone fruits (as they are commonly known) have the same issues. As you will see when you turn to the Stone Fruit Problem-Solving Guide on page 217, there are a lot of pests and diseases to contend with. The most serious problem for cherries is that they are very susceptible to bacterial diseases. But following the guidelines in this plant portrait, reviewing the Introduction, and reading the recommendations in "Change the Growing Conditions" (page 247) will help you keep your cherries healthy.

Chestnut

Nut Problem-Solving Guide, page 179

DESCRIPTION. People in Asia, Europe, and North America have been harvesting, roasting, and eating chestnuts for millennia. Large, handsome trees with bold, beautiful foliage and sweet, tasty nuts, chestnuts add lush grandeur to your landscape.

The American chestnut, *Castanea dentata*, formerly occupied about 25 percent of the eastern deciduous forests of North America, and was an extremely valuable source of nuts and timber. Unfortunately, the chestnut blight fungus, *Cryphonectria parasitica*, was accidentally introduced to America around 1900 and it decimated forests, causing a devastating loss of native chestnut trees. A few survived and are now being crossed in a breeding program to the Chinese chestnut which is highly resistant to the fungus.

Chinese chestnut, *Castanea mollissima*, is the best, most disease-resistant chestnut for home gardens. A big, bold, deciduous tree to 60 feet tall and 40 feet wide, it needs room to develop its full potential. Japanese (*C. crenata*) and European (*C. sativa*) chestnuts can sometimes be grown where chestnut blight is less problematic and where winter temperatures are mild. Hybrids derived from crosses between American and Chinese chestnuts are resistant to the blight fungus and are readily available in nurseries. Complex hybrids involving European and/or Japanese chestnuts in addition to the American and Chinese species are also under development.

Chestnuts flower in summer, about two and a half months after the leaves first unfold in spring. Thousands of long, stiff catkins, each bearing dozens of tiny, white, male flowers, cast their pollen on the wind. These male catkins are the first flowers to form. A little later the bases of these catkins develop spiny green burrs, which house the female flowers. Each burr contains three to seven female flowers; and each female flower, after successful pollination, develops into a fat brown nut still enclosed by the burr. The trees drop their burrs to the ground when the nuts are ripe, in early autumn, making the harvest easy. The spiny burrs are quite sharp, however, and easily capable of puncturing your fingers, so handle them with gloves. After the burrs have dropped to the ground they open naturally to release the nuts.

Most burrs contain three shiny brown nuts, which means that three female flowers were pollinated. When the nuts are fresh the outer covering, or nutshell, within the burr is loose, soft, and flexible, and easily peeled away from the nutmeat. A second, papery covering coats the wrinkled, creamy yellow nutmeat.

TEMPERATURE. Chinese chestnuts are hardy in zones 5 to 9. Their buds can be damaged by late frosts in spring so avoid frost pockets whenever possible. Winter chilling requirement is 300 to 400 hours below 45°F. The maximum heat tolerance for chestnut trees is 150 days per year above 86°F.

SOIL, LIGHT, AND WATER. All fruit needs healthy, biologically active soil, full sun, and regular water. Review the Introduction for guidance on how to provide these three essential elements. Chestnuts have poor tolerance for limestone, that is, alkaline, soils. Maintain soil pH between 5.5 and 6.5, which is slightly acid. Regardless of the pH, the site must be well drained in order to avoid phytophthora root rot.

GARDEN USES. Chestnuts are commanding trees of great stature and high ornamental value. Fall foliage color is brilliant yellow. If you have the space for them, their generous canopy adds complex structure to your garden, and provides habitat for birds and other helpful wildlife. Their thick canopy of large leaves casts dense shade and creates its own cool microclimate below. As we all know from Longfellow, "under a spreading chestnut-tree/ the village smithy stands," implying to us that that microclimate makes a great location for a patio or pergola. Beware the mess that ensues from falling nuts.

To grow a chestnut tree in a container strikes us as a difficult proposition, because these trees get so big. You can do it, of course, if you treat it like a large bonsai and keep it starved, stunted, and pruned. But it's unlikely you'd get any nuts that way.

POLLINATION. Chestnuts are self-incompatible. See the Introduction for an overview of pollination and its terminology.

PRUNING. While your chestnut trees are still young, prune them to a central leader. After that initial shaping, they'll need only basic maintenance pruning. To avoid fungal diseases prune only in early summer, and when it is hot and dry. Have a look at "Prune Properly" (page 264) for more tips.

PROBLEM-SOLVING. Chestnuts, for the most part, are subject to many of the same pests and diseases as walnuts, pecans, and hazelnuts. Following the guidelines in this plant portrait, reviewing the Introduction, and reading the recommendations in "Change the Growing Conditions" (page 247) will help you keep your chestnut trees healthy. If you run into trouble, turn to the Nut Problem-Solving Guide, page 179, for specific information on pests and diseases of chestnuts and other nut trees.

Currant and gooseberry

**Currant and Gooseberry
Problem-Solving Guide, page 138**

DESCRIPTION. Currant and gooseberry bushes are deciduous shrubs, 3 to 5 feet tall and wide. A plethora of species in the genus *Ribes* will generously provide you with valuable and delicious small berries. *Ribes rubrum* yields both red and white currants while *R. nigrum* gives us the distinctively resinous black currant. *Ribes odoratum*, the clove currant, has the prettiest and most fragrant flowers of the bunch in addition to tasty fruit. Another currant cultivated for its berries is *R. petraeum*. And the ferociously spiny gooseberry, *R. uva-crispa*, yields larger berries that are both sweet and tart. The American gooseberry, *R. hirtellum*, is native to North America and is also cultivated for its fruit. All other species discussed here are native to the Old World.

In a few places in the United States it remains illegal to grow all currants and gooseberries, because many are alternate hosts to white pine blister rust, *Cronartium ribicola*, a fungus that kills white pine trees. The fungus lives half its life cycle in currant and gooseberry bushes, and the other half in white pine trees. It does little harm to the currants and gooseberries, but it is lethal to these important timber trees. For many years the United States banned the cultivation of currants and gooseberries, but the ban proved ineffective in controlling the disease. The federal ban was lifted in 1966. Most states have now followed suit and lifted the ban, but a few states still maintain it. The most susceptible of all the species in cultivation is the black currant, *Ribes nigrum*. In some states, New York and Ohio, for example, black currant is still banned, but not its cultivars and hybrids that are known to be resistant to the disease.

Currants and gooseberries flower in mid-spring, but the shrubs could be in full bloom, and you might not notice it. An exception is the clove currant with its bright yellow flowers and pleasant fragrance. By summer the berries are ripe.

The berries of currants are small, but potent. They have four times as much vitamin C as oranges, and black currants have twice the antioxidants of blueberries. Currants are borne in long dangling clusters of tiny gem-like berries. Gooseberries are borne singly or in small clusters of three berries. Both currants and gooseberries should be harvested as soon as they're ripe, otherwise they will shrivel up, or the birds will get them. Red currants are an exception, because they'll hang on the bush in good condition for weeks as long as you keep the birds at bay.

Red, white, and clove currants, as well as gooseberries, fruit best on wood that is one, two, or three years old. Black currant fruits best on one-year-old wood.

TEMPERATURE. Red, white, and black currants, and gooseberries are hardy in zones 3 to 7. Most cultivars need 1,000 to 1,200 hours of winter chilling below 45°F. Maximum heat tolerance is 90 days per year above 86°F.

Clove currants are hardy in zones 4 to 8. Winter chilling requirement is 1,000 hours below 45°F. They tolerate more heat than other currants, taking up to 150 days per year above 86°F.

SOIL, LIGHT, AND WATER. All fruit needs healthy, biologically active soil, full sun, and regular water. Review the Introduction for guidance on how to provide these three essential elements. Currants and gooseberries will tolerate more shade than most other small fruits, making them excellent candidates for growing with or under your fruit trees.

GARDEN USES. Currants and gooseberries don't win any horticultural beauty contests, but they are good, solid, steady workhorses that pump out delicious, healthful berries year after year with minimum effort on your part. They do very well in the shade beneath the canopy of taller trees, giving your fruit garden an understory shrub layer. All currants and gooseberries do very well in containers. We've had a gooseberry in a five-gallon plastic pot for more than five years and it's still going strong. Watch where you place gooseberries, however, because those thorns can blindside you, reaching out and snagging clothing or skin.

POLLINATION. Currants and gooseberries are self-fertile. Clove currant may be an exception and will fruit better with cross-pollination. See the Introduction for an overview of pollination and its terminology.

PRUNING. Prune your bushes every year for best fruit production. Cut all stems older than three years to the ground. Each year plants produce new stems from below ground. Keep some of these new stems as you remove and thin out the old ones. Handle black currant differently because it fruits best on one-year-old wood. For black currant, annually remove stems that are older than one year.

PROBLEM-SOLVING. All currants and gooseberries are subject to the same pests and diseases. Following the guidelines in this plant portrait, reviewing the Introduction, and reading the recommendations in "Change the Growing Conditions" (page 247) will help you keep them healthy. If you run into trouble, see the Currant and Gooseberry Problem-Solving Guide, page 138, for specific information on pests and diseases of these delicious small fruits.

Fig

Fig Problem-Solving Guide, page 144

DESCRIPTION. Soft, juicy, and sweet as honey, fresh figs get top ratings from most people lucky enough to have tried them. If dried figs are the only figs you've ever eaten, you've got to try some fresh figs. Fresh figs are to dried figs as table grapes are to raisins. Both are good but they are so different in texture and flavor that it's hard to imagine what the fresh fruit is like if all you know is the dried product. You rarely find fresh figs in the market, because they are too soft and easily damaged to ship well. You really need to grow your own. Fortunately that's not hard to do.

Figs have been cultivated and eaten by humans for millennia, starting in the Middle East where the species, *Ficus carica*, is native. The first recorded mention of figs was about 5,000 years ago. Since then, we have carried this plant all over the world, from Australia to Zimbabwe, and we harvest more than two billion pounds of fruit each year, worldwide.

Fig plants are large deciduous shrubs or small trees that grow 10 to 30 feet tall depending on cultivar, climate, and pruning. The simple, alternate leaves are large and palmately lobed like a maple leaf. The foliage is extremely ornamental and the plants are interesting year-round.

TEMPERATURE. Figs are hardy in zones 8 to 11. Winter chilling requirement is 100 hours below 45°F for most cultivars. They tolerate more than 210 days per year above 86°F. Some cultivars will fruit well with no days above 86°F.

SOIL, LIGHT, AND WATER. All fruit needs healthy, biologically active soil, full sun, and regular water. Review the Introduction for guidance on how to provide these three essential elements. Give a fig full sun and a warm spot that traps the heat, and you'll be richly rewarded.

GARDEN USES. Figs, with their very large, handsome foliage, create a tropical ambiance wherever they grow. These are very attractive plants that make bold statements in your landscape and provide four-season interest. Even when leafless in winter their thick silvery branches make dramatic silhouettes. Easy to grow in large containers like half whiskey barrels, figs deserve a place on your patio or deck. If you live where winters are cold enough to damage the plants, move containerized figs into a protected space for the winter.

POLLINATION. Some fig cultivars are self-fertile. These are referred to as "home-garden" or "common" types on plant labels and catalog descriptions. To ensure abundant fruit production, choose this type.

San Pedro and Smyrna types, which are not recommended for the home garden, need to be pollinated by a tiny wasp, *Blastophaga psenes*. If you want to grow and get fruit from a San Pedro or Smyrna type fig, you'll need to make sure that the wasp lives in your area. In large commercial fig orchards, growers staple paper bags full of wasps to their trees to guarantee pollination.

The reason for all this rigmarole is that fig flowers are really weird; they are borne inside the "fruit," which is actually swollen stem tissue. San Pedro or Smyrna type's "fruit" has a tiny hole, called an eye, for the wasp to gain access to the flowers. In the self-fertile varieties, that eye is closed. See the Introduction for an overview of pollination and its terminology.

PRUNING. Figs flower in the spring on branches that are one year old, that is, on last season's growth. This spring crop is called the breba crop. The trees flower again in the fall on the current year's new wood. The fall crop is called the main crop. Some fig cultivars mostly produce in fall, that is, they produce a main crop. The more you head back stems in late winter or early spring, the more new side branches and therefore the more main-crop fruit you'll get. Other cultivars produce both a breba and a main crop. Don't head back all the growth on these cultivars.

Truth is you really don't need to prune, because if you just leave them alone figs will produce plenty of fruit. Have a look at "Prune Properly" (page 264) for tips.

PROBLEM-SOLVING. Winter dieback of branch tips is the most common problem. You will probably also encounter birds wanting to eat all your fruit. Otherwise figs are quite easy to grow. Following the guidelines in this plant portrait, reviewing the Introduction, and reading the recommendations in "Change the Growing Conditions" (page 247) will help you keep your trees healthy. See the Fig Problem-Solving Guide, page 144, for specific information on pests and diseases of these delicious fruits.

Fig   53

Grape

Grape Problem-Solving Guide, page 148

DESCRIPTION. Grapes are big, woody, tendril-bearing vines that reach as high as they can, to more than 100 feet tall, for maximum light. They'll even clamber up into the tree tops. These vines flower, and therefore fruit, only on new shoots of the current season that grow from one-year-old canes. New shoots from older canes will not flower or set fruit. Clusters of tiny flowers appear in early summer, after new growth is well underway. Fruits, which are large clusters of sweet berries, develop in late summer and autumn.

The European grape, *Vitis vinifera*, is the wine grape of history, legend, romance, and religion. Recent discoveries show we've been making wine from this grape for 7,400 years, since the Neolithic period. This tender species can be killed in sub-zero weather. The lands where it thrives have a Mediterranean climate— the Mediterranean itself, California, Australia, Chile, and South Africa—the premier wine-growing regions of the world. It is primarily valued for wine, fresh table grapes, and raisins. The skin of this species is firmly attached to the flesh.

American grapes, *Vitis labrusca*, *V. aestivalis*, and others native to the New World, have a shorter but still colorful history. These grapes are very hardy, surviving temperatures as low as -40°F. They also are naturally resistant to certain pests and diseases that decimate the European grape. In the United States, 'Concord', a cultivar of the native fox grape, *V. labrusca*, is widely grown for fresh juice, table grapes, and jams and jellies. It contributes a distinctive and undesirable "foxy" flavor profile to wines made from it. The skin of this species slips easily away from the flesh when squeezed.

Hybrids between the European grape and American grapes, called French hybrids, combine the fruit quality of *Vitis vinifera* with the winter hardiness and pest resistance of American grapes.

French hybrids extend high-quality wine production to regions of the world too cold for European grapes.

When American species of grapes were taken to Europe, a hitchhiker, a tiny but very destructive insect pest of the root system, went along for the ride. The European wine grape lacked natural resistance to the pest, a species of *Phylloxera*. Soon, French vineyards that had been in production for centuries were all but wiped out. Grafting wine-grape cultivars to rootstock of the highly resistant American grapes rescued the wine industry.

The muscadine grape, *Muscadinia rotundifolia*, formerly known as *Vitis rotundifolia*, is native to the southeastern United States. It bears small clusters of large, tough-skinned, bronze, black, or red berries used for wine, juice, and jelly. A variety of these fruit-producing vines is the scuppernong, named for a river in North Carolina.

TEMPERATURE. European grapes are hardy in zones 7 to 10. Most cultivars need 100 to 500 hours of winter chilling below 45°F. These plants prefer the warm, dry summers of Mediterranean climates and can tolerate 150 days annually above 86°F. Some cultivars fruit well with only 60 days per year above 86°F.

American grapes are hardy in zones 3 to 7. Winter chilling requirement is 1,000 to 1,400 hours below 45°F for most cultivars. These plants prefer warm, humid summers, taking up to 150 days per year above 86°F. Some cultivars fruit well with only 7 days per year above 86°F.

French hybrids are hardy in zones 5 to 9. Winter chilling requirement is 500 to 600 hours below 45°F. Heat tolerance varies by cultivar.

Muscadine grapes grow beautifully in zones 7 to 10. Winter chilling requirement is 200 to 600 hours below 45°F for most cultivars. These grapes grow best in regions with high heat and humidity, taking as many as 210 days above 86°F annually. Some cultivars fruit well with only 60 days per year above 86°F.

SOIL, LIGHT, AND WATER. All fruit needs healthy, biologically active soil, full sun, and regular water. Review the Introduction for guidance on how to provide these three essential elements.

GARDEN USES. Grape vines of all types are highly attractive plants in every season. The shaggy trunks twist and turn and develop great character with age. The foliage itself is quite handsome. Some cultivars turn beautiful shades of red, orange, and yellow in fall. Give vines a pergola, arbor, fence, or other structure to climb. Otherwise, given the opportunity they'll latch onto the nearest tree and happily climb to the top, whether the tree likes it or not.

POLLINATION. All grapes, other than certain muscadine cultivars, are self-fertile. If you acquire a muscadine, check the label to see if the cultivar you've chosen requires a different cultivar for successful pollination. See the Introduction for an overview of pollination and its terminology.

PRUNING. Grape vines need to be pruned every year in late winter for best fruit production. Have a look at "Prune Properly" (page 264) for tips on pruning vines.

PROBLEM-SOLVING. Sad to say, grapes can face many hardships, but following the guidelines in this plant portrait, reviewing the Introduction, and reading the recommendations in "Change the Growing Conditions" (page 247) will help you head off trouble before it starts. See the Grape Problem-Solving Guide, page 148, for specific information on pests and diseases.

Grapefruit

Citrus Problem-Solving Guide, page 130

DESCRIPTION. Like all other citrus trees in cultivation, grapefruit trees are evergreens from warm, subtropical climates. The trees grow to 20 feet tall and wide and, when in bloom, the delightful orange-blossom fragrance of their flowers will permeate your yard.

The plant we know as grapefruit, *Citrus paradisi*, is a natural hybrid between the sweet orange (*C. sinensis*) and the pummelo (*C. maxima*). The plant, thought to have originated in Jamaica, was first documented on Barbados in 1750 and was brought to Florida in 1823, as "shaddock"; how it got the name "grapefruit" is something of a mystery. Some believe it's because the large, round fruit hangs on the tree in clusters, like grapes. Others point out that the size and shape of the fruit strongly resemble grapeshot, or cannonballs. Crews of 19th-century sailing ships stacked grapeshot on deck in clusters, again, like grapes.

The parents of the grapefruit contributed some of their best qualities to their offspring. The familiar and ubiquitous orange is juicy and the perfect size for eating fresh. The pummelo is dry, and very large, like a small volleyball. We had a pummelo tree in Hawaii, and we grew to love the fruit in tossed green salads. The grapefruit evidently got its juiciness from the orange and its size from the pummelo. Sugar content, acidity, and bitterness, all components of fruit flavor, are strongly influenced by climate. Grapefruit is sweetest and most flavorful when grown in hot, arid regions. Red grapefruits, which contain lycopene, develop their most intense coloration in the dry heat of desert regions. Grapefruit cultivars that have seeds taste better and are sweeter than seedless varieties.

As with other citrus trees, growth slows in winter and then speeds up when the weather turns warm again in spring. Trees flower in flushes, profusely in spring and again in the fall, but they can flower sporadically all year, as long as temperatures are warm. Fruits ripen on the tree; they can hang there for many weeks without significantly deteriorating in quality.

TEMPERATURE. Grapefruit trees produce better-tasting, sweeter fruit in areas with warmer winters, particularly the frost-free areas of zone 11. They tolerate temperatures down to 24°F, as long as the weather turns cold gradually. Even temperatures of 28°F are cold enough to damage blossoms and fruit, especially during a sudden cold snap. Grapefruit needs a long, hot growing season to fully develop its natural sweetness and flavor, a minimum of 150 days above 86°F annually. Cooler temperatures result in bitter, strongly acid, sour fruit.

SOIL, LIGHT, AND WATER. All fruit needs healthy, biologically active soil, full sun, and regular water. Review the Introduction for guidance on how to provide these three essential elements. Grapefruits need well-drained soil in order to avoid foot, root, and crown rots. Keep mulch 1 foot away from the trunk to avoid these fungal diseases.

GARDEN USES. Grapefruits are handsome evergreens with beautiful leaves. If you have room in your garden, the crown of a grapefruit provides crucial structure and habitat for birds and other beneficial partners. Sedums, strawberries, and impatiens should grow nicely on your "forest" floor beneath grapefruit and other subtropical fruits like guava, passionfruit, and banana. Imitating a natural plant community in a polyculture garden is a rewarding way to keep your plants healthy.

Grapefruits are excellent container plants for a large pot or a half whiskey barrel. Wherever you live, even in colder climates, you can grow citrus outdoors in summer and move them indoors in winter. Because grapefruit requires much more heat than other citrus, you will seldom obtain edible fruit from container-grown grapefruits. Even so, the plants are attractive, the foliage is lovely, and the fragrance of their flowers is heavenly, all of which makes them desirable houseplants that can summer outdoors. Treat them as you would bonsai, trimming 1 inch off the roots each year, and repotting them in fresh potting soil (page 26).

POLLINATION. Grapefruit is self-fertile. See the Introduction for an overview of pollination and its terminology.

PRUNING. Prune for shape and to open the center to light and air. Other than that, grapefruit trees require only basic maintenance pruning. Have a look at "Prune Properly" (page 264) for tips.

PROBLEM-SOLVING. If your climate is hospitable, grapefruit is fairly easy to grow. Following the guidelines in this plant portrait, reviewing the Introduction, and reading the recommendations in "Change the Growing Conditions" (page 247) will help you keep your trees healthy. See the Citrus Problem-Solving Guide, page 130, for specific information on pests and diseases.

Guava

Guava Problem-Solving Guide, page 160

DESCRIPTION. Guava, *Psidium guajava*, is a single or multi-trunked evergreen tree to 20 feet tall and wide. The smooth trunk is attractively mottled with hues of greenish and light brown. Pineapple guava, *Acca sellowiana*, is a large, multi-trunked, thorny shrub or small tree, 10 to 15 feet tall and wide. It is crowned with dense evergreen foliage. Both species belong to the eucalyptus family, Myrtaceae.

Guava is native to tropical regions of Central and South America. It is grown commercially in Hawaii, Puerto Rico, and Florida. There are many named cultivars. Pineapple guava, also from South America, was formerly classified and is often still listed as *Feijoa sellowiana*; in fact, feijoa (fay-*joe*-ah) is another of its common names. There are a few named cultivars, but many plants offered at nurseries have been grown from seed.

Guavas have 1-inch-wide white flowers that appear on vigorous new growth of the current season, usually in spring, but flowering can occur whenever the plant is in active growth. The main crop of fruit matures in the summer with a smaller crop in the spring, but with judicious pruning you can have fruit nearly all year long.

The larger, showier flowers of the pineapple guava also appear in spring. Interestingly, its petals are edible and quite sweet; add them to salads for a textural and tasty treat. If you pull or cut petals off carefully, without damaging the remainder of the flower, you can still harvest fruit when it's ripe. Of course, for every whole flower you pick you won't get a fruit.

Guava fruit is a berry with many small brown seeds. Its shape is usually round but it can be ovoid to pear-shaped. Size ranges from one ounce to as much as three pounds, depending on the cultivar. The peel is green or yellow at maturity and varies in thickness. The flavor of mature fruits differs by cultivar and can be sweet, highly acid, or tart. The aroma of the fruit also varies by cultivar and may be mild and pleasant or strong and penetrating.

Pineapple guava fruit (pictured) is a tasty, strongly aromatic, kiwi-like berry, 1 to 3 inches long. The berries are smooth-skinned and gray-green. The fruit falls off the plant when it's ready to eat. You can pick it early and it will ripen indoors. Some people think the fruit tastes like guava while others detect a combination of pineapple and mint with a hint of strawberry. Ripe fruit is soft and bruises easily, which makes it difficult to ship; thus, it is rarely seen in markets.

TEMPERATURE. Guava is well adapted to warm subtropical and tropical climates, zones 9 to 11. Mature guava trees are killed below 25°F. Young guava trees are even more sensitive and will be killed at 28°F. This tropical plant has no chilling requirement. The ideal temperature range for optimum growth is 73 to 82°F. Temperatures below 60°F cause the plant to stop growing.

Pineapple guava, which grows at fairly high elevation in its native South American habitat, is hardy in zones 8 to 10. Winter chilling requirement is 50 hours below 45°F. It does well in hot climates, with 210 days or more per year above 86°F.

SOIL, LIGHT, AND WATER. All fruit needs healthy, biologically active soil, full sun, and regular water. Review the Introduction for guidance on how to provide these three essential elements. Guava is widely adapted to different soil types and a range of pH. Plants benefit from a good mulch but keep the mulch 1 foot away from the trunk. Pineapple guava prefers full sun but will tolerate partial shade. In desert areas it will need afternoon shade to protect it from intense sunlight.

GARDEN USES. Guava and pineapple guava are both handsome evergreens for home landscapes in those climates to which they are adapted. Grow them among citrus, hibiscus, passionfruit, and figs to gain the benefits of a polyculture garden. Even in cold-winter areas outside their range you can grow either of these plants in large pots, and bring them indoors to a sunny window in winter. As evergreens, they'll need sunlight all winter long. Guava is highly invasive and weedy, however, and should not be grown in South Florida where it can readily escape

cultivation. In our old neighborhood in Hawaii, it now grows wild in vacant lots.

POLLINATION. Guava is self-fertile, but you'll get better crops with cross-pollination between two different cultivars. Some pineapple guava cultivars are self-fertile, but most require cross-pollination. Pineapple guava flowers attract hummingbirds which do a good job of pollinating them. Both kinds of guava attract honeybees. See the Introduction for an overview of pollination and its terminology.

PRUNING. Both guava and pineapple guava should be pruned to an open vase. Continuously head back new growth of guava to induce branching and keep the tree about 6 feet tall. This will stimulate new growth which will then flower and set fruit. Pineapple guava is sometimes clipped into a hedge, but keeping it trimmed reduces the quantity of fruit you can expect. Have a look at "Prune Properly" (page 264) for tips.

PROBLEM-SOLVING. Following the guidelines in this plant portrait, reviewing the Introduction, and reading the recommendations in "Change the Growing Conditions" (page 247) will help you keep your guavas healthy. They are generally trouble-free but occasionally something goes awry. If it does, see the Guava Problem-Solving Guide, page 160, for specific information on pests and diseases.

Hazelnut

Nut Problem-Solving Guide, page 179

DESCRIPTION. Hazels are multi-trunked large shrubs or small trees 10 to 18 feet tall and wide. The plants are deciduous, and shed all their leaves soon after the nut crop matures. Hazels have male flowers borne in 2- to 5-inch-long, dangly catkins in late winter to very early spring. Golden catkins shedding their windborne pollen are one of the very first harbingers of spring. The inconspicuous female flowers are borne inside small leafy cups; only their red stigmas hang out to snag pollen as it drifts by.

The hazel fruit is a true nut: the ovary wall of the female flower matures into the hard shell of the structure we call a nut. The edible portion of the fruit is the seed inside the shell. Each nut forms inside an involucre, a cup formed by frilly, leafy bracts. When they're fully mature, in mid-autumn, the nuts fall to the ground.

All told there are about 15 species in the genus *Corylus*, native to Asia, Europe, and North America. All produce nuts. European hazel, *C. avellana*, native to Europe and western Asia, is the one most commonly cultivated for its large, tasty nuts. The nuts of this species have been harvested by humans for more than 9,000 years, a date confirmed by radiocarbon dating of a Mesolithic Scottish midden pit that was filled with charred hazelnut shells. It is a major nut crop in Oregon and Washington.

Corylus maxima from southeastern Europe and southwest Asia is secondary in importance to European hazel. This species is called filbert in Europe. Native American species include *C. americana*, the American hazel, which has smallish nuts, and *C. cornuta*, the beaked hazel. In the United States the words "hazelnut" and "filbert" are used interchangeably. Many hybrids between these various species of hazelnuts are cultivated for their delicious nuts.

TEMPERATURE. American hazel is hardy to zone 4. European hazel, the source of commercially grown hazelnuts, is hardy only to zone 5. Frequently they're both labeled either hazelnuts or filberts. Find out which species you're looking at before purchasing.

European hazel flowers are damaged at temperatures below -15°F, making them more sensitive to cold than the tree itself. Accordingly, the nut crop is less at risk when grown where the average winter temperature does not go below -10°F. European hazelnuts grow well in zones 6 to 10. Cultivars have a winter chilling requirement of 300 to 1,500 hours below 45°F. Where winters are warm, in zones 11 and 12, it rarely gets cold enough for them to prosper, and you'll have to select low-chill cultivars. European hazels prefer less than 150 days above 86°F per year.

SOIL, LIGHT, AND WATER. All fruit needs healthy, biologically active soil, full sun, and regular water. Review the Introduction for guidance on how to provide these three essential elements. Hazels prefer deep, well-drained soil.

GARDEN USES. Hazels have attractive foliage, and pleasing, but not extraordinary yellow fall color. Their intricate branching patterns give the garden winter interest. Hazels come into their glory as ornamentals in February, when golden catkins of male flowers cover the plants. The dangling catkins shimmy like tinsel in the breeze, and glow in the sunlight. It takes your breath away to chance upon the native hazels lighting up the dark forests of the Pacific Northwest after a long, dreary, wet winter.

Hazels attract friendly wildlife into the garden. Squirrels and jays, especially, love this nut, but keep watch; they may take more than their fair share. A few winters ago we watched through the window as two Steller's jays harvested every single nut from the beaked hazel in the backyard. Each bird carefully picked a nut, flew to the ground, and buried it beneath the duff. After an hour or so, all the nuts had been harvested and stored away for winter.

POLLINATION. Hazelnut trees are monoecious and most cultivars are self-incompatible. You'll need two different cultivars for adequate pollination. Catalogs describe hazelnut cultivars either as producers or pollinators. Both types produce nuts, but producers yield more nuts than pollinators. See the Introduction for an overview of pollination and its terminology.

PRUNING. The natural habit of hazels is a large multi-trunked shrub. If you want your hazel to be a tree rather than a shrub, prune away lower branches to develop a single trunk and prune it to a central leader. Have a look at "Prune Properly" (page 264) for more tips.

PROBLEM-SOLVING. If you live in the right climate, hazels are easy to grow. Your biggest problem may well be sharing the nuts with wildlife. Following the guidelines in this plant portrait, reviewing the Introduction, and reading the recommendations in "Change the Growing Conditions" (page 247) will help you keep your trees healthy. If you run into trouble, be sure to check the Nut Problem-Solving Guide, page 179, for specific information on pests and diseases.

Kiwi

Kiwi Problem-Solving Guide, page 163

DESCRIPTION. All kiwis are large, woody vines to 30 feet tall. Their stems coil around any support they can find, from those you provide to trees, sheds, and clotheslines. Male vines have only male flowers that produce pollen, but bear no fruits. Female vines have only female flowers that produce fruits, but no pollen. You must have both a female and a male of the same species to get fruit.

There are four species from which to choose, depending on your climate. The stems of fuzzy kiwi, *Actinidia deliciosa*, sometimes called Chinese gooseberry, are covered with velvety, red hairs. You will frequently see these fruits in grocery stores. They're the chicken-egg-sized berries with fuzzy brown skin and lime-green flesh. Fruit of the golden kiwi, *A. chinensis*, is very similar, except the brown fuzz is shorter and finer, and the flesh has a yellowish tint. Hardy kiwi, *A. arguta*, has green, smooth-skinned fruit the size of a grape. Pop the whole berry in your mouth, and taste a burst of sweet flavor. Super-hardy kiwi, *A. kolomikta*, also has grape-sized, hairless green fruit. All four species have only recently become popular outside their native range in China and eastern Asia. Only since about 1960 have any been commonly available to U.S. gardeners.

Kiwis flower in summer on new shoots growing from one-year-old stems. The fruit ripens in late summer into autumn depending on species and cultivar. The earliest fruits to ripen are those of the golden kiwi, followed by the super-hardy kiwi, the hardy kiwi, and finally, the fuzzy kiwi. Each species has more than one variety in cultivation, and each of those varies somewhat in flowering and fruiting time.

TEMPERATURE. Fuzzy kiwi is hardy in zones 6 to 9. It tolerates temperatures down to 0°F, as long as the weather turns cold gradually. Temperatures that bounce back and forth from very cold to warm will kill the plant. Winter chilling requirement is 800 hours below 45°F, but low-chill cultivars needing only 300 hours are available. It prefers climates with 45 to 150 days above 86°F annually.

Golden kiwi is hardy in zones 8 to 10. Winter chilling requirement is 700 hours below 45°F. It prefers 90 to 180 days per year above 86°F.

Hardy kiwi is hardy in zones 4 to 9. Its winter chilling requirement is unknown, but plants seem to produce well in both low- and high-chill climates. It prefers less than 150 days per year above 86°F.

Super-hardy kiwi does well in zones 3 to 6. Its winter chilling requirement has not been established. It prefers less than 90 days per year above 86°F.

SOIL, LIGHT, AND WATER. All fruit needs healthy, biologically active soil, full sun, and regular water. Review the Introduction for guidance on how to provide these three essential elements. Make sure kiwi vines have good drainage, because they're quite susceptible to crown rot.

GARDEN USES. Kiwi vines are handsome ornamental additions to any garden. We've grown fuzzy kiwi in Hawaii and hardy kiwi in the Pacific Northwest, and relished them both. Most are very large, rampant growers that need a strong support to climb on. It can take as long as five years after planting for a kiwi vine to flower. In that time vines can succumb to winter cold, be gnawed to the ground by your cat, or grow so rampantly that you can't tell which vine is which. Many gardeners, after waiting patiently for years, have completely lost track of which vines are female and which ones are male. Sometimes the female has died, and the grower is disappointed that there's no fruit. Careful pruning and observation will mitigate this problem.

POLLINATION. Kiwi vines are dioecious. You need a female and a male plant of the same species. Because of this, many gardeners end up asking themselves, "Is my vine a boy or a girl?" Here's how to tell. In female flowers, the ovary and its stigmas are clearly visible in the center of the flower, as seen in the portrait photo. The ovary, a fuzzy, white, round structure, is crowned by white tentacles, the stigmas, and is surrounded by stamens that are nonfunctional. Male flowers, on a separate vine, have a powder puff spray of golden yellow stamens; they are fully functional and produce abundant pollen, but they have no ovary. You need only one male vine to pollinate as many as eight female vines. See the Introduction for an overview of pollination and its terminology.

PRUNING. Prune every year, in late winter, for best fruit production. Prune again in summer to control vigorous growth. Have a look at "Prune Properly" (page 264) for tips on pruning vines.

PROBLEM-SOLVING. Aside from crown rot, birds' taste for the fruit may well be the biggest trouble you face with kiwis. By following the guidelines in this plant portrait, reviewing the Introduction, and reading the recommendations in "Change the Growing Conditions" (page 247) you should be able to keep your kiwis healthy. See the Kiwi Problem-Solving Guide, page 163, for specific information on pests and diseases.

Lemon

Citrus Problem-Solving Guide, page 130

DESCRIPTION. Lemon trees grow 10 to 20 feet tall and wide, depending on the cultivar. Some varieties have wickedly sharp, stout thorns. Others are thornless. Lemons are subtropical, evergreen, woody plants that never really go dormant.

The lemon, *Citrus limon*, is probably a natural hybrid between pummelo (*C. maxima*) and citron (*C. medica*), but no one really knows, because most citrus trees in cultivation are ancient hybrids. *Citrus* species hybridize freely in the wild within their native ranges in Southeast Asia and adjacent areas of China and India. Accidental hybrids, discovered in the wild thousands of years ago, have been nurtured by humans and carried all over the world.

Botanically, lemon fruits, like all citrus, are a special kind of berry called a hesperidium; they have a thick, soft rind and a juicy interior divided into 10 or more segments. The rind of the fruit contains aromatic oils that give it its characteristic fresh, zesty bouquet. Bright yellow, and shaped rather like a fat football, the fruit is slightly tapered at both ends. Each is about 3 inches long and 2 inches wide, but size and shape varies by cultivar.

Many cultivars have a nipple-like protuberance on the blossom end of the fruit. Some are seedless; but others have seeds. The Meyer types (lemon × sweet orange hybrids) are smaller and rounder, with a deep yellow, orange-toned hue. They are also much softer, making them more difficult to ship, which explains why they are more expensive than regular lemons. An excellent reason to grow your own.

Lemon flowers are mildly fragrant, less so than other citrus, but still have that wonderful, sensuous orange-blossom scent. Star-shaped flowers, up to 1½ inches wide, are borne in small clusters at the ends of twigs. Flowers are white, but flower buds are often purple on the outside.

TEMPERATURE. Lemons thrive in zones 9b through 11. In zones 10 and 11, trees will grow, flower, and fruit all year long. When it gets cold they just slow down rather than going fully dormant. Trees tolerate temperatures down to 27°F, as long as the weather turns cold gradually. Sudden cold snaps damage them. Slightly higher temperatures, up to 31°F, are still cold enough to damage blossoms and fruit. Because their fruit is not sugary sweet, lemons do not require heat to produce high-quality fruit. They grow and fruit well in both cool- and warm-summer climates.

SOIL, LIGHT, AND WATER. All fruit needs healthy, biologically active soil, full sun, and regular water. Review the Introduction for guidance on how to provide these three essential elements. Lemon trees suffer from foot, root, and crown rots in wet, poorly drained soils. Make sure they have good drainage and keep mulch 1 foot away from the trunk.

GARDEN USES. Lemons are lovely trees to have in your fruit garden. As the folk song says, "Lemon tree very pretty, and the lemon flower is sweet/but the fruit of the poor lemon is impossible to eat." Not. The scent of the large lemon tree that once graced our yard in Southern California wafted through the windows on warm evenings. Friends and relatives clamored for the delicious fruit. One spring a friend from New Mexico visited. He happily stripped the tree of every fruit, juiced them, made lemon curd, lemonade, and lemon meringue pie, and had gin and tonics with a twist of lemon ready when we arrived home from work. What a houseguest. By fall we had another bumper crop.

Lemons are excellent container plants for a large pot or a half whiskey barrel. Make sure the pot has good drainage and never let the container sit in a saucer of water. The roots will rot if the potting soil is too wet for too long. Wherever you live, even in colder climates, you can easily grow citrus outdoors in summer and move them indoors to a sunny window in winter. Our 'Improved Meyer' lemon is perfectly happy in its pot and produces fruit for us every year. Because lemon requires very little heat compared to other citrus, you will easily obtain edible fruit from container-grown lemons. Besides, the plants are handsome, the foliage adds a tropical note, and the fragrance of their flowers is heavenly, all of which makes them desirable houseplants that can summer outdoors.

POLLINATION. All lemons are self-fertile. See the Introduction for an overview of pollination and its terminology.

PRUNING. Prune for shape and to open the center to light and air. Beyond that, lemon trees require only basic maintenance pruning. Have a look at "Prune Properly" (page 264) for tips.

PROBLEM-SOLVING. All the lemons we've grown in Hawaii, California, Mallorca, and in the Pacific Northwest have been nearly trouble-free. The most frequent problem we've encountered is scale insects. Follow the guidelines in this plant portrait, review the Introduction, and read the recommendations in "Change the Growing Conditions" (page 247) to keep your trees just as healthy. See the Citrus Problem-Solving Guide, page 130, for specific information on pests and diseases.

Lime

Citrus Problem-Solving Guide, page 130

DESCRIPTION. Lime, *Citrus aurantiifolia*, is a shrubby, small tree to about 16 feet tall and wide, with many stout thorns. It is usually multi-trunked, with numerous branches sprouting from the base of the plant. The trunks never grow straight; they zig-zag. It's a very attractive plant, with leaves that resemble those of the sour orange, *C. aurantium* (thus *aurantiifolia*, "foliage like an orange").

Bartenders commonly use 'Mexican Lime', aka Key lime or West Indian lime, for margaritas and other drinks. 'Bearss Lime' is a type of Persian lime, aka Tahitian lime; these are seedless, thornless, and have a mild flavor.

The lime, a natural hybrid like most cultivated citrus species, originated in Southeast Asia or India so long ago that its putative parents cannot be determined with certainty. It is mentioned in a 2,000-year-old Indian medical work. Lime trees evidently made their way through the Arabic world but are not mentioned in Western literature until 1677.

Citrus species intercross quite readily, and the resulting hybrids maintain their distinctive characteristics by producing seedlings that are clones, which is to say exact duplicates of the mother plant. You can grow your own lime trees from seeds of this plant, and most of the seedlings will come true to type.

Limes flower and fruit all year long. Flowering is most abundant from May to September, but will continue sporadically all winter long. The white flowers, purplish in bud, are about 1 inch across and richly fragrant with the alluring scent of orange blossoms. Lime fruits are round or ovoid and 1 to 2 inches in diameter. They are usually picked while green, but when fully mature they are yellow. Even when fully mature the fruit is not sweet. It is very tart, with high acidity and a strong, distinctively "limey" aroma. The rind of the fruit is also aromatic, and thin, with a strong, pleasant flavor. The delicious Key lime pie is made from this fruit.

TEMPERATURE. Limes grow beautifully in zone 11 and higher. They do not like cold weather. The trees will tolerate low temperatures down to 28°F, as long as the weather turns cold gradually. Slightly higher temperatures, up to 32°F, are still cold enough to damage blossoms and fruit. Limes prefer at least 150 days above 86°F annually. Cultivars differ somewhat in their temperature needs.

SOIL, LIGHT, AND WATER. All fruit needs healthy, biologically active soil, full sun, and regular water. Review the Introduction for guidance on how to provide these three essential elements. Limes suffer from foot, root, and crown rots in wet, poorly drained soils. Make sure they have good drainage to avoid this problem, and keep mulch 1 foot away from the trunk of the tree.

GARDEN USES. Limes are handsome plants with beautiful evergreen foliage; remember that they are thorny and need to be sited in the home landscape with care to avoid snagging passersby. In the polyculture garden, plant limes with bananas, guavas, and avocados. Use melons, basil, and tarragon on the ground level. Attract beneficial insects with cosmos, Queen Anne's lace, and catmint.

Lime trees, especially those grafted onto dwarfing rootstocks, are excellent container subjects for a large pot or a half whiskey barrel. Just make sure your pot has good drainage, and never let your pot sit in a saucer of water. The roots will rot if the potting soil is too wet for too long. Wherever you live, even in colder climates, you can easily grow your potted lime tree outdoors in summer and move it indoors to a sunny window in winter. Be sure to give it as much sunlight as possible. Because limes require very little heat to mature their fruit compared to other citrus, you will easily obtain edible fruit from container-grown limes. Besides, the plants are handsome, the foliage adds a tropical note, and the fragrance of their flowers is heavenly, all of which makes them desirable houseplants that can summer outdoors.

POLLINATION. All limes are self-fertile. See the Introduction for an overview of pollination and its terminology.

PRUNING. Prune for shape and to open the center to light and air. Other than that, lime trees need only basic maintenance pruning. Have a look at "Prune Properly" (page 264) for tips.

PROBLEM-SOLVING. Insects, such as scale and aphids, will likely be your biggest concern when growing limes, but following the guidelines in this plant portrait, reviewing the Introduction, and reading the recommendations in "Change the Growing Conditions" (page 247) will help you keep your trees healthy. See the Citrus Problem-Solving Guide, page 130, for specific information on pests and diseases.

Loquat

Pome Fruit Problem-Solving Guide, page 198

DESCRIPTION. Loquat, *Eriobotrya japonica*, is a shrubby evergreen tree from 15 to 30 feet tall and wide. It branches freely low on the trunk, becoming multi-trunked with age. The plant is extremely attractive with leathery, tropical-looking foliage. The leaves are as much as 1 foot long and 4 inches wide, deep green, shiny on the upper surface and woolly white to rust-colored on the undersides. New growth is woolly, and the delicious fruits are also fuzzy.

The loquat has been cultivated in its native southeastern China from ancient times. It was introduced to Japan, and has been grown there for at least 1,000 years. People carried it from Asia to the rest of the world, where it has escaped cultivation and naturalized in the Mediterranean, the Middle East, and many other areas. It is grown for fruit production in India, Israel, Australia, New Zealand, South Africa, and Brazil. In the United States it is commonly grown in Florida, California, and Hawaii.

Loquat trees are unusual in that they begin to flower in autumn or early winter. The flowers are about 3/4 inch in diameter, five-petaled, white, fragrant, and borne in clusters of 30 to 100 on woolly white or rust-colored stems.

The fruit ripens three months after flowering, in late winter or early spring, at a time when most other fruit plants are only just beginning to flower. The fruit is 1 to 2 inches long, about the same size as a small apricot, and round to pear-shaped. It is a thin-fleshed pome, like an apple or pear, and is borne in clusters of four to 30 fruits. The fruit is yellow to apricot-colored when fully ripe. The succulent flesh is white, yellow, or orange. You will find three to five large, shiny, brown seeds inside each fruit. The fruit is soft, bruises easily, and does not ship well, so it's seldom seen in markets. But the taste is superb, a delicious, refreshing combination of tartness and sweetness, and the tree is well worth growing in the home garden.

TEMPERATURE. Loquat trees survive winter freezes down to 15°F. But their flowers and fruit are damaged at 28°F. Grow them for fruit production in the warm-winter climates of zone 10 and higher. You can grow them as ornamental plants to zone 8b, but don't expect any fruit. As subtropical to warm-temperate plants, loquats have no chilling requirement and prefer a minimum of 90 days per year above 86°F.

SOIL, LIGHT, AND WATER. All fruit needs healthy, biologically active soil, full sun, and regular water. Review the Introduction for guidance on how to provide these three essential elements. Loquat tolerates a wide range of different soil types, but good drainage is essential.

GARDEN USES. This very beautiful tree richly deserves a place in any home landscape where the climate is suitable. It is highly valued and widely planted as an ornamental. To grow it for its wonderful fruit, choose a cultivar developed for that purpose. Loquats grow very nicely with bananas, citrus, avocados, and birds of paradise. Attract pollinators and beneficial predators with Queen Emma and ginger lilies, marigolds, and red hot pokers.

Plants are shallow-rooted and readily adapt to container culture in a large, wide pot like a half whiskey barrel. Dwarf cultivars are the preferred choice for this purpose. Placed on your deck or patio, a potted loquat is a beautiful addition to your landscape. Just be sure you bring it indoors to a sunny window if you live in a cold-winter climate.

POLLINATION. Most loquat cultivars are at least partially self-fertile. Some are self-incompatible. Regardless, you'll get bigger and better crops of fruit if you have two different cultivars. Honeybees love the flowers and do a great job of pollinating the plants for you. See the Introduction for an overview of pollination and its terminology.

PRUNING. Keep the center open to light and air. Beyond that, loquats require only basic maintenance pruning. Have a look at "Prune Properly" (page 264) for tips.

PROBLEM-SOLVING. Loquats are low maintenance and nearly trouble-free, which is why they are common street trees throughout Southern California. Following the guidelines in this plant portrait, reviewing the Introduction, and reading the recommendations in "Change the Growing Conditions" (page 247) will help you keep your trees healthy. See the Pome Fruit Problem-Solving Guide, page 198, for specific information on pests and diseases of loquats and their relatives.

Mandarin

Citrus Problem-Solving Guide, page 130

DESCRIPTION. Mandarins are smallish trees, 10 to 20 feet tall and wide. As a group they vary tremendously, so the mature size of a tree differs within that range from one cultivar to the next. All have attractive, dense, deep green foliage, with leaf size and shape varying by cultivar. Most do not have thorns, but some are thorny. Our mandarin trees in Hawaii had been planted by a previous owner and we never knew which cultivar we had. The trees were stunted, but gave us delectable fruit. What a joy it was to walk out into the garden first thing in the morning and harvest a handful of ripe, fragrant, delicious mandarins for breakfast.

The common mandarin, *Citrus reticulata*, probably originated in northwestern India and southwestern China; humans have cultivated it for at least 3,000 years. Varieties of the species include seedless satsumas, seedy clementines, and tangerines, those with an orange-red peel. Hybrids include tangors, *C. nobilis* (mandarin × sweet orange), and tangelos, *C. ×tangelo* (mandarin × grapefruit). All mandarins share some wonderful features. The juicy flesh of the fruit is only loosely attached to the peel, and separates easily into 10 sections. These attributes make the fruit easy to peel and eat.

Mandarins flower in spring, sporting white, five-petal blossoms, about 1 inch wide, and wonderfully fragrant. Bees work the flowers for pollen to feed their offspring, and for nectar to make honey, efficiently moving pollen from one flower to another, and bestowing effective pollination.

Mandarin fruits look like small, flat oranges and are 2 to 3 inches in diameter. The fruit tastes sweet and tart and has a distinctive, easily recognized flavor and aroma. Most do not store well on the tree and need to be harvested when they are mature. Left on the tree too long they become puffy and dry. Some cultivars, however, will keep their fruit hanging on the tree in good condition much longer than others. Fruits mature in fall and winter in a subtropical climate. It takes longer for fruit to mature where the climate is cooler. Many varieties mature at Christmastime and are sometimes called Christmas oranges. Pay close attention to catalog descriptions and plant labels to find cultivars that suit your needs.

TEMPERATURE. Mandarin trees tolerate low temperatures down to 23°F, as long as the weather turns cold gradually. Slightly higher temperatures, up to 27°F, are still cold enough to damage blossoms and fruit. Mandarins perform better in zone 10 and higher, especially in the frost-free areas of zone 11. Mandarins also need a long, warm growing season to fully develop their sweetness and rich flavor, at least 90 days per year above 86°F. Commercial cultivars in Florida also seem to love the humidity. Maybe that's why ours did so well on Maui.

SOIL, LIGHT, AND WATER. All fruit needs healthy, biologically active soil, full sun, and regular water. Review the Introduction for guidance on how to provide these three essential elements. Mandarins, like all citrus, are susceptible to foot, root, and crown rots in waterlogged soil, which can kill the tree, so be certain that drainage is good and keep mulch 1 foot away from the trunk.

GARDEN USES. Mandarin flower scent is heady, and the orange-colored fruits against the deep evergreen background of foliage beautiful, giving these trees all-season interest. If your cultivar happens to be a thorny one you'll need to put it in a location where it won't harm passersby. The polyculture garden benefits from the presence of these trees because they attract pollinators and other beneficial partners from the wild.

Mandarins are excellent container subjects. Dwarf plants grafted to dwarfing rootstocks are perhaps best for this purpose. Put them in a large pot or a half whiskey barrel. Plant them in a good-quality potting soil with excellent drainage and never let the pot sit in a saucer of water. The roots will rot if they are waterlogged and deprived of oxygen for too long. Wherever you live, you can grow your potted mandarin tree outdoors in summer, and then bring it indoors to a sunny window for the winter. A sunny window is essential. The plant requires full sun and warmth all year in order for the fruit to be sweet.

POLLINATION. Plant labels or catalog descriptions should tell you whether the cultivar you are considering is self-fertile or self-incompatible. Mandarins can be either. See the Introduction for an overview of pollination and its terminology.

PRUNING. Prune for shape and to open the center to light and air. Beyond that, mandarins require only basic maintenance pruning. Have a look at "Prune Properly" (page 264) for tips.

PROBLEM-SOLVING. Following the guidelines in this plant portrait, reviewing the Introduction, and reading the recommendations in "Change the Growing Conditions" (page 247) will help you keep your mandarin trees healthy. See the Citrus Problem-Solving Guide, page 130, for specific information on pests and diseases.

Melon

Melon Problem-Solving Guide, page 167

DESCRIPTION. Cantaloupe, muskmelon, honeydew, casaba, crenshaw, Persian—all belong to one species, *Cucumis melo*. Watermelon, *Citrullus lanatus*, is a different plant altogether, and has its own plant portrait. Melon plants are frost-sensitive annual vines that climb by means of tendrils. They have rounded, lobed, hairy leaves. Vines grow about 2 feet high and sprawl over 30 to 40 square feet. They can climb up a 6-foot-tall A-frame or trellis, or crawl across the ground. Compact "bush" types, about 2 feet high and 3 to 4 feet across, work well in containers.

The melon is native to sub-Saharan Africa through the Middle East to Afghanistan. It was probably domesticated in Asia, and we know it has been an important crop in China for at least 2,000 years. People in the Mediterranean region began to cultivate it near the end of the Roman era. Today it is grown worldwide; major commercial producers include China, France, India, Spain, Turkey, and the United States.

There are many cultivars. All have fruit that is a large, round or oblong berry with juicy, sweet flesh. The muskmelons, with their characteristic musky aroma, have a network of pale, raised, corky ridges covering the surface of the fruit. Honeydews and other winter melons have smooth, whitish to greenish skins; these typically have green flesh. A third group, the cantaloupes, have scaly skin, but lack the network of veins covering the fruit. They usually have orange flesh.

Melons need a long, warm growing season with plenty of heat to develop maximum sweetness. When the fruits reach baseball size, put two bricks or stones, side by side, beside the fruit and place the young fruit on top. The stones absorb heat during the day and keep the fruit warm at night. In addition, they keep the fruit up off the soil, helping to avoid soilborne diseases. You can also suspend fruits in net slings or old nylon stockings, and hang them from a support structure to keep them off the ground.

Many gardeners prefer to plant melons on a little hill or mound about 1 foot across. Poke a hole in the soil with your finger or a stick, and put two or three seeds in the hole. Make only one planting hole, about 1 inch deep, per hill or container. Seeds should germinate in four to seven days. Thin to one robust seedling per planting hole.

TEMPERATURE. Melons are killed by frost. Seeds that are planted in soil that is too cool generally fail to germinate and rot. Make sure you plant in spring after all danger of frost is past and the soil has warmed up. Melons thrive where summer daytime high temperatures average 65 to 75°F and the soil temperature is at least 60°F. They seem to do well no matter how hot it gets, but give them some dappled shade, if afternoons are over 98°F and sunny.

Pay attention to the days to maturity for the cultivars you're considering to be certain your growing season is long enough for fruits to mature before the first frost of autumn.

SOIL, LIGHT, AND WATER. All fruit needs healthy, biologically active soil, full sun, and regular water. Review the Introduction for guidance on how to provide these three essential elements. In addition, feed melons well with a complete balanced organic fertilizer and compost at the beginning of each growing season. Feed them additional organic fertilizer once during the growing season; gently rake the nutrients into the soil around the plants. Control weeds, conserve moisture, and protect fruit lying on the ground by mulching to a depth of 3 inches after the plants are growing well. Maintain soil pH between 6.0 and 6.5. Increase the amount of water to as much as 2 inches a week when the vines support a heavy fruit crop. Make sure your planting site is well drained. Plant your melons in raised beds or large containers if your drainage is poor or the water table is high.

GARDEN USES. Melons are generally grown sprawling across the ground but smaller-fruited varieties can be grown on a support. Be sure to prepare the structure they're going to climb before you plant the seeds. You can use sturdy stakes, tripods of bamboo, or tree limbs arranged in a teepee fashion; or you can grow them on a net, chain-link fence, A-frame, or trellis. Space them well apart from each other and interplant flowers that attract beneficial insects to help combat pests. Good companions for melons include corn and beans.

To grow melons in a container, select a compact or bush-type variety and start with either a five-gallon pot or a half whiskey barrel. Make sure there is a drainage hole. Inside the pot place a small square of window screen over the hole. Then fill the pot with potting soil, not garden soil.

POLLINATION. Melons are monoecious. The first flowers produced in early summer will always be male and cannot produce fruit. Be patient and as the plant gets a little older it will make female flowers and produce a generous crop of fruit after the bees have done their job. See the Introduction for an overview of pollination and its terminology.

PRUNING. Melons do not need to be pruned.

PROBLEM-SOLVING. Following the guidelines in this plant portrait, reviewing the Introduction, and reading the recommendations in "Change the Growing Conditions" (page 247) will help you keep your melons healthy. Be on the lookout for powdery mildew, the most common problem. See the Melon Problem-Solving Guide, page 167, for specific information on pests and diseases.

Mulberry

Mulberry Problem-Solving Guide, page 175

DESCRIPTION. All three species of mulberries are deciduous trees with milky sap, like their relatives the figs. Black mulberry, *Morus nigra*, is 15 to 30 feet tall and wide. Red mulberry (*M. rubra*) and white mulberry (*M. alba*) can both grow to 50 feet tall and wide. Leaf shape varies widely on the same plant. Some leaves are lobed and some are not. Yellow fall foliage can be very bright or rather pale.

Black mulberry has been in cultivation for thousands of years. Its precise origin is lost in time, but it's probably native to southwestern Asia, where it is still grown for its delicious fruits. Red mulberry, a relative newcomer to cultivation, is native to the eastern United States. White mulberry hails from China where it has long been in cultivation, not for the berries, but for silk. Silkworms feed exclusively on the leaves of white mulberry. When they spin their cocoons, humans carefully unwind the threads of silk and spin it into thread.

The petal-less flowers of all three mulberries are borne in small unisexual catkins. Picture a fuzzless pussy willow and you've got the idea. The plant can be in full flower in the spring and you might never notice it. Fruit ripens in summer, and looks a lot like blackberries. Another fruit we call a berry, but isn't, a mulberry fruit is, botanically, a syncarp because it's composed of a collection of tiny individual fruits aggregated into a single unit. You'd think that black mulberry fruits would be black, red mulberry fruits red, and white mulberry fruits white. And sometimes you'd be right. White mulberry fruits are often white, but also pink or dark purple. Black mulberry fruits are dark red to purple-black, but sometimes white. Red mulberry fruits are red or black.

TEMPERATURE. Black mulberry is hardy in zones 7 to 10. It does especially well in summer-dry, winter-wet Mediterranean climates like the Mediterranean itself, the Pacific coasts of North and South America, South Africa, and Australia. Chilling requirement is 400 to 450 hours below 45°F. It prefers less than 150 days per year above 86°F.

Red and white mulberry and their hybrids are hardy in zones 5 to 8. Chilling requirement is the same as for black mulberry, 400 to 450 hours below 45°F. They tolerate somewhat cooler summer temperatures than black mulberry.

SOIL, LIGHT, AND WATER. All fruit needs healthy, biologically active soil, full sun, and regular water. Review the Introduction for guidance on how to provide these three essential elements.

GARDEN USES. Mulberries are valuable ornamental trees, often grown as shade trees rather than for fruit. As a shade tree, many people prefer to plant a male tree, because it gives no fruit, which can stain sidewalks or clothing, or carpets when tracked into the house. Black mulberry sets the standard for delectable flavor by which all other mulberries are judged. Its fruit has a combination of sweetness and tartness mixed with intense flavor that explodes on the tongue. Other mulberries may be less flavorful or merely sweet but not tart, so it pays to search out specific cultivars known to have excellent tasting fruit. White mulberry has gone wild in many parts of the United States and can be an invasive weed.

Mulberries can be grown in tubs or large pots. Dwarf cultivars are excellent for this purpose. Growing in containers allows you to consider having a black mulberry in a colder winter climate than it prefers. Just remember to bring it indoors to a sheltered garage or basement for the winter. Because it's deciduous it won't need light over the winter.

POLLINATION. Mulberries are wind-pollinated, and red mulberry hybridizes freely with white mulberry. An individual tree might be dioecious, monoecious, or even parthenocarpic, which means it can set fruit without pollination. Read labels and catalog descriptions to find out which type of tree you're considering, and whether you will need two trees to get fruit. See the Introduction for an overview of pollination and its terminology.

PRUNING. Train mulberries to an open vase. Other than that, they'll require only basic maintenance pruning. Have a look at "Prune Properly" (page 264) for tips.

PROBLEM-SOLVING. Following the guidelines in this plant portrait, reviewing the Introduction, and reading the recommendations in "Change the Growing Conditions" (page 247) will help you keep your mulberry trees healthy. See the Mulberry Problem-Solving Guide, page 175, for specific information on pests and diseases.

Olive

Olive Problem-Solving Guide, page 188

DESCRIPTION. Olives, *Olea europaea*, are long-lived, small trees to 25 to 30 feet high with willow-like evergreen leaves. The simple, opposite, 2- to 4-inch-long leaves are gray-green on the upper surface and silvery gray on the lower surface. The overall effect is a fine-textured, soft, neutral gray that blends very well with other colors in the landscape. As youngsters the trees grow fairly fast, but as they age, they grow slowly and become twisted and picturesque.

Native to the Mediterranean, the olive tree has been in cultivation since the dawn of western civilization by the peoples of the region, from the Assyrians and Egyptians to the ancient Greeks. It was cultivated on the island of Crete at least 5,500 years ago. Today, all the great Mediterranean climates of the world, from the Mediterranean itself to California, Australia, South Africa, and Chile, sport extensive olive groves. Basically, olives thrive wherever wine grapes and citrus trees flourish, and the cultivation of this tree has become a massive industry. Cultivars, developed either for oil or eating, number in the thousands.

Olive trees bloom in the spring in the axils of leaves on last year's branches. Flowers are small, whitish, and borne in loose clusters. Some are perfect, which means they have both male and female sex parts. Other flowers are male only. Breeders have developed male cultivars to be fruitless, or nearly so. Male trees have landscape value wherever ripe, falling fruit is unwanted because it stains pavement and might harm lawns.

Olives are, botanically, drupes like a peach or plum, with a stony pit that contains the seed. The fruits are smooth and green and gradually turn black as they ripen. Green table olives are harvested in early fall, before they ripen. Black table olives and oil cultivars are harvested in late fall or early winter, after they ripen. Green fruits contain a very bitter compound, oleuropein, which is neutralized by soaking in an alkaline solution such as lye. The fruits are then leached in clean water for about a month. After that they are pickled and fermented in a strong brine solution. You have to wonder how in the world ancient peoples figured out this very complex procedure.

TEMPERATURE. Olive trees are hardy in zones 8b to 10. Winter chilling requirement is 200 to 300 hours below 45°F. The trees do best with 90 to 180 days above 86°F annually.

SOIL, LIGHT, AND WATER. All fruit needs healthy, biologically active soil, full sun, and regular water. Review the Introduction for guidance on how to provide these three essential elements. Olive trees grow well on a variety of soil types, including shallow, stony, and infertile, but they'll do their best on deep, rich soils.

GARDEN USES. The beauty of the olive tree has been extolled through the ages. If you live in a climate appropriate for this tree, incorporate it into your home landscape. You'll be glad you did. Grow it as an ornamental, or a tree from which you want to harvest the fruit, or both. Their gnarled trunks and silvery gray leaves give olive trees a commanding presence. In the polyculture garden where the goal is to imitate the complexity of a natural plant community, grow them with plants that have similar needs. Excellent companions include sage, rosemary, lavender, pineapple guava, bay laurel, grapes, yarrow, and daffodils.

In addition to their great beauty as ornamentals olives bear an extremely valuable fruit which yields, when cold-pressed, the rich, healthful, and delicious extra virgin olive oil so often featured in contemporary cuisine. Commercial breeders have developed many oil-rich cultivars, grown primarily for their oil. Several cultivars grown primarily for table olives are also available. Either type of tree works beautifully in a home garden. Keep in mind that if you grow olives to consume, they are far too bitter to be eaten fresh. They must be processed before you can eat them. Brined and pickled in a hundred different ways, olives are good as condiments, in salads, and of course, in martinis.

Olive trees grow well in tubs and large pots making them useful to gardeners even in cold-winter climates. Keep them on the deck or patio in the summer and bring them indoors for the winter. Remember they are evergreen, and, therefore, need a sunny window all winter long. You may or may not obtain any fruit from potted olive trees, but they can still be exceedingly handsome specimens. Large, picturesque trees are sometimes dug up from old olive groves and planted in large wooden boxes for sale to landscape designers and homeowners. Olives seem to tolerate this treatment very well if given reasonable handling and care.

POLLINATION. Olives are wind-pollinated and many cultivars are self-fertile, though some are self-incompatible. All cultivars will likely produce larger crops if cross-pollinated with another cultivar. See the Introduction for an overview of pollination and its terminology.

PRUNING. Olive trees withstand heavy pruning, so you can shape them easily to show off their dramatic, gnarled trunks and branches. Have a look at "Prune Properly" (page 264) for tips.

PROBLEM-SOLVING. Olives are easy to grow if you live in the right climate. Following the guidelines in this plant portrait, reviewing the Introduction, and reading the recommendations in "Change the Growing Conditions" (page 247) will help you keep your trees healthy. If you run into trouble, see the Olive Problem-Solving Guide, page 188, for specific information on pests and diseases.

Orange

Citrus Problem-Solving Guide, page 130

DESCRIPTION. The sweet orange, *Citrus sinensis*, is an evergreen tree that grows 20 to 25 feet tall and wide. Dwarf orange trees, grafted to a dwarfing rootstock, get 8 to 12 feet high and wide. Some orange cultivars are thorny and others are not. More orange trees are grown today, worldwide, than any other fruit tree on the planet. Numerous cultivars exist, including navel oranges, blood oranges, and Valencia oranges.

This plant is an ancient natural hybrid. Possible parents are the pummelo (*Citrus maxima*) and the mandarin (*C. reticulata*), but no one knows for sure. The original homeland of the sweet orange is presumed to be Southeast Asia, but the tree no longer occurs in the wild there. Cultivated in China for at least 4,500 years, it made its way to the Mediterranean by 1450 and from there to the rest of the world.

Orange blossoms are legendary for their fragrance, an attribute shared by most citrus. Borne singly or in small clusters, the flowers are 1½ to 2 inches across, white on the inside, sometimes purple in bud. Trees flower most profusely in spring, but they may flower sporadically at almost any time of year. Honeybees diligently work the flowers to get their nectar and provide pollination services in the process. The resulting honey has floral and fruity notes that make it a gourmet treat.

It can take up to 10 months or more from flower to mature fruit. A globose berry, from 3 to 4 inches in diameter, it has a thick rind that is relatively easy to peel. Most orange cultivars produce harvestable fruit by late autumn or winter, but some won't mature until spring. The fruit ripens only on the tree, but can hang there for weeks, or even months, in good condition. Once you pick the fruit the ripening process ceases. The only way to tell if the fruit is fully mature is to taste it, because you can't rely on color. The color of mature, ripe oranges varies by climate. Fruit grown in warm areas like Hawaii tends to be green, sweet, and not very acid. In cooler regions the fruit is orange, sweet, and tart due to higher acidity. The fleshy interior is divided into 10 segments separated by membranous material. Each segment has fusiform fibers filled with delectable juice. Navel oranges are seedless, while blood and Valencia oranges have seeds.

The sweet orange does not come true from seed. Although you might be able to grow plants from seeds, it may have no fruit, or its fruit may not resemble the parent at all. If you want to try growing any citrus from seed, don't let the seed dry out. Keep it in damp paper towels till it germinates and then plant it.

TEMPERATURE. Orange trees tolerate low temperatures down to 24°F, as long as the weather turns cold gradually. Slightly higher temperatures, up to 28°F, are still cold enough to damage blossoms and fruit. They perform better in zone 10 and higher and really thrive in the frost-free areas of zone 11. Oranges need less heat to fully develop their natural sweetness and flavor than most other citrus, ideally 120 to 180 days annually above 86°F.

SOIL, LIGHT, AND WATER. All fruit needs healthy, biologically active soil, full sun, and regular water. Review the Introduction for guidance on how to provide these three essential elements. Orange trees are susceptible to foot, root, and crown rots in waterlogged soil, so be certain that drainage is good. Keep mulch 1 foot away from the trunk to avoid moist conditions at the soil line.

GARDEN USES. These beautiful trees, highly valued as ornamentals and for fruit production, give your garden all-season interest. The foliage is attractive, the flowers strongly scented, and the orange fruits, hanging like Christmas ornaments against the background of green foliage, are striking. You can harvest fruit for as long as 10 months of the year, if you choose cultivars that flower and fruit at different times. Site any thorny cultivars where they won't latch onto people walking past.

Orange trees are excellent container subjects. Dwarf plants grafted to dwarfing rootstocks are best for this purpose. Plant them in a large pot or a half whiskey barrel, using a good-quality potting soil with excellent drainage. Never let the container sit in a saucer of water. The roots will rot if they are waterlogged and deprived of oxygen for too long. Wherever you live, you can grow your potted orange tree outdoors in summer and bring it indoors to a sunny window for the winter, but a sunny window is essential. And orange fruit requires both warmth and sunlight to develop its sugar content.

POLLINATION. Oranges are self-fertile. See the Introduction for an overview of pollination and its terminology.

PRUNING. For commercial propagation, oranges are usually grafted to a rootstock that is a different plant. If you know or suspect your plant is grafted, watch for shoots developing from below the graft union and remove them. Prune for shape and to open the center to light and air. Otherwise, oranges require little more than basic maintenance pruning. Have a look at "Prune Properly" (page 264) for tips.

PROBLEM-SOLVING. Following the guidelines in this plant portrait, reviewing the Introduction, and reading the recommendations in "Change the Growing Conditions" (page 247) will help you keep your orange trees healthy. See the Citrus Problem-Solving Guide, page 130, for specific information on pests and diseases.

Passionfruit

**Passionfruit
Problem-Solving Guide, page 192**

DESCRIPTION. Passionfruits are evergreen or semi-evergreen vines, 20 to 30 feet tall. They are robust, and need a strong support to climb, which they do by means of tendrils. The light yellowish green, somewhat leathery leaves have three lobes. There are about 500 species in this genus of vines and shrubs. Some have aromatic fruit pulp with a unique flavor profile that complements many cuisines. Other species are poisonous. And some are noxious weeds that overwhelm and smother neighboring trees and invade the landscape. Many are grown either as beautiful ornamental flowering vines, or for their delicious fruit, or both, but we're only going to concern ourselves with two species.

Passiflora edulis, the passionfruit, or, in Hawaii, lilikoi, is native to southern Brazil, Paraguay, and northern Argentina. The Spanish brought it to the world's attention, and it is now the most commonly cultivated species, worldwide, for its aromatic sweet/tart fruit. The purple and white flowers are 3 to 5 inches in diameter. Each lasts only one day. Spanish missionaries called them "passion flower" because the complex flower structure provided convenient symbols of the Passion of Christ. Different parts of the flower represent the crown of thorns, the whips, the nails or wounds, and the apostles present at the crucifixion. *Passiflora mollissima*, the banana passionfruit or curuba, is increasingly known and cultivated for its flavorful fruit as well.

The typical form of *Passiflora edulis* has purple fruits. The form with yellow fruits is *P. edulis* f. *flavicarpa*, yellow passionfruit or golden lilikoi. The two forms are distinct in other ways. Purple passionfruit is sweeter, yellow passionfruit more tart. The purple form flowers in spring, the yellow form flowers sporadically spring to fall. Both are pollinated efficiently by carpenter bees and the fruits mature 70 to 80 days after pollination.

Passionfruits are round, from tennis-ball-sized up to grapefruit-sized, fragrant, speckled with whitish dots, and either purple or yellow at maturity. The fruit is a berry with a hard rind, rather like a gourd, and has a center filled with seeds. Each seed is surrounded by an aril, a globule of orange liquid that is strongly aromatic, sweet and tart, and mouthwateringly delicious. Cut the fruit in half and scoop out the seeds with a spoon into a strainer. Strain out the seeds and preserve the orange liquid. Use the fragrant juice to make all manner of wonderful edibles, such as lilikoi cheesecake or butter.

TEMPERATURE. Passionfruit vines are hardy to 26°F but will die to the ground below 32°F and resprout in spring. Where winter temperatures rarely dip below 32°F, the plants may shed some leaves in cold weather but, again, will not be killed. These subtropical and tropical vines have no chilling requirement and produce more fruit in frost-free areas, zone 10 and higher. They do best where the heat load is not excessive, preferring 45 to 150 days annually above 86°F.

SOIL, LIGHT, AND WATER. All fruit needs healthy, biologically active soil, full sun, and regular water. Review the Introduction for guidance on how to provide these three essential elements.

GARDEN USES. As ornamentals, the big, showy, complex flowers of passionfruit are gorgeous and make the vines worth growing for the flowers alone. Training the vine on a support of wire or wood against a wall or fence displays the flowers to best advantage. It also makes the fruit easier to harvest. These plants function as trees in a polyculture garden, creating complex structure and habitat for pollinators and beneficial predators. For species

diversity, which helps keep your garden healthy, grow them with other subtropical plants: citrus, guava, banana, ginger and calla lilies, and fatsia.

Passionfruit vines can also be grown in large tubs or pots and taken indoors for the winter. There's a good chance they'll flower off and on all winter, but you need to hand pollinate the flowers to get fruit. You'll still need to provide a trellis or some other kind of support for it to climb on. Fit the trellis inside the pot or attach it to the side of the container. Remember these vines are evergreen and, indoors, they'll need a sunny window all winter long.

POLLINATION. Some cultivars of both purple and yellow passionfruit are self-incompatible. Others are self-fertile. Read labels and catalog descriptions to determine the pollination needs of the cultivar you choose. See the Introduction for an overview of pollination and its terminology.

PRUNING. Light, judicious pruning once a year stimulates new growth as well as fruit production. Have a look at "Prune Properly" (page 264) for tips on pruning vines.

PROBLEM-SOLVING. The most likely problem you will encounter is winter cold, so following the guidelines in this plant portrait, reviewing the Introduction, and reading the recommendations in "Change the Growing Conditions" (page 247) is important. If your climate is right and you still encounter problems, see the Passionfruit Problem-Solving Guide on page 192, for specific information on pests and diseases.

Peach and nectarine

Stone Fruit Problem-Solving Guide, page 217

DESCRIPTION. Small, spreading trees to about 10 feet tall and wide, the peach or nectarine fits easily into the home landscape. Trees are deciduous and the leaves color beautifully in autumn in bright yellow and orange. Of all the homegrown, tree-ripened fruit you could grow, the peach rewards you more than any other with its fragrant, juicy, golden deliciousness. The flavor of a store-bought peach is nothing compared to a tree-ripened peach. Tree-ripened peaches are too soft to ship to grocery stores, so the only way you can get the good stuff is to grow it yourself or get yourself to a farmer's market.

The original home of the wild peach, *Prunus persica*, is China, not Persia as its epithet implies. Thousands of years ago humans carried the peach west to Asia Minor, then to Europe, and then to the rest of the world. As the portrait photo shows, a nectarine (var. *nucipersica*) is basically a fuzzless peach; its smooth skin is due to a simple mutation of a single gene.

Peaches and nectarines cover themselves with large, showy pink flowers in early spring. If the weather cooperates and bees are active, you will harvest baskets of luscious fruit in summer. In a cling peach or nectarine, the flesh of the fruit clings to the pit; in a freestone fruit, the flesh separates easily from the pit. Our favorites are freestones, but many people swear by clings because they are more firm and stand up well to canning. The mouthwatering, complex flavor of the peach derives from a combination of aroma, juiciness, sweetness, and acidity.

TEMPERATURE. The branches of peach and nectarine trees can be seriously damaged if the temperature drops below -20°F. At -10°F to -15°F the flower buds can be killed; this results in no fruit, even though the tree's branches may be unharmed. Zone 6 is the more reliable limit for peach production in most years. The chilling requirement varies by cultivar, from a low of 150 to 200 hours, to a high of 1,050 hours, with most needing 750 to 950 hours.

Peaches and nectarines like 30 to 150 days annually above 86°F and prefer warm, but not too hot, summers. Regions with dry summer weather avoid some of the fungal and bacterial diseases to which they are prone.

SOIL, LIGHT, AND WATER. All fruit needs healthy, biologically active soil, full sun, and regular water. Review the Introduction for guidance on how to provide these three essential elements.

GARDEN USES. The peach or nectarine is a highly ornamental small tree with beautiful large pink flowers in spring and attractive yellow and orange fall foliage color. In fact, landscape value is so high, their delicious fruit might almost be considered a bonus. All trees create a canopy layer, and thus complex habitat structure, for pollinators, predators, and parasitoids, beneficial organisms that contribute to your success in growing organic fruit. Grow a wide variety of other plants—strawberries, yarrow, four o'clocks, daylilies, santolina, echinacea, garlic, chives, onion, sage, rue, dill, fennel—under and around your fruit trees to create high species diversity and emulate natural plant communities.

Peaches and nectarines can also be grown in large containers like half whiskey barrels. Genetic dwarfs that get only 3 feet high are perfect for this purpose. Whether a dwarf or a standard-sized tree, it must be root pruned eventually in order to remain in the same pot year after year (page 26).

POLLINATION. Most peach and nectarine cultivars are self-fertile. See the Introduction for an overview of pollination and its terminology.

PRUNING. Peaches and nectarines bear fruit only on one-year-old shoots. This means you have to prune them every year to stimulate new growth for next year's crop. Have a look at "Prune Properly" (page 264) for tips.

PROBLEM-SOLVING. Almonds, apricots, cherries, peaches, plums, and nectarines are species in the genus *Prunus*, and all these stone fruits (as they are commonly known) have the same issues. As you will see when you turn to the Stone Fruit Problem-Solving Guide on page 217, there are a lot of pests and diseases to contend with, but following the guidelines in this plant portrait, reviewing the Introduction, and reading the recommendations in "Change the Growing Conditions" (page 247) will help you keep your trees healthy.

Pear

Pome Fruit Problem-Solving Guide, page 198

DESCRIPTION. The European pear, *Pyrus communis*, is the most commonly encountered pear tree in North American home gardens. But Asian pears, *P. pyrifolia*, *P. ussuriensis*, and their hybrids, are gaining in popularity. All are deciduous. Standard cultivars that have not been grafted to dwarfing rootstocks grow to 40 feet tall. Semi-dwarf cultivars are half that size, and fully dwarf varieties may reach only 8 feet. European pears are usually taller than they are wide, because their branches tend to grow vertically. Asian pears, with wider spreading branches, are nearly as wide as they are tall.

We know that European pears, native to Europe and Southwest Asia, were harvested from the wild in the Neolithic period, some 10,000 years ago. The earliest written record of the deliberate cultivation of pears comes to us from Theophrastus in ancient Greece. So we know that humans have been enjoying pears for a very long time. Asian pears, native to China and Siberia, have a similar history in China, Korea, and Japan, where they have been harvested, cultivated, and grafted for thousands of years.

Asian pears are sometimes called apple-pears, which suggests they're hybrids between apples and pears, but they're not. This misnomer comes about because of their round shape. They're also more crisp, watery, and gritty, and less sweet, than European pears. When properly ripened a European pear is soft, juicy, sweet, fragrant, and unabashedly hedonistic, more so than its Asian counterpart.

Both Asian and European pears flower in very early spring, before the leaves unfold. The five-petaled flowers are white, have many stamens, and resemble their apple-blossom cousins. Pear flowers are usually borne in small clusters on specialized shoots called spurs. Fruits ripen in the autumn, at about the same time as apples.

European pears are harvested when mature, but before they are fully ripe. They soften as they ripen, so pick them slightly green and hard, and ripen them off the tree for a higher percentage of quality fruit. Another oddity of these pears is that they'll ripen to buttery sweet perfection only if you store them at 30°F after you harvest them. The time they need to spend in cold storage varies from a few days to a few weeks, depending on the cultivar. Asian pears do not need any special ripening process, and can be ripened on the tree.

TEMPERATURE. European pears are hardy in zones 3 to 9, sometimes surviving even zone 2 winters. Winter chilling requirement is 700 to 800 hours below 45°F. Their preferred heat load is less than 150 days above 86°F annually.

Asian pears are more tender, hardy in zones 4 to 9. Winter chilling requirement is 350 to 450 hours below 45°F. Their preferred annual heat load is the same as European pears.

SOIL, LIGHT, AND WATER. All fruit needs healthy, biologically active soil, full sun, and regular water. Review the Introduction for guidance on how to provide these three essential elements.

GARDEN USES. Pear trees, especially when in full spring flower, can be beautiful ornamental subjects. Then there is the bonus of luscious fruit. All pears are especially amenable to espalier training along a fence or wall, a very handy and space-saving way to grow fruit in small spaces. Pears, especially dwarf cultivars, can also be grown in tubs or large pots. In most cases they are so hardy you don't have to worry about providing them with winter protection.

POLLINATION. All pears are self-incompatible, and some cultivars, 'Seckel' and 'Bartlett' for example, are incapable of cross-pollinating each other. Asian and European pears flower at different times, so you can't rely on them to pollinate each other. Pay attention to labels and catalog descriptions to know which cultivars will pollinate each other. See the Introduction for an overview of pollination and its terminology.

PRUNING. Prune pears every year in winter while they're dormant. Prune European pears to a central leader, or modified central leader, because of their upright growth habit. Do not head back or thin more than a third of the branches in any given year, because pruning stimulates the growth of water sprouts. Prune Asian pears to an open vase or modified central leader; head back or thin about half the new shoots. Have a look at "Prune Properly" (page 264) for tips and terminology.

PROBLEM-SOLVING. Pears do best in summer-dry Mediterranean climates, where there is less risk of exposure to the fire blight bacterium, which can be a common problem. Following the guidelines in this plant portrait, reviewing the Introduction, and reading the recommendations in "Change the Growing Conditions" (page 247) will help you keep your trees healthy. See the Pome Fruit Problem-Solving Guide, page 198, for specific information on pests and diseases.

Pecan and walnut

Nut Problem-Solving Guide, page 179

DESCRIPTION. Substantial, attractive, deciduous trees, pecans get 70 feet tall and wide and walnuts easily reach 60 feet tall and wide. Both have big, pinnately compound leaves. Aromatic, flavorful, and oil-rich seeds of these two trees are commonly called nuts. Technically, however, their fruit is a drupe, like a peach or almond, with the edible portion being the seed inside the pit. The seeds are eaten raw or roasted and salted.

Walnut, *Juglans regia*, is native to southeastern Europe and western and central Asia, and has been cultivated for thousands of years by Chinese, Persian, Greek, and Roman civilizations. There are two strains of walnut in cultivation. One is the English, Persian, or common walnut. The second strain, the Carpathian walnut, is significantly more tolerant of cold winters than the English walnut. Black walnut, *J. nigra*, commonly grows in the wild in North America.

The pecan, in contrast, is a relative newcomer to the world stage. A native American species, *Carya illinoinensis*, pecans originally hail from south-central United States and Mexico. The nuts were harvested from the wild by the indigenous peoples of North America and brought into cultivation in the 18th century.

Pecan and walnut are in the same botanical family, the Juglandaceae. Both are monoecious with dozens of tiny male flowers in 4-inch-long dangly catkins, and female flowers in small upright clusters of three to five at branch tips. The male catkins develop on one-year-old branches and mature simultaneously with the unfolding of the leaves in early spring. Female flowers, seen in the portrait photo, appear later, at the tips of branches of new growth of the current season. Fruits develop over the course of the summer and mature in autumn.

They look like small, green, smooth eggs at the tips of branches. When they're ripe they fall to the ground. The seed, which is inside the fruit, or husk, is the part we eat. If the husk doesn't break open on its own, remove it by hand. Rake up the fruits as they fall, peel away the husks, and dry the nuts for storage.

TEMPERATURE. Carpathian walnuts are hardy in zones 5 to 7. English/Persian walnuts generally survive zone 7 winters but they prosper in zones 8 and 9. Depending on the cultivar, winter chilling requirement for walnuts is 400 to 1,500 hours below 45°F.

Pecan trees are generally hardy to zone 6, but they thrive in regions with warmer winters, zones 7 to 9. Winter chilling requirement is 500 to 1,000 hours below 45°F. Some low-chill cultivars need only 300 to 400 hours. Both walnuts and pecans can take as much as 150 days above 86°F per year.

SOIL, LIGHT, AND WATER. All fruit needs healthy, biologically active soil, full sun, and regular water. Review the Introduction for guidance on how to provide these three essential elements.

GARDEN USES. Both walnuts and pecans are big trees that can be difficult to include in small home gardens. But they are well worth growing if you have the space. Just imagine all the good things you can do with a fresh crop of homegrown nuts at Thanksgiving. One cautionary note: walnuts exude chemicals from their root systems which inhibit the growth of other plants. Keep your other plants out from under the canopy of a walnut tree. Don't try to grow anything closer to the trunk than the drip-line, that is, the outer edge of the canopy.

POLLINATION. Pecans and walnuts are wind-pollinated. There are two types of pecan trees based on when the female flowers become receptive to pollen. In type-one trees, male flowers shed their pollen first; several days to a week later the type-one female flowers become receptive. This makes it less likely that the type-one tree will pollinate itself. In type-two trees, the female flowers become receptive before the type-two male flowers shed their pollen. Because the male and female flowers on the same tree or type of tree are out of phase with each other, you will only get a few nuts if you have only one type of tree. For a decent crop you'll need a type-one tree and a type-two tree, so that they can cross-pollinate each other.

Male and female flowers of walnuts are also out of phase with each other. But there are so many types that each tree is practically its own type. Some walnut cultivars are self-fertile and some are self-incompatible. All, even the self-fertile ones, will have higher yields with cross-pollination between two different cultivars. Read labels and catalog descriptions. See the Introduction for an overview of pollination and its terminology.

PRUNING. Prune suckers growing from below the graft union. Other than that, trees will require only basic maintenance pruning. Have a look at "Prune Properly" (page 264) for tips.

PROBLEM-SOLVING. Following the guidelines in this plant portrait, reviewing the Introduction, and reading the recommendations in "Change the Growing Conditions" (page 247) will help you keep your pecan and walnut trees healthy. See the Nut Problem-Solving Guide, page 179, for specific information on pests and diseases.

Persimmon

Persimmon Problem-Solving Guide, page 195

DESCRIPTION. The American persimmon, *Diospyros virginiana*, and Asian persimmon, *D. kaki*, are deciduous trees with beautiful, vivid autumn foliage color in yellow and orange to red. American persimmons are 15 to 30 feet tall and wide. Asian persimmons get 30 or more feet tall and wide. Both species have handsome branching patterns. And the fruit? The name of the genus translated from ancient Greek means "fruit of the gods." People who know and love persimmons certainly agree. Their divine flavor is complex, sweet, and a little tangy.

American persimmon is Kathryn's mother's favorite fruit. The species is native to the eastern United States, where it still grows wild. On our travels one September, we saw it thriving, loaded with fruit, along Interstate 66 in Virginia. This is good news, for its wood is so durable that it was nearly wiped out by logging many generations ago. Black ebony, famous for its presence in piano keyboards, is also a member of this genus. Asian or kaki persimmon hails from China, where it has been cultivated for millenia. It is still widely grown in China, Korea, and Japan, and was introduced to California in the 1800s. Hybrids between Asian and American persimmons were developed in Russia, and cultivars such as 'Russian Beauty' and 'Nikita's Gift' are now available in the United States.

Relatively small, inconspicuous flowers appear in spring. Both American and Asian persimmon flowers are 1 inch wide with four petals and four persistent sepals. Female flowers tend to be yellowish white, and are often borne singly; male flowers tend to be pinkish white, with three flowers to an inflorescence.

Persimmon fruits are berries with one to eight seeds. American persimmon fruits are 1½ to 2 inches in diameter and yellow-orange when ripe.

Asian persimmon fruits are 3 to 4 inches in diameter and orange-red when ripe. If you've tried a persimmon, you may know that there are two types: astringent and non-astringent. The astringent fruits are loaded with very bitter, mouth-puckering tannins that make them inedible until they have been subjected to frost or allowed to soften naturally. The tannins disappear eventually and then the fruit becomes soft and jelly-like. Wait until they're fully ripe and soft, then cut them open, and eat them with a spoon. Non-astringent fruits lack tannins and can be eaten when they are firm and crunchy, like an apple.

TEMPERATURE. American persimmons are hardy in zones 4 to 10. Winter chilling requirement is 200 to 400 hours below 45°F. They can take 150 days per year above 86°F.

Asian persimmons are hardy in zones 7 to 10. Winter chilling requirement is 100 to 200 hours below 45°F. Their preferred heat load is 60 to 180 days per year above 86°F.

Hybrid persimmons combine the cold hardiness of American persimmons with the larger fruit of the Asian.

SOIL, LIGHT, AND WATER. All fruit needs healthy, biologically active soil, full sun, and regular water. Review the Introduction for guidance on how to provide these three essential elements.

GARDEN USES. Persimmon trees are highly ornamental and deserve a place in the home landscape. They are low maintenance, not fussy, and relatively easy to grow. Their flamboyant fall color, followed by vivid fruits hanging on bare branches, is a dramatic annual show. Persimmons have tap roots that make them challenging to grow in a pot. If you want to try one in a large tub or pot, cut the tap root to force the plant to develop side roots.

POLLINATION. Both species are dioecious, though rare flowers will have both female and male sex parts. You'll generally need two trees, one female for the fruit and one male for the pollen. Some persimmons, however, are parthenocarpic, which means they can set fruit without pollination. Go figure. With parthenocarpic cultivars you'll need only one tree. Hybrid persimmons are self-fertile. See the Introduction for an overview of pollination and its terminology.

PRUNING. Prune to open the center to light and air. Other than that, persimmon trees require only basic maintenance pruning. Have a look at "Prune Properly" (page 264) for tips.

PROBLEM-SOLVING. Following the guidelines in this plant portrait, reviewing the Introduction, and reading the recommendations in "Change the Growing Conditions" (page 247) will help you keep your trees healthy. See the Persimmon Problem-Solving Guide, page 195, for specific information on pests and diseases.

Plum

Stone Fruit Problem-Solving Guide, page 217

DESCRIPTION. The fruits we call plums are a hodge-podge derived from a number of species and, as a result, vary enormously in color, size, taste, and texture. All are in the genus *Prunus*, and all are stone fruits, which include almonds, apricots, cherries, peaches, and nectarines.

American plums, *Prunus americana*, are shrubby plants that grow to about 6 feet tall and wide. Japanese (*P. salicina*) and European (*P. domestica*) plums are 15 to 20 feet tall and somewhat wider than that at maturity. European plums (aka damsons), native to Europe, are probably ancient natural hybrids between *P. spinosa* and *P. cerasifera*. They are the sweetest of the bunch, delicious eaten fresh and with a high enough sugar content to dry in the sun to become prunes. They flower about the same time as apple trees, later in spring than Japanese plums.

Japanese plums make the largest fruits; they're sweet-tart and very juicy, and are generally eaten fresh rather than dried. We think you can guess where they come from. Trees flower in very early spring and can be damaged by late frosts. American plums, the smallest of the group, bear fruits that are often very tart, and cooked rather than eaten fresh. They are extremely hardy, tolerating much lower temperatures than other plums. Japanese-American hybrids combine features of both parents.

Depending on the cultivar and climate, plum fruits mature from early summer through fall. Plum skins may be nearly black, red, purple, blue, green, or yellow with flesh that can be red, green, or yellow. They can be very sweet, sweet and tart, or merely tart and good for cooking.

TEMPERATURE. European plums are hardy to zone 4. Winter chilling requirement is 700 to 1,000 hours below 45°F for most cultivars. Low-chill cultivars need 250 to 400 hours of winter chilling. Heat tolerance is less than 120 days per year above 86°F.

American plums are hardy to zone 3. Their winter chilling needs can be as much as 3,600 hours below 45°F. Low-chill cultivars require 800 hours. Many American plums tolerate hot summers very well, even though they too prefer less than 120 days per year above 86°F.

Japanese plums are hardy to zone 6. Most need 500 to 900 hours of winter chilling below 45°F. Low-chill cultivars require only 250 to 400 hours. Heat tolerance is up to 150 days annually above 86°F.

SOIL, LIGHT, AND WATER. All fruit needs healthy, biologically active soil, full sun, and regular water. Review the Introduction for guidance on how to provide these three essential elements.

GARDEN USES. Like all their stone fruit cousins, plums are valuable ornamental flowering trees. The small flowers are either pink or white, have five petals, and are borne in great profusion. The trees are small enough to be easily accommodated in the home landscape. Mixing a wide variety of plants with your fruit trees provides the complex structure, high species diversity, and biologically active soil that emulate natural plant communities. A tree's canopy provides habitat for wild partners such as pollinators, predators, and parasitoids, all beneficial organisms that contribute to your success in growing organic fruit. Plants to grow under and around your plum tree include strawberries, yarrow, four o'clocks, daylilies, santolina, echinacea, garlic, chives, onion, sage, rue, dill, and fennel.

A plum tree can be grown in a large container such as a half whiskey barrel, but you will need to trim the roots (page 26).

POLLINATION. Most European and American plums are self-fertile. But fruit yield is often better with cross-pollination by another cultivar. Some Japanese plums are self-fertile, and others require cross-pollination, often with specific varieties. European and Japanese plums will not cross-pollinate each other. Hybrids need to be crossed to another variety of the same type of hybrid or back to a parent. Read labels and pollination charts available at most garden centers and in plant catalogs to learn which varieties pollinate each other. See the Introduction for an overview of pollination and its terminology.

PRUNING. Plums bear fruit on one-year-old shoots and on spurs on older wood. This means you only need to prune them lightly to stimulate new growth for next year's crop. Have a look at "Prune Properly" (page 264) for tips.

PROBLEM-SOLVING. Aphids, scale, and raccoons may well be your biggest headaches with plum trees, but following the guidelines in this plant portrait, reviewing the Introduction, and reading the recommendations in "Change the Growing Conditions" (page 247) will help you keep them healthy. They and all species in the genus *Prunus* are, for the most part, subject to the same pests and diseases; see the Stone Fruit Problem-Solving Guide, page 217, for specifics.

Pomegranate

Pomegranate Problem-Solving Guide, page 213

DESCRIPTION. The pomegranate, *Punica granatum*, has long been an integral part of human history, steeped in myth and legend of the western world from Persephone to the present. The plant is a twiggy bush or shrubby, multi-trunked tree, 15 to 20 feet tall and wide. Plants are often kept pruned to about 10 feet tall and wide. Dwarf cultivars are available. Leaves are narrow, opposite or nearly so, and about 1 ¼ inches long. Plants are somewhat thorny and deciduous. The yellow leaves of autumn often hang on into November. The peculiar fruit, which contains lycopene, is a frequent symbol of fertility. Its deep red juice is used to make grenadine, a familiar ingredient in cocktails.

Pomegranate is native from Iran to northern India but humans carried it to the Mediterranean region a very long time ago, and it is widely naturalized there. Archeological remains of the fruit have been found in early Bronze Age sites in Israel; written records of its cultivation in the Middle East date back some 4,500 years, and some scholars think this is the original "Tree of Knowledge" in the Bible. It was brought to California and Latin America in 1769 by the Spanish.

The plant is not wanton in its flowering. It does not completely cover itself in thousands of blossoms the way an apple tree does. Instead, it chastely produces a few flowers at a time over a long season, beginning in spring. Flower color varies by cultivar, and may be orange, yellow, pink, or white, but the typical color is an intense orange-red. Large, vermilion flowers that glow like neon are unusual for plants that produce fruit. The flowers have five to seven crinkly, crepe-like petals that are very attractive to hummingbirds. Flowers are followed some five to seven months later by the fruits.

Pomegranate fruits are round, 3 to 5 inches in diameter; they are usually some shade of red. Each fruit is topped by thick, leathery sepals, like the crown of some fairy-tale king. In fact, the pomegranate fruit is thought to be the original design inspiration for the crowns of European royalty. The leathery rind of the fruit encloses hundreds of sparkling ruby-like globules of red juice, each surrounding a seed. Pomegranate fruits mature in September and October. They last in good condition on the plant but are likely to split open and rot in wet weather.

TEMPERATURE. The pomegranate is hardy in zones 7 to 10. Winter chilling requirement is 150 hours below 45°F. It can tolerate anything from zero to more than 210 days annually above 86°F but fruits best where summers are long, hot, and dry. We have even seen it thriving in Portland, Oregon, a location not famous for long, hot summers.

SOIL, LIGHT, AND WATER. All fruit needs healthy, biologically active soil, full sun, and regular water. Review the Introduction for guidance on how to provide these three essential elements. Consistent soil moisture helps to keep the fruit from cracking open.

GARDEN USES. Pomegranates are attractive ornamentals, especially when they are in flower or in fruit. Old plants develop craggy, twisted trunks that can be beautiful in winter when plants are leafless. Emerging new foliage in spring is often colorful and fall color is a pleasant yellow. Grow your pomegranate in a polyculture with a variety of companion plants that attract honeybees and beneficial predators to your garden. Chamomile, Queen Anne's lace, fennel, hyssop, and lavender all attract beneficial insects such as lady beetles and lacewings in addition to honeybees. You need pollinators to pollinate

the flowers or you'll have no fruit. Honeybees and hummingbirds both do a good job of pollination for this plant. Other good plants that will lure hummingbirds into your garden: red flowering currant, beebalm, agastaches, penstemons, and fuchsias.

Pomegranates, especially dwarf cultivars, are excellent in containers or large tubs. Set them out on your deck or patio during the growing season. Because they're thorny, place them where they won't snag passersby. If you live in a colder climate than they prefer, bring them indoors for the winter. Since they are deciduous they don't need sunshine indoors in winter.

POLLINATION. Pomegranate is self-fertile. See the Introduction for an overview of pollination and its terminology.

PRUNING. Pomegranates need only light annual pruning. The plant naturally produces new stems from underground which can be useful in case replacements are needed for any older stems damaged by winter freezes. Allowing the plant to develop three to five trunks provides insurance against such losses and is in keeping with its natural habit. Have a look at "Prune Properly" (page 264) for tips.

PROBLEM-SOLVING. Following the guidelines in this plant portrait, reviewing the Introduction, and reading the recommendations in "Change the Growing Conditions" (page 247) will help you keep your trees healthy. See the Pomegranate Problem-Solving Guide, page 213, for specific information on pests and diseases.

Raspberry

Bramble Problem-Solving Guide, page 123

DESCRIPTION. All raspberry cultivars are freestanding perennial bushes that can grow to about 6 feet tall, with erect, self-supporting stems, also called canes, and branches. They bear weak prickles all along their canes. Red raspberry, *Rubus idaeus*, has berries that range from red to orange or yellow. Plants generate new canes from both the crown and roots every year. These new canes are liable to pop up in unexpected places, so red raspberries can be invasive. Black raspberry, *R. occidentalis*, produces deep black berries with a distinctive flavor. Plants grow new canes only from their crowns, and do not spread. Purple raspberries are hybrids between the red and the black. All raspberries produce berries generously, so you'll get an abundance of flavorful, delicious fruit for freezing, for baking, and for making jams, jellies, wine, beer, or spirits.

In addition to considering the color and taste of berries, you can also choose cultivars that bear fruit at different times of the year. Summer-bearing raspberries—red or black—are so named because each cane fruits only once in its lifetime, in the summer of its second year. The new, first-year canes (aka primocanes) are non-fruiting. They grow throughout spring and summer without flowering, and persist through the winter. Primocanes will lose all their leaves, however, so don't panic and think they are dead. In its second summer, each primocane becomes a floricane: it flowers, sets fruit, and then dies.

Ever-bearing raspberries fruit twice a year, in summer and fall. Their primocanes debut their first fruits in the autumn of their first year. They reprise their performance in the summer of their second year. You get two crops of fruit from each cane over two growing seasons.

TEMPERATURE. Red and purple raspberries are hardy to zone 5, black raspberries to zone 6. Winter chilling requirement ranges from 250 to 1,400 hours below 45°F, depending on the cultivar. Heat tolerance also varies by cultivar but, in general, raspberries don't thrive where temperatures go above 86°F for more than 14 days a year. An average summer temperature of 70°F is optimum. However, we've had good luck with red raspberries in hot summer climates by planting them where they get full sun all morning but are shaded by trees in the afternoon.

SOIL, LIGHT, AND WATER. All fruit needs healthy, biologically active soil, full sun, and regular water. Review the Introduction for guidance on how to provide these three essential elements. Red raspberries need a slightly alkaline soil, pH 7.5, so add dolomite lime, following label directions, if necessary.

GARDEN USES. Raspberry shrubs contribute to the complexity of a fruit garden's structure by adding an understory layer. They also provide habitat for beneficial wildlife, especially birds that are likely to eat insect pests. Interplant with garlic, yarrow, and various other herbs and flowers in the mint, carrot, and daisy families to increase species diversity and to attract beneficial predators and pollinators. We plant our raspberries in small patches rather than the traditional rows. Either way, the berries are much easier to harvest, and the canes are easier to prune, if you provide a support structure.

POLLINATION. All raspberries are self-fertile. See the Introduction for an overview of pollination and its terminology.

PRUNING. When summer-bearing canes have finished fruiting they die. You can prune them to the ground in the fall or winter, whenever it's most convenient. For ever-bearing raspberries prune away the top third of the cane when first-year fruiting is finished in the autumn. In its second year that same cane will produce a summer crop on the bottom two-thirds and then it will die. Have a look at "Prune Properly" (page 264) for more on pruning brambles.

PROBLEM-SOLVING. Our biggest problem with raspberries is that the birds get the fruit before we do. The berries can also succumb to fruit rots, but following the guidelines in this plant portrait, reviewing the Introduction, and reading the recommendations in "Change the Growing Conditions" (page 247) will help you keep your raspberries healthy. See the Bramble Problem-Solving Guide, page 123, for specific information on pests and diseases.

Strawberry

Strawberry Problem-Solving Guide, page 234

DESCRIPTION. Strawberry plants are evergreen perennials to about 8 inches tall and 12 inches wide. They have two different kinds of stems. One kind is strongly compressed into a crown—a nubbin, with a whorl of compound leaves at its apex. The second kind of stem is a stolon. Each plant's crown generates several of these long, thin, string-like runners, and each stolon sprouts new plants at its tip that then root and grow on their own. The new plants that grow from the runners are genetically identical to the mother plant, making it very easy to multiply your plants and renovate decrepit strawberry beds. Left unchecked, strawberry plants spread.

People have grown or harvested strawberries from the wild for millennia. Alpine strawberry, *Fragaria vesca*, is native throughout the Northern Hemisphere. Musk strawberry, *F. moschata*, is native to Europe. Both species have very small, aromatic fruits, and are still cultivated to some extent. But the subject of this portrait, *F. ×ananassa*, is a relative newcomer to our tables and gardens. It is an accidental hybrid between two wild species, both native to the Americas. One, *F. virginiana*, came from the Atlantic coast of North America and the other, *F. chiloensis*, came from the Pacific coast of South America. By about 1750 they found themselves nestled side by side in European gardens. Bees moved the pollen back and forth and chance hybrid seedlings were discovered with bigger and better fruits than either parent. Most cultivated strawberries worldwide are these delectable, large-fruited natural hybrids.

Most cultivars flower in spring and the fruit ripens in June. These June-bearing strawberries produce a prodigious quantity of fruit all at once—a distinct advantage if you're looking to make jams, preserves, and pies. Another group of cultivars, ever-bearing strawberries, produce a small quantity of fruit in June, and then again in September. A third group developed in the early 1980s, the day-neutrals, are truly ever-bearing, with small quantities of ripe fruits throughout the growing season.

That lovely, bright red, heart-shaped structure we call a strawberry is not a berry. In fact it's technically not even a fruit. Botanically, the fruits of a strawberry are achenes, those tiny "seeds" that speckle the outside of the "berry." The edible, luscious, red flesh is actually the greatly enlarged flower receptacle—where sepals, petals, stamens, and ovaries are attached. Botanists term it an accessory fruit because a true fruit is a mature, ripened ovary.

TEMPERATURE. Strawberries are hardy in zones 3 to 10. Winter chilling requirement is 200 to 300 hours below 45°F. Preferred heat load is less than 180 days above 86°F annually.

SOIL, LIGHT, AND WATER. All fruit needs healthy, biologically active soil, full sun, and regular water. Review the Introduction for guidance on how to provide these three essential elements. Strawberry fruits naturally lie on the ground. This makes them subject to pests like slugs and snails and soilborne fungus infections like mold. Mulch your plants with straw to keep fruits up off the ground. This mulching technique gives the fruit its name.

GARDEN USES. Strawberries are highly ornamental, and are welcome additions to any landscape. Shallow-rooted, they make an excellent ground cover anywhere. And they are possibly the easiest of all fruit-bearing plants to grow in a container. People often plant them in hanging baskets or the traditional "strawberry jar," which is a ceramic container with small pouches on the outside. You plant strawberries in each of the pouches and in the top

of the jar. We've never had luck with this type of planter, but they are very decorative and some people swear by them. We grow strawberries in ordinary pots. In the polyculture garden, grow strawberries under and around fruit trees, as long as the trees do not shade the ground completely. Combine them with borage, lettuce, garden mums, and marigolds, plants that attract a wide variety of beneficial predators and pollinators.

POLLINATION. *Fragaria ×ananassa* is self-fertile. See the Introduction for an overview of pollination and its terminology.

PRUNING. Strawberries do not require pruning. Some people like to snip off the runners the first year after planting in order to build a stronger plant.

PROBLEM-SOLVING. Strawberries are so rambunctious that we've rarely had a problem getting all the berries we can eat. Following the guidelines in this plant portrait, reviewing the Introduction, and reading the recommendations in "Change the Growing Conditions" (page 247) will help you keep your plants just as healthy. See the Strawberry Problem-Solving Guide, page 234, for specific information on pests and diseases.

Watermelon

Melon Problem-Solving Guide, page 167

DESCRIPTION. Watermelon, *Citrullus lanatus*, is an annual vine that climbs by means of tendrils. The large, hairy leaves are deeply lobed. Most plants grow 2 to 3 feet tall and spread out over 64 square feet. Because they climb you can also grow them on an A-frame, trellis, or some other sort of structure. But plants with large fruits will break unless you support the fruit in a sling or net.

Native to subtropical Africa, wild plants still thrive in the Kalahari Desert. This plant was domesticated and brought into cultivation several hundred years ago around the Mediterranean and in India. It is very popular in China, Southeast Asia, Japan, and North America.

Plants begin to flower in early summer and fruits mature three to four months later. The fruit is a round or elongated oval. Most weigh between 5 and 40 pounds. One record-breaker clocked in at 268.8 pounds. Now that's a big watermelon. The flesh is very sweet, juicy, crisp, and delicious, and may be red, orange, or yellow. Nearly all watermelons have lots of rich, nutritious, black or white seeds. In many cultures these are an important part of the diet, being 30 to 40 percent protein and 45 percent edible oil. There are many different cultivars available with fruits that vary in size, flesh color, days to maturity, and whether they have seeds or are seedless. In one interesting heirloom strain, 'Moon and Stars', both fruits and leaves are dotted with bright yellow spots. For tips on planting and growing, refer to the melon portrait on page 72.

TEMPERATURE. Watermelons need long, hot summers to do well. They thrive where summer daytime highs average 70 to 80°F, and the soil temperature is at least 70°F. Make sure you plant in spring after all danger of frost is past and the soil has warmed up.

Seeds planted in soil that is too cool generally fail to germinate and rot. Also make sure your summer planting allows enough time for the fruit to mature before the first killing frost of autumn.

SOIL, LIGHT, AND WATER. All fruit needs healthy, biologically active soil, full sun, and regular water. Review the Introduction for guidance on how to provide these three essential elements. In addition, feed watermelons well with a complete balanced organic fertilizer and compost at the beginning of each growing season. Feed them additional organic fertilizer once during the growing season, and gently rake it into the soil around the plants. Control weeds, conserve moisture, and protect fruit lying on the ground by mulching to a depth of 3 inches after the plants are growing well. Maintain soil pH between 6.0 and 6.5. Increase the amount of water to as much as 2 inches a week when the vines support a heavy fruit crop. Make sure your planting site is well drained. Plant your watermelons in raised beds or large containers if your drainage is poor or the water table is high.

GARDEN USES. Watermelons are generally grown sprawling across the ground but smaller-fruited varieties can be grown on a support. Be sure to prepare the structure they're going to climb before you plant the seeds. You can use sturdy stakes, tripods of bamboo, or tree limbs arranged in a teepee fashion, or you can grow them on a net, chain-link fence, A-frame, or trellis. Support the fruit in a sling or net. Good companions include corn and beans. Space vines well apart from each other and interplant flowers that attract beneficial insects to help combat pests.

To grow watermelons in a container, select a compact or bush-type variety and start with either a five-gallon pot or a half whiskey barrel. Make sure there is a drainage hole. Inside the pot place a small square of window screen over the hole. Then fill the pot with potting soil, not garden soil.

POLLINATION. Watermelons are monoecious. The first flowers produced in early summer will always be male and cannot produce fruit. Be patient and as the plant gets a little older it will make female flowers and produce a generous crop of fruit after the bees have done their job.

PRUNING. Watermelons do not need to be pruned.

PROBLEM-SOLVING. Following the guidelines in this plant portrait, reviewing the Introduction, and reading the recommendations in "Change the Growing Conditions" (page 247) will help you keep your watermelons healthy. See the Melon Problem-Solving Guide, page 167, for specific information on pests and diseases.

Plant Problem-Solving Guides

Avocado Problem-Solving Guide

Symptom	Diagnosis	Solution
Small, reddish brown, yellow, gray-white, or black lumps stick to upper and lower leaf surfaces or stems. You can easily remove them with your thumbnail. These insects coat the upper surfaces of leaves and fruit with clear, sticky, varnish-like honeydew. A gray-black coating that easily rubs off (sooty mold) forms on the honeydew.	Scale insects	Plant polycultures, page 258 Encourage beneficial organisms, page 260 Hand-pick pests, page 277 Sticky bands, page 278 Beneficial predators, page 280 Insecticidal soap, page 285 Horticultural oil, page 286 Sulfur, page 287 Pyrethrin, page 287
You discover fluffy grayish white lumps clustered where leaves attach to stems and on the undersides of leaves. These insects do not fly. They coat the upper surfaces of leaves and fruit with sticky, varnish-like honeydew. A gray-black coating that easily rubs off (sooty mold) forms on the honeydew.	Mealybugs	Plant polycultures, page 258 Encourage beneficial organisms, page 260 Blast with hose, page 278 Sticky bands, page 278 Beneficial predators, page 280 Insecticidal soap, page 285 Neem, page 286 Horticultural oil, page 286 Sulfur, page 287 Pyrethrin, page 287
You watch ants scurry over deformed leaves and march up and down the trunk. They are tending the aphids, scale insects, or mealybugs they bring to your tree. Ants feed on the sweet, sticky honeydew produced by these insects.	Ants and aphids, mealybugs, or scale	Plant polycultures, page 258 Sticky bands, page 278 Diatomaceous earth, page 285

You see small, bright white insects fly away when you disturb your plant. Large colonies on the undersides of leaves deposit patches of white residue. These insects coat the upper surfaces of leaves and fruit with a clear, sticky, varnish-like honeydew. A gray-black coating that easily rubs off (sooty mold) forms on the honeydew.

Whitefly

Encourage beneficial organisms, page 260
Move the air, page 264
Row covers, page 274
Blast with hose, page 278
Vacuum, page 278
Sticky cards, page 279
Beneficial predators, page 280
Insecticidal soap, page 285
Neem, page 286
Horticultural oil, page 286
Sulfur, page 287
Pyrethrin, page 287

You find scars on the fruit with patches and streaks of raised, rough, corky yellow-brown or silvery tissue. Leaves look silvery. Some damaged leaves roll up and drop off. Tiny (1/20 inch long) yellow to orangish insects congregate on flower petals, leaves, and young fruit.

Thrips

Plant polycultures, page 258
Encourage beneficial organisms, page 260
Weed, page 262
Sanitize, page 263
Kaolin spray, page 277
Blast with hose, page 278
Beneficial predators, page 280
Insecticidal soap, page 285
Spinosad, page 286
Neem, page 286
Horticultural oil, page 286
Pyrethrin, page 287

If you see caterpillars on your plants, you know what the problem is. But you may find that leaves have been skeletonized, or rolled and sewn together with silk, or have large irregular holes. Look for black pellets of caterpillar poop. The caterpillars bore holes into the fruit and eat flower buds and the foliage, depriving the fruit of shade. Fruit may develop dark sunburned patches.

Caterpillars

Plant polycultures, page 258
Encourage beneficial organisms, page 260
Hand-pick pests, page 277
Beneficial predators, page 280
BTK, page 283
Insecticidal soap, page 285
Spinosad, page 286
Neem, page 286
Horticultural oil, page 286
Pyrethrin, page 287

Symptom	Diagnosis	Solution

You discover notches on edges of leaves nearest the ground. This is your main clue that gray-brown snout beetles (weevils) have crawled up the trunk and branches to eat the edges of the lower leaves on the trees. Their larvae are white grubs with brown heads that live in the soil and eat plant roots.

Weevils

Soil solutions, page 248
Plant polycultures, page 258
Encourage beneficial organisms, page 260
Chickens and ducks, page 282
Beneficial nematodes, page 282
Beauveria bassiana, page 285
Insecticidal soap, page 285
Diatomaceous earth, page 285
Spinosad, page 286
Neem, page 286
Horticultural oil, page 286
Sulfur, page 287
Pyrethrin, page 287

You see large (to 1½ inches long) brown and white striped beetles and/ or large (to 1 inch long) metallic green beetles eating holes in leaves or fruit. Larvae of these beetles are whitish grubs (to 2 inches long) that live in the soil and eat plant roots. The grubs have three pairs of jointed legs and a brown head. They curl into a C shape when disturbed.

Ten-lined and green June beetles, figeater beetles

Soil solutions, page 248
Plant polycultures, page 258
Encourage beneficial organisms, page 260
Hand-pick pests, page 277
Jug traps, page 279
Beneficial predators, page 280
Chickens and ducks, page 282
Beneficial nematodes, page 282
BTSD, page 284
Beauveria bassiana, page 285
Insecticidal soap, page 285
Spinosad, page 286
Neem, page 286
Horticultural oil, page 286
Pyrethrin, page 287

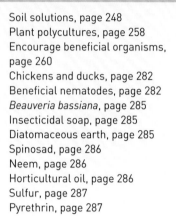

Numerous tiny holes in the bark and wood indicate borer beetles are active in your tree. Borer larvae excavate tunnels under damaged bark. The bark sometimes cracks open.

Borers

Plant polycultures, page 258
Encourage beneficial organisms, page 260
Sanitize, page 263
Hand-pick pests, page 277
Beneficial predators, page 280
Beauveria bassiana, page 285
Spinosad, page 286
Neem, page 286
Pyrethrin, page 287

You find shield-shaped insects sucking sap out of stems, flower buds, and fruit. These insects are true bugs and have mouthparts like hypodermic needles. Fruit becomes blemished, discolored, or deformed (cat-faced). Pits or pustules may develop on the fruit. Leaves become twisted, wilt, and turn brown.

Stink bugs, lygus bugs, tarnished plant bugs, boxelder bugs, leaffooted bugs, avocado lace bugs

Plant polycultures, page 258
Encourage beneficial organisms, page 260
Bags, page 277
Kaolin spray, page 277
Hand-pick pests, page 277
Beneficial predators, page 280
Chickens and ducks, page 282
Garlic spray, page 283
Pepper spray, page 283
Beauveria bassiana, page 285
Insecticidal soap, page 285
Spinosad, page 286
Neem, page 286
Horticultural oil, page 286
Pyrethrin, page 287

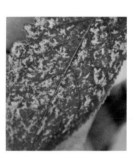

Tiny white specks stipple the leaves. Leaf edges may yellow and turn brown. Wedge-shaped, greenish blue or brownish gray insects (to ½inch long) hide on the undersides of leaves. Fast fliers, they fly away when disturbed. These insects transmit serious bacterial and viral diseases to your plants.

Leafhoppers, sharpshooters, psyllids

Plant polycultures, page 258
Encourage beneficial organisms, page 260
Weed, page 262
Kaolin spray, page 277
Beneficial predators, page 280
Beauveria bassiana, page 285
Insecticidal soap, page 285
Neem, page 286
Horticultural oil, page 286
Pyrethrin, page 287

Grasshoppers and katydids hop and fly about the garden during the day. You see large holes on the edges and in the middle of leaves. Crickets hide during the day and do their damage at night.

Grasshoppers, katydids, crickets

Soil solutions, page 248
Plant polycultures, page 258
Encourage beneficial organisms, page 260
Beneficial predators, page 280
Chickens and ducks, page 282
Nosema spore, page 283
Beauveria bassiana, page 285
Insecticidal soap, page 285
Spinosad, page 286
Neem, page 286
Horticultural oil, page 286
Pyrethrin, page 287

Symptom	Diagnosis	Solution

You notice leaves stippled with tiny pale dots that sometimes turn the whole leaf bronze-colored. Fine webbing, like spider silk, covers leaves and twigs. Badly infested leaves turn yellow or red and drop off.

Spider mites

Plant polycultures, page 258
Encourage beneficial organisms, page 260
Sanitize, page 263
Kaolin spray, page 277
Blast with hose, page 278
Beneficial predators, page 280
Garlic spray, page 283
Pepper spray, page 283
Beauveria bassiana, page 285
Insecticidal soap, page 285
Spinosad, page 286
Neem, page 286
Horticultural oil, page 286
Sulfur, page 287
Pyrethrin, page 287

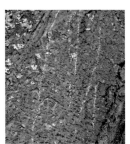

Slime trails criss-cross trunks, leaves, and fruit. You find large irregular holes in leaves or fruit.

Slugs and snails

Plant polycultures, page 258
Encourage beneficial organisms, page 260
Weed, page 262
Mulch, page 262
Hand-pick pests, page 277
Copper tape, page 278
Slug and snail traps, page 279
Beneficial predators, page 280
Chickens and ducks, page 282
Iron phosphate, page 285
Diatomaceous earth, page 285

Brown spots appear on leaves; leaves turn yellow. The spots enlarge, coalesce, and become dry. Leaves wilt, dry, and drop off. Sometimes the dead tissue falls out of the leaf.

Anthracnose

Manage water, page 253
Plant polycultures, page 258
Sanitize, page 263
Move the air, page 264
Bacillus subtilis, page 289
Reynoutria sachalinensis, page 289
Baking soda, page 290
Neem, page 290
Sulfur, page 291
Copper, page 291

Symptom	Diagnosis	Solution
 Fruit develops raised, brown, corky spots and patches. Leaves also get brown spots. Fruit may become deformed.	Scab	Manage water, page 253 Plant polycultures, page 258 Mulch, page 262 Sanitize, page 263 Move the air, page 264 *Bacillus pumilus*, page 289 *Bacillus subtilis*, page 289 *Reynoutria sachalinensis*, page 289 Baking soda, page 290 Neem, page 290 Copper, page 291
 You find branches dying back or weakened above brown, sunken patches of dead bark, known as cankers, on stems. Dark amber-colored gum oozes from the cankers and dries white.	Canker	Manage water, page 253 Plant polycultures, page 258 Sanitize, page 263 Move the air, page 264 Prune properly, page 264 *Bacillus subtilis*, page 289 Baking soda, page 290 Neem, page 290 Copper, page 291
 Leaves drop off and trees wilt and die. You discover dark patches oozing gum or dark sap at the base of the trunk. Reddish brown streaks occur in the inner bark and outer layers of wood.	Phytophthora root rot, crown rot	Soil solutions, page 248 Manage water, page 253 Plant polycultures, page 258 Sanitize, page 263 *Bacillus subtilis*, page 289 *Reynoutria sachalinensis*, page 289 *Streptomyces lydicus*, page 290 *Trichoderma harzianum*, page 290

Pale mushrooms sprout at the base of your tree. They are the fruiting bodies of a destructive fungus. You notice leaves are small and yellowish, and growth is slow. Shoots die back from the tips. Trees may develop autumn color early. Peel back the bark from the trunk just below the soil line to find leathery white patches that smell like fresh mushrooms. Look at the roots to find blackish, root-like structures (rhizomorphs) adjacent to them.

Armillaria root rot

Soil solutions, page 248
Manage water, page 253
Plant polycultures, page 258
Sanitize, page 263
Bacillus subtilis, page 289
Reynoutria sachalinensis, page 289
Streptomyces lydicus, page 290
Trichoderma harzianum, page 290

The lower leaves turn yellow and develop brown blotches on their tips. Often, this symptom appears on only one side of the plant. The leaves curl and die. The plant's growth slows. Look for black spots on the stems near the soil line. To confirm your diagnosis, cut stems in half lengthwise to see dark streaks inside.

Fusarium wilt, verticillium wilt

Soil solutions, page 248
Manage water, page 253
Plant polycultures, page 258
Sanitize, page 263
Reynoutria sachalinensis, page 289
Streptomyces lydicus, page 290
Trichoderma harzianum, page 290

Banana Problem-Solving Guide

Symptom	Diagnosis	Solution
 Tiny, black, soft-bodied, pear-shaped insects (look for two tubes on their rear ends) cluster on the undersides of leaves and on pseudostems. These insects coat the upper surfaces of leaves and fruit with clear, sticky, varnish-like honeydew. A gray-black coating that easily rubs off (sooty mold) forms on the honeydew.	Aphids	Plant polycultures, page 258 Encourage beneficial organisms, page 260 Blast with hose, page 278 Sticky bands, page 278 Beneficial predators, page 280 Insecticidal soap, page 285 Neem, page 286 Horticultural oil, page 286 Sulfur, page 287 Pyrethrin, page 287
 Small, gray-white or yellowish lumps stick to upper and lower leaf surfaces and pseudostems. You easily remove them with your thumbnail. These insects coat the upper surfaces of leaves and fruit with clear, sticky, varnish-like honeydew. A gray-black coating that easily rubs off (sooty mold) forms on the honeydew.	Scale insects	Plant polycultures, page 258 Encourage beneficial organisms, page 260 Hand-pick pests, page 277 Sticky bands, page 278 Beneficial predators, page 280 Insecticidal soap, page 285 Horticultural oil, page 286 Sulfur, page 287 Pyrethrin, page 287
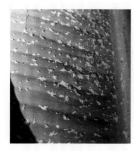 You discover fluffy grayish white lumps clustered on the undersides of leaves and on pseudostems. These insects do not fly. They coat the upper surfaces of leaves and fruit with clear, sticky, varnish-like honeydew. A gray-black coating that easily rubs off (sooty mold) develops on the honeydew.	Mealybugs	Plant polycultures, page 258 Encourage beneficial organisms, page 260 Blast with hose, page 278 Sticky bands, page 278 Beneficial predators, page 280 Insecticidal soap, page 285 Neem, page 286 Horticultural oil, page 286 Sulfur, page 287 Pyrethrin, page 287

Symptom	Diagnosis	Solution
You watch ants scurry over deformed leaves and march up and down the trunk. They are tending the aphids, scale insects, or mealybugs they bring to your plant. Ants feed on the sweet, sticky honeydew produced by these insects.	**Ants and aphids, mealybugs, or scale**	Plant polycultures, page 258 Sticky bands, page 278 Diatomaceous earth, page 285
You see small, bright white insects fly away when you disturb your plant. Large colonies on the undersides of leaves deposit patches of white residue. These insects coat the upper surfaces of leaves and fruit with a clear, sticky, varnish-like honeydew. A gray-black coating that easily rubs off (sooty mold) forms on the honeydew.	**Whitefly**	Encourage beneficial organisms, page 260 Move the air, page 264 Row covers, page 274 Blast with hose, page 278 Vacuum, page 278 Sticky cards, page 279 Beneficial predators, page 280 Insecticidal soap, page 285 Neem, page 286 Horticultural oil, page 286 Sulfur, page 287 Pyrethrin, page 287
Fruit is scarred with patches and streaks of corky russet-brown tissue. Tiny (1/20 inch long) yellow to orangish insects congregate on flower petals, leaves, and young fruit.	**Thrips**	Plant polycultures, page 258 Encourage beneficial organisms, page 260 Weed, page 262 Sanitize, page 263 Kaolin spray, page 277 Blast with hose, page 278 Beneficial predators, page 280 Insecticidal soap, page 285 Spinosad, page 286 Neem, page 286 Horticultural oil, page 286 Pyrethrin, page 287

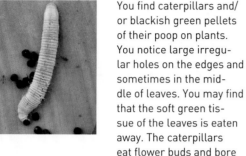

You find caterpillars and/or blackish green pellets of their poop on plants. You notice large irregular holes on the edges and sometimes in the middle of leaves. You may find that the soft green tissue of the leaves is eaten away. The caterpillars eat flower buds and bore holes into the fruit.

Caterpillars

Plant polycultures, page 258
Encourage beneficial organisms, page 260
Hand-pick pests, page 277
Beneficial predators, page 280
BTK, page 283
Insecticidal soap, page 285
Spinosad, page 286
Neem, page 286
Horticultural oil, page 286
Pyrethrin, page 287

Holes between the veins near the edges give leaves a ragged or serrated appearance. Gray-brown beetles eat the leaves.

Chinese rose beetle

Soil solutions, page 248
Plant polycultures, page 258
Encourage beneficial organisms, page 260
Chickens and ducks, page 282
Beneficial nematodes, page 282
Beauveria bassiana, page 285
Insecticidal soap, page 285
Diatomaceous earth, page 285
Spinosad, page 286
Neem, page 286
Horticultural oil, page 286
Sulfur, page 287
Pyrethrin, page 287

You find holes in the pseudostems. Sawdust-like material (frass) may exude from these holes as well as holes in the rhizomes. Plants are stunted and wilt easily. Leaves turn yellow. Weevils (snout beetles) live inside the plant and tunnel through the tissue. Plants die or topple over in wind or with a heavy load of fruit.

Weevils

Soil solutions, page 248
Plant polycultures, page 258
Encourage beneficial organisms, page 260
Chickens and ducks, page 282
Beneficial nematodes, page 282
Beauveria bassiana, page 285
Insecticidal soap, page 285
Diatomaceous earth, page 285
Spinosad, page 286
Neem, page 286
Horticultural oil, page 286
Sulfur, page 287
Pyrethrin, page 287

Symptom	Diagnosis	Solution
Fruit is gnawed open and left hanging in the tree. The flesh is gouged out with parallel grooves like little chisel marks.	**Rats, squirrels, mice**	Metal collars, page 276 Trunk guards, page 276 Bags, page 277 Fright tactics, page 278 Rodent traps, page 279 Garlic spray, page 283 Pepper spray, page 283
Bananas are stripped off your plants and partially eaten. Plants are broken and debris litters the ground.	**Raccoons, opossums**	Metal collars, page 276 Nets, page 277 Fright tactics, page 278 Garlic spray, page 283 Pepper spray, page 283
Plants wilt in the heat of the day even when adequate moisture is available. They lack vigor and grow slowly. Leaves turn yellow. Plants eventually die, turn black, and topple over. The roots are all dead. Nematodes are microscopic. Send samples to a lab to confirm your diagnosis.	**Nematodes**	Soil solutions, page 248 Solarize the soil, page 252 Plant polycultures, page 258 Sanitize, page 263 *Paecilomyces lilacinus*, page 284
Large light brown spots with pronounced yellow haloes occur on leaves. This fungus is a minor leaf-spot pathogen of banana.	**Cordana leaf-spot**	Manage water, page 253 Plant polycultures, page 258 Sanitize, page 263 Move the air, page 264 *Bacillus subtilis*, page 289 *Reynoutria sachalinensis*, page 289 Baking soda, page 290 Neem, page 290 Sulfur, page 291 Copper, page 291

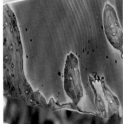

Symptom	Diagnosis	Solution

Narrow reddish brown streaks on the undersides of leaves are the first symptom. The spots enlarge and turn black with yellow haloes on both surfaces. The centers of the spots turn gray. The spots are not confined by the veins of the leaf. The spots coalesce into large patches of dead tissue. Entire leaves are killed by this fungus.

Black sigatoka

Manage water, page 253
Plant polycultures, page 258
Sanitize, page 263
Move the air, page 264
Bacillus subtilis, page 289
Reynoutria sachalinensis, page 289
Baking soda, page 290
Neem, page 290
Sulfur, page 291
Copper, page 291

Leaves wilt, turn brown, and die. Pseudostems turn brown and eventually topple over. All the roots are dead and the internal tissue of the rhizome is brown and dead. Several different soil-dwelling fungi attack and kill banana root systems when the soil is too wet and too cold.

Root rot, crown rot, Panama disease, erwinia soft rot

Soil solutions, page 248
Manage water, page 253
Plant polycultures, page 258
Sanitize, page 263
Bacillus subtilis, page 289
Reynoutria sachalinensis, page 289
Streptomyces lydicus, page 290
Trichoderma harzianum, page 290

The outer leaf sheaths of the pseudostem wither and decay. Leaves become stunted and pseudostems crack open. Plants are stunted, blacken, and die. White mushrooms sprout along the cracks in the pseudostems.

Marasmiellus stem rot

Soil solutions, page 248
Manage water, page 253
Plant polycultures, page 258
Sanitize, page 263
Bacillus subtilis, page 289
Reynoutria sachalinensis, page 289
Streptomyces lydicus, page 290
Trichoderma harzianum, page 290

Symptom	Diagnosis	Solution
 Leaves are mottled with pale streaks between the veins. Plants are stunted. These viruses are spread by mealybugs, which must be controlled. There is no cure for the virus; it can only be prevented.	Mosaic viruses, cucumber mosaic	Plant polycultures, page 258 Encourage beneficial organisms, page 260 Sanitize, page 263 Sterilize tools, page 263 Blast with hose, page 278 Sticky bands, page 278 Beneficial predators, page 280 Insecticidal soap, page 285 Neem, page 286 Horticultural oil, page 286 Sulfur, page 287 Pyrethrin, page 287
 The leaves at the top of the plant become tightly bunched together and their edges turn pale green. This virus is spread by aphids. Control the aphids to prevent the virus. There is no cure for the virus.	Bunchy top	Plant polycultures, page 258 Encourage beneficial organisms, page 260 Sanitize, page 263 Sterilize tools, page 263 Blast with hose, page 278 Sticky bands, page 278 Beneficial predators, page 280 Insecticidal soap, page 285 Neem, page 286 Horticultural oil, page 286 Sulfur, page 287 Pyrethrin, page 287

Blueberry Problem-Solving Guide

Symptom	Diagnosis	Solution
 Tiny, green, woolly-gray, black, or brown, soft-bodied, pear-shaped insects (look for two tubes on their rear ends) cluster on the undersides of leaves. Tips of branches have curled, cupped, or deformed leaves. These insects coat the upper surfaces of leaves and fruit with clear, sticky, varnish-like honeydew. A gray-black coating that easily rubs off (sooty mold) forms on the honeydew.	Aphids	Plant polycultures, page 258 Encourage beneficial organisms, page 260 Blast with hose, page 278 Sticky bands, page 278 Beneficial predators, page 280 Insecticidal soap, page 285 Neem, page 286 Horticultural oil, page 286 Sulfur, page 287 Pyrethrin, page 287
 Small, reddish brown, yellow-brown, or black lumps stick to stems and upper and lower leaf surfaces. You can easily remove them with your thumbnail. These insects coat leaves and fruit with clear, sticky, varnish-like honeydew. A gray-black coating that easily rubs off (sooty mold) forms on the honeydew.	Scale insects	Plant polycultures, page 258 Encourage beneficial organisms, page 260 Hand-pick pests, page 277 Sticky bands, page 278 Beneficial predators, page 280 Insecticidal soap, page 285 Horticultural oil, page 286 Sulfur, page 287 Pyrethrin, page 287
 Ants scurry over deformed leaves and march up and down stems to tend the aphids or scale insects they bring to your bush. They feed on the sweet, sticky honeydew produced by these insects.	Ants and aphids or scale	Plant polycultures, page 258 Sticky bands, page 278 Diatomaceous earth, page 285

You find shrunken berries and sawdust-like material (frass). Small caterpillars bore holes into the fruit and feed inside it. Berries are sometimes webbed together in a mass. Look inside the berries to find caterpillars and confirm your diagnosis.	**Cherry fruitworm, cranberry fruitworm**	Plant polycultures, page 258 Encourage beneficial organisms, page 260 Hand-pick pests, page 277 Beneficial predators, page 280 BTK, page 283 Insecticidal soap, page 285 Spinosad, page 286 Neem, page 286 Horticultural oil, page 286 Pyrethrin, page 287

You spot leaves with their edges rolled into tubes and sewn together with silk. Look inside to find a caterpillar hiding and eating the leaf tissue. Young leafrollers skeletonize leaves because they can only eat the soft green tissue and leave the tough veins behind. Older, stronger leafrollers eat large holes in the leaves.	**Leafrollers**	Plant polycultures, page 258 Encourage beneficial organisms, page 260 Hand-pick pests, page 277 Beneficial predators, page 280 BTK, page 283 Insecticidal soap, page 285 Spinosad, page 286 Neem, page 286 Horticultural oil, page 286 Pyrethrin, page 287

Webs in the branches house large colonies of caterpillars that devour every leaf in sight. Tent caterpillars occur in spring. Watch for fall webworms in mid to late summer.	**Tent caterpillars, fall webworms**	Plant polycultures, page 258 Encourage beneficial organisms, page 260 Hand-pick pests, page 277 Beneficial predators, page 280 BTK, page 283 Insecticidal soap, page 285 Spinosad, page 286 Neem, page 286 Horticultural oil, page 286 Pyrethrin, page 287

Symptom	Diagnosis	Solution

You discover notches in leaves nearest the ground. This is your main clue that gray-brown snout beetles (weevils) have crawled up the trunk and branches to eat the edges of the lower leaves on the bushes. Their larvae are white grubs with brown heads that live in the soil and eat plant roots.

Weevils

Soil solutions, page 248
Plant polycultures, page 258
Encourage beneficial organisms, page 260
Chickens and ducks, page 282
Beneficial nematodes, page 282
Beauveria bassiana, page 285
Insecticidal soap, page 285
Diatomaceous earth, page 285
Spinosad, page 286
Neem, page 286
Horticultural oil, page 286
Sulfur, page 287
Pyrethrin, page 287

You spot metallic green and copper-colored beetles (to ½ inch long) with black legs chewing holes in leaves, flowers, and fruit. Larvae are whitish grubs (to 1 inch long) that live in the soil and eat plant roots. The grubs have three pairs of jointed legs and a brown head. They curl into a C shape when disturbed.

Japanese beetles

Soil solutions, page 248
Plant polycultures, page 258
Encourage beneficial organisms, page 260
Hand-pick pests, page 277
Jug traps, page 279
Beneficial predators, page 280
Chickens and ducks, page 282
Beneficial nematodes, page 282
BTSD, page 284
Milky spore, page 284
Beauveria bassiana, page 285
Insecticidal soap, page 285
Spinosad, page 286
Neem, page 286
Horticultural oil, page 286
Pyrethrin, page 287

You see withering fruit that turns soft and leaks juice from sunken areas. Tiny, white, headless and legless worms (maggots) tunnel through the flesh of the fruit. When mature the maggots drop to the soil to pupate.

Fruit flies and maggots

Soil solutions, page 248
Plant polycultures, page 258
Encourage beneficial organisms, page 260
Sanitize, page 263
Bags, page 277
Kaolin spray, page 277
Traps, page 278
Beneficial predators, page 280
Chickens and ducks, page 282
Beneficial nematodes, page 282
BTI, page 283

Symptom	Diagnosis	Solution

You think thieves have stolen your berries. You could be right. Birds pick off fruit and eat it whole.

Birds

Nets, page 277
Bags, page 277
Fright tactics, page 278
Garlic spray, page 283
Pepper spray, page 283

Marauders invade your garden. They strip berries off your plants. Broken branches and partially eaten berries litter the ground.

Raccoons, opossums

Nets, page 277
Fright tactics, page 278
Garlic spray, page 283
Pepper spray, page 283

Your bushes lack vigor, leaves turn yellowish, and plants grow slowly. Examine the roots for lumps (galls) that are firmly attached and cannot be rubbed off. Nematodes are microscopic. Send samples to a lab to confirm your diagnosis.

Nematodes

Soil solutions, page 248
Solarize the soil, page 252
Plant polycultures, page 258
Sanitize, page 263
Paecilomyces lilacinus, page 284

The leaves of new shoots wilt, turn pale green, then brown and die. The shoot dies back from the tip. Cankers develop on shoots. Fruit becomes infected. Fuzzy, buff-colored mold grows on infected areas.

Botrytis blossom and twig blight

Manage water, page 253
Plant polycultures, page 258
Sanitize, page 263
Move the air, page 264
Bacillus amyloliquefaciens, page 288
Bacillus subtilis, page 289
Reynoutria sachalinensis, page 289
Streptomyces lydicus, page 290
Baking soda, page 290
Neem, page 290
Sulfur, page 291
Copper, page 291

Symptom	Diagnosis	Solution

You notice fruit begin to turn blue very early, then shrivel, and mummify, becoming hard, dry, grayish white, and inedible. Young leaves turn violet, wilt, turn brown, and die. Flower buds, leaves, and stems wilt, turn brown and black, then die.

Mummyberry

Manage water, page 253
Plant polycultures, page 258
Sanitize, page 263
Move the air, page 264
Bacillus amyloliquefaciens, page 288
Bacillus subtilis, page 289
Reynoutria sachalinensis, page 289
Streptomyces lydicus, page 290
Baking soda, page 290
Neem, page 290
Sulfur, page 291
Copper, page 291

You observe brown spots on leaves. Flowers wilt, turn brown, and die. Young stems and twigs develop dark brown spots with concentric rings of pimple-like black bumps. Masses of orange spores grow on last year's infected stems. Infected fruit becomes sunken and puckered as it ripens. All above-ground plant parts are susceptible to this fungal infection.

Anthracnose

Manage water, page 253
Plant polycultures, page 258
Sanitize, page 263
Move the air, page 264
Bacillus subtilis, page 289
Reynoutria sachalinensis, page 289
Baking soda, page 290
Neem, page 290
Sulfur, page 291
Copper, page 291

White or grayish white powdery patches develop on leaves, stems, and fruit. You can easily rub the fungus off the plant tissue. New growth becomes distorted.

Powdery mildew

Manage water, page 253
Plant polycultures, page 258
Sanitize, page 263
Move the air, page 264
Bacillus amyloliquefaciens, page 288
Bacillus pumilus, page 289
Bacillus subtilis, page 289
Reynoutria sachalinensis, page 289
Streptomyces lydicus, page 290
Baking soda, page 290
Neem, page 290
Sulfur, page 291
Copper, page 291

Symptom	Diagnosis	Solution

Yellow spots develop on the upper surfaces of new leaves. Later in the season the spots enlarge, turn reddish brown, and develop orange pustules on the undersides of leaves. You may see whole leaves turn brown, die, and drop prematurely. The alternate host is hemlock trees (*Tsuga* species).

Rust

Manage water, page 253
Plant polycultures, page 258
Mulch, page 262
Sanitize, page 263
Move the air, page 264
Bacillus pumilus, page 289
Bacillus subtilis, page 289
Reynoutria sachalinensis, page 289
Streptomyces lydicus, page 290
Baking soda, page 290
Neem, page 290
Sulfur, page 291
Copper, page 291

Oblong swellings at the tips of the stems develop anytime during the growing season. Tiny maggots live inside the galls.

Stem galls

Soil solutions, page 248
Plant polycultures, page 258
Encourage beneficial organisms, page 260
Sanitize, page 263
Bags, page 277
Kaolin spray, page 277
Traps, page 278
Beneficial predators, page 280
Chickens and ducks, page 282
Beneficial nematodes, page 282
BTI, page 283

You spot swollen, black twigs twisted in dense clusters like a broom. The alternate host of this rust fungus is fir trees (*Abies* species).

Witches' broom

Manage water, page 253
Plant polycultures, page 258
Sanitize, page 263
Move the air, page 264
Bacillus subtilis, page 289
Reynoutria sachalinensis, page 289
Baking soda, page 290
Neem, page 290
Sulfur, page 291
Copper, page 291

New stems suddenly wilt and die in summer. Look for cankers, patches of dark red-brown tissue around or near buds, on the stems near the ground. Some cankers develop a bull's eye pattern of concentric rings. Cankers turn gray with age.

Canker

Manage water, page 253
Plant polycultures, page 258
Sanitize, page 263
Move the air, page 264
Prune properly, page 264
Bacillus subtilis, page 289
Baking soda, page 290
Neem, page 290
Copper, page 291

Long, flat, gray cankers develop on older stems. You observe older shoots wilt, turn bright orange-brown, and die back from the tips toward the crown. One or two stems on a healthy bush suddenly die. The rest of the stems are not affected.

Phomopsis twig blight

Manage water, page 253
Plant polycultures, page 258
Sanitize, page 263
Move the air, page 264
Prune properly, page 264
Bacillus subtilis, page 289
Baking soda, page 290
Neem, page 290
Copper, page 291

Red-brown, irregular-shaped cankers develop on stems of the previous season. Buds in the area of infection die. When these cankers girdle the stem, the stem above them dies.

Bacterial blight and canker

Manage water, page 253
Plant polycultures, page 258
Encourage beneficial organisms, page 260
Sanitize, page 263
Sterilize tools, page 263
Move the air, page 264
Prune properly, page 264
Bacillus amyloliquefaciens, page 288
Bacillus subtilis, page 289
Pseudomonas fluorescens, page 289
Reynoutria sachalinensis, page 289
Streptomyces lydicus, page 290
Copper, page 291

Symptom	Diagnosis	Solution
 You discover rough, warty tumors on larger roots near the base of the trunk. Tumors may also develop on smaller roots underground.	**Crown gall, root gall, hairy root**	Soil solutions, page 248 Manage water, page 253 Plant polycultures, page 258 Sanitize, page 263 *Reynoutria sachalinensis*, page 289 *Trichoderma harzianum*, page 290 Baking soda, page 290 Copper, page 291
 Leaves develop red-brown mottled spots sometimes shaped like an oak leaf with jagged edges. Blossoms wilt, turn brown, and become gray. New growth blackens and dies back. Plant health declines and yield drops rapidly. This virus is spread by aphids. Control aphids to prevent the disease, for which there is no cure.	**Blueberry scorch virus**	Plant polycultures, page 258 Encourage beneficial organisms, page 260 Sanitize, page 263 Sterilize tools, page 263 Blast with hose, page 278 Sticky bands, page 278 Beneficial predators, page 280 Insecticidal soap, page 285 Neem, page 286 Horticultural oil, page 286 Sulfur, page 287 Pyrethrin, page 287
Young leaves turn black and older leaves turn orange. Leaves and developing flowers wither and drop off. Plants grow new foliage but produce no fruit in the first year of infection. Plants recover in subsequent years but remain infected. This virus, which is incurable, is pollen-borne and spread by pollinators.	**Blueberry shock virus**	Plant polycultures, page 258 Encourage beneficial organisms, page 260 Sanitize, page 263 Sterilize tools, page 263

Bramble Problem-Solving Guide

Symptom	Diagnosis	Solution
Tiny, green, woolly-gray, black, or brown, soft-bodied, pear-shaped insects (look for two tubes on their rear ends) cluster on the undersides of leaves. Tips of branches have curled, cupped, or deformed leaves. These insects coat the upper surfaces of leaves and fruit with clear, sticky, varnish-like honeydew. A gray-black coating that easily rubs off (sooty mold) forms on the honeydew.	Aphids	Plant polycultures, page 258 Encourage beneficial organisms, page 260 Blast with hose, page 278 Sticky bands, page 278 Beneficial predators, page 280 Insecticidal soap, page 285 Neem, page 286 Horticultural oil, page 286 Sulfur, page 287 Pyrethrin, page 287
You watch ants scurry over deformed leaves and march up and down the canes. They are tending the aphids they bring to your bramble bushes. Ants feed on the sweet, sticky honeydew produced by aphids.	Ants and aphids	Plant polycultures, page 258 Sticky bands, page 278 Diatomaceous earth, page 285
Leaves turn yellow and the edges curl downward. Small green insects on the undersides of leaves scurry sideways. Adults are green, wedge-shaped, and fast flyers.	Leafhoppers	Plant polycultures, page 258 Encourage beneficial organisms, page 260 Weed, page 262 Kaolin spray, page 277 Beneficial predators, page 280 *Beauveria bassiana*, page 285 Insecticidal soap, page 285 Neem, page 286 Horticultural oil, page 286 Pyrethrin, page 287

Symptom	Diagnosis	Solution
 You spot metallic green and copper-colored beetles (to ½ inch long) with black legs chewing holes in leaves, flowers, and fruit. Larvae are whitish grubs (to 1 inch long) that live in the soil and eat plant roots. The grubs have three pairs of jointed legs and a brown head. They curl into a C shape when disturbed.	Japanese beetles	Soil solutions, page 248 Plant polycultures, page 258 Encourage beneficial organisms, page 260 Hand-pick pests, page 277 Jug traps, page 279 Beneficial predators, page 280 Chickens and ducks, page 282 Beneficial nematodes, page 282 BTSD, page 284 Milky spore, page 284 *Beauveria bassiana*, page 285 Insecticidal soap, page 285 Spinosad, page 286 Neem, page 286 Horticultural oil, page 286 Pyrethrin, page 287
 Large holes appear in leaves. You see small black beetles with a reddish thorax on the plants. Canes develop swellings near the base where larvae are feeding inside. Damaged canes may break off.	Red-necked cane borers	Plant polycultures, page 258 Encourage beneficial organisms, page 260 Sanitize, page 263 Hand-pick pests, page 277 Beneficial predators, page 280 *Beauveria bassiana*, page 285 Spinosad, page 286 Neem, page 286 Pyrethrin, page 287
 Small, beige to brown beetles are present on the plants and inside the flowers. You find holes in foliage and flower buds. Grubs may be present inside the fruit.	Rose chafer, raspberry fruitworm	Plant polycultures, page 258 Encourage beneficial organisms, page 260 Sanitize, page 263 Hand-pick pests, page 277 Beneficial predators, page 280 *Beauveria bassiana*, page 285 Spinosad, page 286 Neem, page 286 Pyrethrin, page 287

Symptom	Diagnosis	Solution
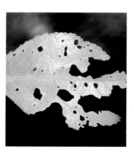 You find shield-shaped insects sucking sap out of canes, flower buds, and fruit. These insects are true bugs and have mouthparts like hypodermic needles. Fruit becomes blemished, discolored, or deformed (cat-faced). Pits or pustules may develop on the fruit. Leaves become twisted, wilt, and turn brown.	**Stink bugs, tarnished plant bugs**	Plant polycultures, page 258 Encourage beneficial organisms, page 260 Bags, page 277 Kaolin spray, page 277 Hand-pick pests, page 277 Beneficial predators, page 280 Chickens and ducks, page 282 Garlic spray, page 283 Pepper spray, page 283 *Beauveria bassiana*, page 285 Insecticidal soap, page 285 Spinosad, page 286 Neem, page 286 Horticultural oil, page 286 Pyrethrin, page 287
 Caterpillars eat large ragged holes in leaves and/or leaves are skeletonized. They sew leaves together with silk and hide inside the rolled leaves.	**Winter moth**	Plant polycultures, page 258 Encourage beneficial organisms, page 260 Hand-pick pests, page 277 Beneficial predators, page 280 BTK, page 283 Insecticidal soap, page 285 Spinosad, page 286 Neem, page 286 Horticultural oil, page 286 Pyrethrin, page 287
Leaves turn yellow, then brown. You find that canes are weak, die back, and break off at the crown. Caterpillars are inside the crown, chewing and tunneling their way through and making lots of frass.	**Crown borers, cane borers**	Plant polycultures, page 258 Encourage beneficial organisms, page 260 Sanitize, page 263 Hand-pick pests, page 277 Beneficial predators, page 280 Beneficial nematodes, page 282 *Beauveria bassiana*, page 285 Spinosad, page 286 Neem, page 286 Pyrethrin, page 287

Symptom	Diagnosis	Solution
 You notice leaves stippled with tiny pale dots that sometimes turn the whole leaf bronze-colored. Fine webbing, like spider silk, covers leaves and twigs. Badly infested leaves turn yellow or red and drop off.	Spider mites	Plant polycultures, page 258 Encourage beneficial organisms, page 260 Sanitize, page 263 Kaolin spray, page 277 Blast with hose, page 278 Beneficial predators, page 280 Garlic spray, page 283 Pepper spray, page 283 *Beauveria bassiana*, page 285 Insecticidal soap, page 285 Spinosad, page 286 Neem, page 286 Horticultural oil, page 286 Sulfur, page 287 Pyrethrin, page 287
 Ripe fruit is picked off the plants and eaten whole. Birds are shameless as they devour your crop.	Birds	Nets, page 277 Bags, page 277 Fright tactics, page 278 Garlic spray, page 283 Pepper spray, page 283
Brown spots appear on leaves, and then leaves turn yellow. The spots become dry and may fall out of the leaf. Leaves wilt, dry, and drop off.	Anthracnose	Manage water, page 253 Plant polycultures, page 258 Sanitize, page 263 Move the air, page 264 *Bacillus subtilis*, page 289 *Reynoutria sachalinensis*, page 289 Baking soda, page 290 Neem, page 290 Sulfur, page 291 Copper, page 291

Symptom	Diagnosis	Solution

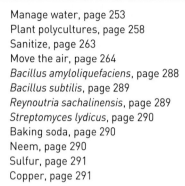

Developing fruit turns gray, rots, and sprouts tufts of grayish brown spores. Flower petals turn brown, shrivel, and decay.

Botrytis blight

Manage water, page 253
Plant polycultures, page 258
Sanitize, page 263
Move the air, page 264
Bacillus amyloliquefaciens, page 288
Bacillus subtilis, page 289
Reynoutria sachalinensis, page 289
Streptomyces lydicus, page 290
Baking soda, page 290
Neem, page 290
Sulfur, page 291
Copper, page 291

You notice leaves turning yellow-brown to bronze. Flowers are more pink, purplish, or reddish than normal. Blossoms are twisted and distorted. Fruit fails to develop. Foliage and lateral stems are congested and look bunched up.

Blackberry rosette, double blossom

Manage water, page 253
Plant polycultures, page 258
Sanitize, page 263
Move the air, page 264
Bacillus subtilis, page 289
Reynoutria sachalinensis, page 289
Baking soda, page 290
Neem, page 290
Sulfur, page 291
Copper, page 291

Small yellow spots appear on the upper surface of leaves in early summer. Small bright orange bumps form on the undersides of leaves. You get orange dust on your fingertips when you touch the bumps.

Rust

Manage water, page 253
Plant polycultures, page 258
Mulch, page 262
Sanitize, page 263
Move the air, page 264
Bacillus pumilus, page 289
Bacillus subtilis, page 289
Reynoutria sachalinensis, page 289
Streptomyces lydicus, page 290
Baking soda, page 290
Neem, page 290
Sulfur, page 291
Copper, page 291

Symptom	Diagnosis	Solution
Leaves turn yellow and plants wilt and die quickly when the weather turns warm in spring. Dark patches oozing gum or dark sap develop at the base of the canes. Reddish brown streaks occur in the inner bark and outer layers of wood.	**Phytophthora root rot, crown rot**	Soil solutions, page 248 Manage water, page 253 Plant polycultures, page 258 Sanitize, page 263 *Bacillus subtilis*, page 289 *Reynoutria sachalinensis*, page 289 *Streptomyces lydicus*, page 290 *Trichoderma harzianum*, page 290
The lower leaves turn yellow and develop brown blotches on their tips. Often, this symptom appears on only one side of the plant. The leaves curl and die. The plant's growth slows. Look for black spots on the stems near the soil line. To confirm your diagnosis, cut stems in half lengthwise to see dark streaks inside.	**Verticillium wilt**	Soil solutions, page 248 Manage water, page 253 Plant polycultures, page 258 Sanitize, page 263 *Reynoutria sachalinensis*, page 289 *Streptomyces lydicus*, page 290 *Trichoderma harzianum*, page 290
Rough, warty tumors occur on the base of canes or on larger roots near the crown. Tumors may also develop on smaller roots underground.	**Crown gall, root gall, hairy root**	Soil solutions, page 248 Manage water, page 253 Plant polycultures, page 258 Sanitize, page 263 *Reynoutria sachalinensis*, page 289 *Trichoderma harzianum*, page 290 Baking soda, page 290 Copper, page 291

Symptom	Diagnosis	Solution
 Leaves are mottled with yellow. Plants are stunted. These viruses are spread by aphids, which must be controlled to prevent the disease. Viruses have no cure.	**Mosaic viruses**	Plant polycultures, page 258 Encourage beneficial organisms, page 260 Sanitize, page 263 Sterilize tools, page 263 Blast with hose, page 278 Sticky bands, page 278 Beneficial predators, page 280 Insecticidal soap, page 285 Neem, page 286 Horticultural oil, page 286 Sulfur, page 287 Pyrethrin, page 287

Citrus Problem-Solving Guide

Symptom	Diagnosis	Solution
Tiny, green, woolly-gray, black, or brown, soft-bodied, pear-shaped insects (look for two tubes on their rear ends) cluster on the undersides of leaves. Tips of branches have curled, cupped, or deformed leaves. A clear, sticky substance coats the upper surfaces of leaves and fruit. A gray-black coating that easily rubs off (sooty mold) may occur on top of the honeydew.	Aphids	Plant polycultures, page 258 Encourage beneficial organisms, page 260 Blast with hose, page 278 Sticky bands, page 278 Beneficial predators, page 280 Insecticidal soap, page 285 Neem, page 286 Horticultural oil, page 286 Sulfur, page 287 Pyrethrin, page 287
Small, gray-white, reddish brown, yellow, or black lumps stick to upper and lower leaf surfaces, or stems. You can easily remove them with your thumbnail. These insects coat the upper surfaces of leaves and fruit with clear, sticky, varnish-like honeydew. A gray-black coating that easily rubs off (sooty mold) forms on the honeydew.	Scale insects	Plant polycultures, page 258 Encourage beneficial organisms, page 260 Hand-pick pests, page 277 Sticky bands, page 278 Beneficial predators, page 280 Insecticidal soap, page 285 Horticultural oil, page 286 Sulfur, page 287 Pyrethrin, page 287
You discover fluffy grayish white lumps clustered where leaves attach to stems and on the undersides of leaves. These insects do not fly. They coat the upper surfaces of leaves and fruit with clear, sticky, varnish-like honeydew. A gray-black coating that easily rubs off (sooty mold) forms on the honeydew.	Mealybugs	Plant polycultures, page 258 Encourage beneficial organisms, page 260 Blast with hose, page 278 Sticky bands, page 278 Beneficial predators, page 280 Insecticidal soap, page 285 Neem, page 286 Horticultural oil, page 286 Sulfur, page 287 Pyrethrin, page 287

Symptom	Diagnosis	Solution
 You watch ants scurry over deformed leaves and march up and down the trunk. They are tending the aphids, scale insects, or mealybugs they bring to your tree. Ants feed on the sweet, sticky honeydew produced by these insects.	**Ants and aphids, mealybugs, or scale**	Plant polycultures, page 258 Sticky bands, page 278 Diatomaceous earth, page 285
 You see small, bright white insects fly away when you disturb your plant. Large colonies on the undersides of leaves deposit patches of white residue. These insects coat the upper surfaces of leaves and fruit with a clear, sticky, varnish-like honeydew. A gray-black coating that easily rubs off (sooty mold) forms on the honeydew.	**Whitefly**	Encourage beneficial organisms, page 260 Move the air, page 264 Blast with hose, page 278 Vacuum, page 278 Sticky cards, page 279 Beneficial predators, page 280 Insecticidal soap, page 285 Neem, page 286 Horticultural oil, page 286 Sulfur, page 287 Pyrethrin, page 287
 You find scars on the fruit with patches and streaks of raised, rough, corky yellow-brown or silvery tissue. Leaves look silvery. Some damaged leaves roll up and drop off. Tiny (1/20 inch long) yellow to orangish insects congregate on flower petals, leaves, and young fruit.	**Thrips**	Plant polycultures, page 258 Encourage beneficial organisms, page 260 Weed, page 262 Sanitize, page 263 Kaolin spray, page 277 Blast with hose, page 278 Beneficial predators, page 280 Insecticidal soap, page 285 Spinosad, page 286 Neem, page 286 Horticultural oil, page 286 Pyrethrin, page 287

Tiny white specks stipple the leaves. Leaf edges may yellow and turn brown. Wedge-shaped, greenish blue or brownish gray insects (to ½ inch long) hide on the undersides of leaves. Fast fliers, they fly away when disturbed. These insects transmit serious bacterial and viral diseases to your plants.

Leafhoppers, sharpshooters

Plant polycultures, page 258
Encourage beneficial organisms, page 260
Weed, page 262
Kaolin spray, page 277
Beneficial predators, page 280
Beauveria bassiana, page 285
Insecticidal soap, page 285
Neem, page 286
Horticultural oil, page 286
Pyrethrin, page 287

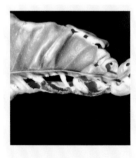

You spot metallic green and copper-colored beetles (to ½ inch long) with black legs chewing holes in leaves, flowers, and fruit. Larvae are whitish grubs (to 1 inch long) that live in the soil and eat plant roots. The grubs have three pairs of jointed legs and a brown head. They curl into a C shape when disturbed.

Japanese beetles

Soil solutions, page 248
Plant polycultures, page 258
Encourage beneficial organisms, page 260
Hand-pick pests, page 277
Jug traps, page 279
Beneficial predators, page 280
Chickens and ducks, page 282
Beneficial nematodes, page 282
BTSD, page 284
Milky spore, page 284
Beauveria bassiana, page 285
Insecticidal soap, page 285
Spinosad, page 286
Neem, page 286
Horticultural oil, page 286
Pyrethrin, page 287

You notice large irregular holes on the edges and sometimes in the middle of leaves. You may find that the soft green tissue of the leaves is eaten away. You may also find blackish green pellets of caterpillar poop. The caterpillars eat flower buds and bore holes into the fruit. Look for caterpillars on your plants to confirm your diagnosis.

Caterpillars

Plant polycultures, page 258
Encourage beneficial organisms, page 260
Hand-pick pests, page 277
Beneficial predators, page 280
BTK, page 283
Insecticidal soap, page 285
Spinosad, page 286
Neem, page 286
Horticultural oil, page 286
Pyrethrin, page 287

Symptom	Diagnosis	Solution
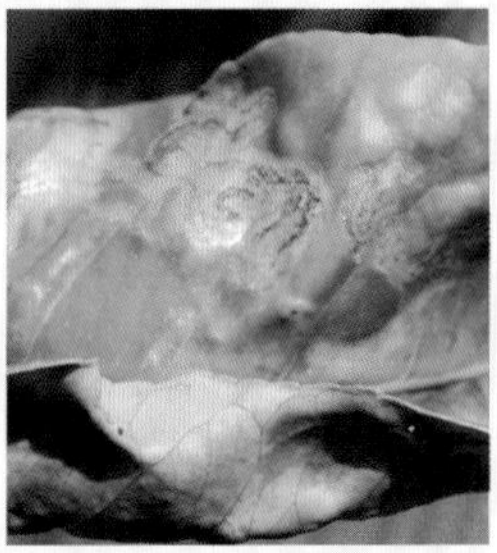 Insect larvae inside the leaf munch tunnels and create discolored blotches and looping trails. The leaves curl and twist. The larvae crawl out of the leaf and drop to the soil to pupate.	Leafminers	Soil solutions, page 248 Plant polycultures, page 258 Encourage beneficial organisms, page 260 Sanitize, page 263 Beneficial predators, page 280 Chickens and ducks, page 282 Beneficial nematodes, page 282 *Beauveria bassiana*, page 285 Neem, page 286 Horticultural oil, page 286 Pyrethrin, page 287
 Grasshoppers and katy-dids hop and fly about the garden during the day. You see large holes on the edges and in the middle of leaves. Crickets hide during the day and do their damage at night.	Grasshoppers, katydids, crickets	Soil solutions, page 248 Plant polycultures, page 258 Encourage beneficial organisms, page 260 Beneficial predators, page 280 Chickens and ducks, page 282 Nosema spore, page 283 *Beauveria bassiana*, page 285 Insecticidal soap, page 285 Spinosad, page 286 Neem, page 286 Horticultural oil, page 286 Pyrethrin, page 287
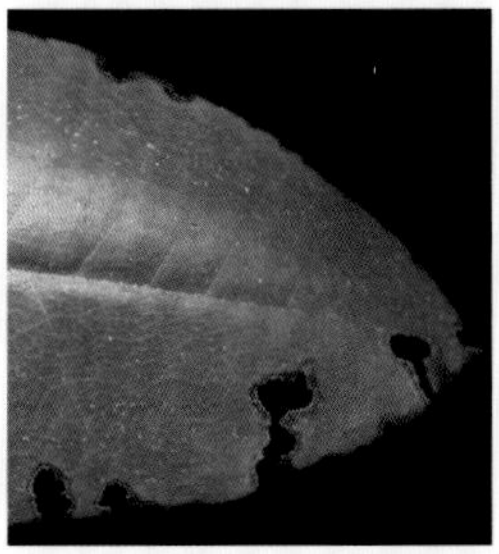 You discover notches on edges of leaves nearest the ground. This is your main clue that gray-brown snout beetles (weevils) have crawled up the trunk and branches to eat the edges of the lower leaves on the trees. Their larvae are white grubs with brown heads that live in the soil and eat plant roots.	Weevils	Soil solutions, page 248 Plant polycultures, page 258 Encourage beneficial organisms, page 260 Chickens and ducks, page 282 Beneficial nematodes, page 282 *Beauveria bassiana*, page 285 Insecticidal soap, page 285 Diatomaceous earth, page 285 Spinosad, page 286 Neem, page 286 Horticultural oil, page 286 Sulfur, page 287 Pyrethrin, page 287

Symptom	Diagnosis	Solution
 You notice leaves stippled with tiny pale dots that sometimes turn the whole leaf bronze-colored. Fine webbing, like spider silk, covers leaves and twigs. Badly infested leaves turn yellow or red and drop off.	**Spider mites, European red mites, brown mites**	Plant polycultures, page 258 Encourage beneficial organisms, page 260 Sanitize, page 263 Kaolin spray, page 277 Blast with hose, page 278 Beneficial predators, page 280 Garlic spray, page 283 Pepper spray, page 283 *Beauveria bassiana*, page 285 Insecticidal soap, page 285 Spinosad, page 286 Neem, page 286 Horticultural oil, page 286 Sulfur, page 287 Pyrethrin, page 287
 Fruit is nipped off the tree, thrown on the ground, and partially eaten. Fruit may also be half-eaten while still hanging on the tree.	**Squirrels, rats**	Metal collars, page 276 Bags, page 277 Fright tactics, page 278 Rodent traps, page 279 Garlic spray, page 283 Pepper spray, page 283
 Slime trails criss-cross trunks, leaves, and fruit. You find large irregular holes in leaves or fruit.	**Slugs and snails**	Plant polycultures, page 258 Encourage beneficial organisms, page 260 Weed, page 262 Mulch, page 262 Hand-pick pests, page 277 Copper tape, page 278 Slug and snail traps, page 279 Beneficial predators, page 280 Chickens and ducks, page 282 Iron phosphate, page 285 Diatomaceous earth, page 285

 Leaves turn yellow. Trees wilt in the heat of the day even when adequate moisture is available. They lack vigor and grow slowly. Examine the roots for lumps (galls) that are firmly attached and cannot be rubbed off. Nematodes are microscopic. Send samples to a lab to confirm your diagnosis.	Nematodes	Soil solutions, page 248 Solarize the soil, page 252 Plant polycultures, page 258 Sanitize, page 263 *Paecilomyces lilacinus*, page 284
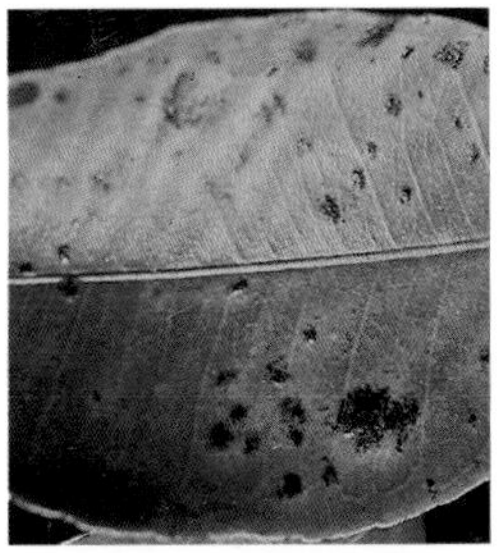 Black greasy-looking spots appear on leaves. Leaves wilt, dry, and drop off.	Greasy spot	Manage water, page 253 Plant polycultures, page 258 Sanitize, page 263 Move the air, page 264 *Bacillus subtilis*, page 289 *Reynoutria sachalinensis*, page 289 Baking soda, page 290 Neem, page 290 Sulfur, page 291 Copper, page 291
 Dark fungal spores cover leaves and twigs. Twigs die back and leaves drop prematurely. You find dull red-brown or greenish brown streaks on the fruit.	Anthracnose	Manage water, page 253 Plant polycultures, page 258 Sanitize, page 263 Move the air, page 264 *Bacillus subtilis*, page 289 *Reynoutria sachalinensis*, page 289 Baking soda, page 290 Neem, page 290 Sulfur, page 291 Copper, page 291

Symptom	Diagnosis	Solution
Raised, brown, corky spots and warts develop on leaves. Warts occur on fruit. Fruit may become deformed.	**Scab**	Manage water, page 253 Plant polycultures, page 258 Mulch, page 262 Sanitize, page 263 Move the air, page 264 *Bacillus pumilus*, page 289 *Bacillus subtilis*, page 289 *Reynoutria sachalinensis*, page 289 Baking soda, page 290 Neem, page 290 Copper, page 291
Brown spots on fruit enlarge rapidly. Fruit turns brown and withers. Fruit mummifies and hangs on the tree.	**Phytophthora brown rot**	Manage water, page 253 Plant polycultures, page 258 Sanitize, page 263 Move the air, page 264 Prune properly, page 264 *Bacillus subtilis*, page 289 *Reynoutria sachalinensis*, page 289 Baking soda, page 290 Neem, page 290 Sulfur, page 291 Copper, page 291
Leaves turn yellowish and drop off. Trees slowly decline. Growth is poor and fruit production declines. You discover dark patches oozing gum or dark sap at the base of the trunk. Reddish brown streaks occur in the inner bark and outer layers of wood.	**Phytophthora foot rot, crown rot**	Soil solutions, page 248 Manage water, page 253 Plant polycultures, page 258 Sanitize, page 263 *Bacillus subtilis*, page 289 *Reynoutria sachalinensis*, page 289 *Streptomyces lydicus*, page 290 *Trichoderma harzianum*, page 290

Symptom	Diagnosis	Solution

Honey-colored mushrooms sprout at the base of your tree. They are the fruiting bodies of a destructive fungus. Leaves are small and yellowish, and growth is slow. Shoots die back from the tips. Peel back the bark from the trunk just below the soil line to find leathery white patches that smell like fresh mushrooms. Look at the roots to find blackish, root-like structures (rhizomorphs) adjacent to them.

Armillaria root rot

Soil solutions, page 248
Manage water, page 253
Plant polycultures, page 258
Sanitize, page 263
Bacillus subtilis, page 289
Reynoutria sachalinensis, page 289
Streptomyces lydicus, page 290
Trichoderma harzianum, page 290

Leaves become brown and crispy dry as if burned by fire. Leaf stalks turn black and whole twigs may die back. Fruit has small black spots.

Citrus blast

Manage water, page 253
Plant polycultures, page 258
Encourage beneficial organisms, page 260
Sanitize, page 263
Sterilize tools, page 263
Move the air, page 264
Prune properly, page 264
Bacillus amyloliquefaciens, page 288
Bacillus subtilis, page 289
Pseudomonas fluorescens, page 289
Reynoutria sachalinensis, page 289
Streptomyces lydicus, page 290
Copper, page 291

Leaves are mottled with yellow. Plants are stunted. These viruses are spread by aphids, pruning, and grafting. Control aphids to prevent this incurable virus.

Mosaic viruses

Plant polycultures, page 258
Encourage beneficial organisms, page 260
Sanitize, page 263
Sterilize tools, page 263
Blast with hose, page 278
Sticky bands, page 278
Beneficial predators, page 280
Insecticidal soap, page 285
Neem, page 286
Horticultural oil, page 286
Sulfur, page 287
Pyrethrin, page 287

Currant and Gooseberry Problem-Solving Guide

Symptom	Diagnosis	Solution
   Tips of branches have curled, cupped, or deformed leaves with bright red patches. Tiny, pale green, soft-bodied, pear-shaped insects (look for two tubes on their rear ends) cluster on the undersides of leaves. These insects coat the upper surfaces of leaves and fruit with clear, sticky, varnish-like honeydew. A gray-black coating that easily rubs off (sooty mold) forms on the honeydew.	**Aphids**	Plant polycultures, page 258 Encourage beneficial organisms, page 260 Blast with hose, page 278 Sticky bands, page 278 Beneficial predators, page 280 Insecticidal soap, page 285 Neem, page 286 Horticultural oil, page 286 Sulfur, page 287 Pyrethrin, page 287
Small, gray-white, reddish brown, yellow, or black lumps stick to upper and lower leaf surfaces, or stems. You can easily remove them with your thumbnail. These insects coat the upper surfaces of leaves and fruit with clear, sticky, varnish-like honeydew. A gray-black coating that easily rubs off (sooty mold) forms on the honeydew.	**Scale insects**	Plant polycultures, page 258 Encourage beneficial organisms, page 260 Hand-pick pests, page 277 Sticky bands, page 278 Beneficial predators, page 280 Insecticidal soap, page 285 Horticultural oil, page 286 Sulfur, page 287 Pyrethrin, page 287

Symptom	Diagnosis	Solution
 You watch ants scurry over deformed leaves and march up and down the stems. They are tending the aphids, scale insects, or mealybugs they bring to your plant. Ants feed on the sweet, sticky honeydew produced by these insects.	Ants and aphids, mealybugs, or scale	Plant polycultures, page 258 Sticky bands, page 278 Diatomaceous earth, page 285
 Caterpillars burrow into the fruit and ruin it. They tie clusters of berries together with silk webbing. When mature they drop to the soil to pupate. Look for caterpillars on your plants to confirm your diagnosis.	Gooseberry fruitworm	Plant polycultures, page 258 Encourage beneficial organisms, page 260 Hand-pick pests, page 277 Beneficial predators, page 280 BTK, page 283 Insecticidal soap, page 285 Spinosad, page 286 Neem, page 286 Horticultural oil, page 286 Pyrethrin, page 287
 Leaves have large holes or have been eaten completely away. You find bright green caterpillar-like larvae on your plants. These are sawfly larvae, not caterpillars, and BTK will not kill them.	Imported currant worm	Soil solutions, page 248 Plant polycultures, page 258 Encourage beneficial organisms, page 260 Kaolin spray, page 277 Hand-pick pests, page 277 Beneficial predators, page 280 Chickens and ducks, page 282 Beneficial nematodes, page 282 *Beauveria bassiana*, page 285 Spinosad, page 286 Neem, page 286 Horticultural oil, page 286 Sulfur, page 287 Pyrethrin, page 287

Symptom	Diagnosis	Solution
 Webs in the branches house large colonies of caterpillars that devour the leaves. Tent caterpillars occur in spring. Fall webworms show up in mid to late summer.	**Tent caterpillars, fall webworms**	Plant polycultures, page 258 Encourage beneficial organisms, page 260 Hand-pick pests, page 277 Beneficial predators, page 280 BTK, page 283 Insecticidal soap, page 285 Spinosad, page 286 Neem, page 286 Horticultural oil, page 286 Pyrethrin, page 287
 You spot metallic green and copper-colored beetles (to ½ inch long) with black legs chewing holes in leaves, flowers, and fruit. Larvae are whitish grubs (to 1 inch long) that live in the soil and eat plant roots. The grubs have three pairs of jointed legs and a brown head. They curl into a C shape when disturbed.	**Japanese beetles**	Soil solutions, page 248 Plant polycultures, page 258 Encourage beneficial organisms, page 260 Hand-pick pests, page 277 Jug traps, page 279 Beneficial predators, page 280 Chickens and ducks, page 282 Beneficial nematodes, page 282 BTSD, page 284 Milky spore, page 284 *Beauveria bassiana*, page 285 Insecticidal soap, page 285 Spinosad, page 286 Neem, page 286 Horticultural oil, page 286 Pyrethrin, page 287
 Shoot tips die. Maggot-like insect larvae hide inside succulent shoot tips and eat the tissue.	**Stem girdler**	Plant polycultures, page 258 Encourage beneficial organisms, page 260 Sanitize, page 263 Hand-pick pests, page 277 Beneficial predators, page 280 Beneficial nematodes, page 282 *Beauveria bassiana*, page 285 Spinosad, page 286 Neem, page 286 Pyrethrin, page 287

Symptom	Diagnosis	Solution
 Leaves turn yellow and stems wilt and die in summer and fall. A pale yellow caterpillar lives inside the stem eating the soft pith.	Currant borer	Plant polycultures, page 258 Encourage beneficial organisms, page 260 Sanitize, page 263 Hand-pick pests, page 277 Beneficial predators, page 280 Beneficial nematodes, page 282 *Beauveria bassiana*, page 285 Spinosad, page 286 Neem, page 286 Pyrethrin, page 287
 You see withering fruit that turns soft and leaks juice from sunken areas. Tiny, white, headless and legless worms (maggots) tunnel through the flesh of the fruit. When mature the maggots drop to the soil to pupate.	Fruit flies and maggots	Soil solutions, page 248 Plant polycultures, page 258 Encourage beneficial organisms, page 260 Sanitize, page 263 Bags, page 277 Kaolin spray, page 277 Traps, page 278 Beneficial predators, page 280 Chickens and ducks, page 282 Beneficial nematodes, page 282 BTI, page 283
 You notice leaves stippled with tiny pale dots that sometimes turn the whole leaf bronze-colored. Fine webbing, like spider silk, covers leaves and twigs. Badly infested leaves turn yellow or red and drop off.	Spider mites	Plant polycultures, page 258 Encourage beneficial organisms, page 260 Sanitize, page 263 Kaolin spray, page 277 Blast with hose, page 278 Beneficial predators, page 280 Garlic spray, page 283 Pepper spray, page 283 *Beauveria bassiana*, page 285 Insecticidal soap, page 285 Spinosad, page 286 Neem, page 286 Horticultural oil, page 286 Sulfur, page 287 Pyrethrin, page 287

Symptom	Diagnosis	Solution
 Slime trails criss-cross stems, leaves, and fruit. You find large irregular holes in leaves or fruit. Look for snails or slugs on your plants or hiding nearby.	Slugs and snails	Plant polycultures, page 258 Encourage beneficial organisms, page 260 Weed, page 262 Mulch, page 262 Hand-pick pests, page 277 Copper tape, page 278 Slug and snail traps, page 279 Beneficial predators, page 280 Chickens and ducks, page 282 Iron phosphate, page 285 Diatomaceous earth, page 285
 Berries are stripped off your plants and partially eaten. Branches are broken, plants crushed, and debris litters the ground.	Raccoons, opossums	Nets, page 277 Fright tactics, page 278 Garlic spray, page 283 Pepper spray, page 283
 Berries are gnawed open and left hanging in the bush or have simply been removed. Partially eaten berries litter the ground.	Rats, squirrels, mice	Bags, page 277 Fright tactics, page 278 Rodent traps, page 279 Garlic spray, page 283 Pepper spray, page 283
Brown spots appear on leaves. The spots enlarge. Pinpoint black or gray bumps develop on the surface of the spots. Black specks may occur on fruit as well.	Anthracnose	Manage water, page 253 Plant polycultures, page 258 Sanitize, page 263 Move the air, page 264 *Bacillus subtilis*, page 289 *Reynoutria sachalinensis*, page 289 Baking soda, page 290 Neem, page 290 Sulfur, page 291 Copper, page 291

White or grayish white powdery patches develop on leaves, stems, and fruit. You can easily rub the fungus off the plant tissue. New growth becomes distorted. Fruit develops web-like scars of russetted corky tissue. | **Powdery mildew** | Manage water, page 253
Plant polycultures, page 258
Sanitize, page 263
Move the air, page 264
Bacillus amyloliquefaciens, page 288
Bacillus pumilus, page 289
Bacillus subtilis, page 289
Reynoutria sachalinensis, page 289
Streptomyces lydicus, page 290
Baking soda, page 290
Neem, page 290
Sulfur, page 291
Copper, page 291

Small yellow spots appear on the upper surface of leaves in early summer. Small brown bumps form on the undersides of leaves. You get a colorful dust on your fingertips when you touch the bumps. | **Rust** | Manage water, page 253
Plant polycultures, page 258
Mulch, page 262
Sanitize, page 263
Move the air, page 264
Bacillus pumilus, page 289
Bacillus subtilis, page 289
Reynoutria sachalinensis, page 289
Streptomyces lydicus, page 290
Baking soda, page 290
Neem, page 290
Sulfur, page 291
Copper, page 291

Leaves of currants (not gooseberries) turn yellow and young shoots wilt in spring or summer. No larvae are inside the stem and there are no exit holes present. Black pinpoint bumps appear near the tips of old stems. | **Currant cane blight, botryosphaeria canker** | Manage water, page 253
Plant polycultures, page 258
Sanitize, page 263
Move the air, page 264
Prune properly, page 264
Bacillus subtilis, page 289
Baking soda, page 290
Neem, page 290
Copper, page 291

Fig Problem-Solving Guide

Symptom	Diagnosis	Solution
Small brown lumps stick to stems, leaves, and fruit. You can easily remove them with your thumbnail. These insects coat the upper surfaces of leaves and fruit with clear, sticky, varnish-like honeydew. A gray-black coating that easily rubs off (sooty mold) forms on the honeydew.	Scale insects	Plant polycultures, page 258 Encourage beneficial organisms, page 260 Hand-pick pests, page 277 Sticky bands, page 278 Beneficial predators, page 280 Insecticidal soap, page 285 Horticultural oil, page 286 Sulfur, page 287 Pyrethrin, page 287
You find fluffy grayish white lumps clustered where leaves attach to stems and on the undersides of leaves. These insects do not fly. They coat the upper surfaces of leaves and fruit with clear, sticky, varnish-like honeydew. A gray-black coating that easily rubs off (sooty mold) forms on the honeydew.	Mealybugs	Plant polycultures, page 258 Encourage beneficial organisms, page 260 Blast with hose, page 278 Sticky bands, page 278 Beneficial predators, page 280 Insecticidal soap, page 285 Neem, page 286 Horticultural oil, page 286 Sulfur, page 287 Pyrethrin, page 287
Ants scurry over deformed leaves and march up and down the trunk to tend the scale insects or mealybugs they bring to your tree. Ants feed on the sweet, sticky honeydew produced by these insects.	Ants and mealybugs or scale	Plant polycultures, page 258 Sticky bands, page 278 Diatomaceous earth, page 285

Symptom	Diagnosis	Solution
Large (to 1 inch long) metallic green and copper-colored beetles eat holes in fruit. Larvae are whitish grubs (to 2 inches long) that live in the soil and eat plant roots. The grubs have three pairs of jointed legs and a brown head. They curl into a C shape when disturbed.	**Figeater beetles**	Soil solutions, page 248 Plant polycultures, page 258 Encourage beneficial organisms, page 260 Hand-pick pests, page 277 Jug traps, page 279 Beneficial predators, page 280 Chickens and ducks, page 282 Beneficial nematodes, page 282 BTSD, page 284 *Beauveria bassiana*, page 285 Insecticidal soap, page 285 Spinosad, page 286 Neem, page 286 Horticultural oil, page 286 Pyrethrin, page 287
You notice leaves stippled with tiny pale dots that sometimes turn the whole leaf bronze-colored. Fine webbing, like spider silk, covers leaves and twigs. Badly infested leaves turn yellow or red and drop off.	**Spider mites**	Plant polycultures, page 258 Encourage beneficial organisms, page 260 Sanitize, page 263 Kaolin spray, page 277 Blast with hose, page 278 Beneficial predators, page 280 Garlic spray, page 283 Pepper spray, page 283 *Beauveria bassiana*, page 285 Insecticidal soap, page 285 Spinosad, page 286 Neem, page 286 Horticultural oil, page 286 Sulfur, page 287 Pyrethrin, page 287
Holes in the ground beside what's left of your fig tree indicate gophers are present. Roots are missing or seriously damaged. Trees are wilting and dying.	**Gophers**	Weed, page 262 Mulch, page 262 Wire mesh, page 274 Rodent traps, page 279 Garlic spray, page 283 Pepper spray, page 283

Symptom	Diagnosis	Solution
Fruit hanging on the tree is half-eaten. Triangular holes are pecked into the edges of the damaged area. Pointed holes poke into the flesh.	Birds	Nets, page 277 Bags, page 277 Fright tactics, page 278 Garlic spray, page 283 Pepper spray, page 283
Trees wilt in the heat of the day even when adequate moisture is available. They lack vigor and grow slowly. Leaves turn yellow. Examine the roots for lumps (galls) that are firmly attached and cannot be rubbed off. Nematodes are microscopic. Send samples to a lab to confirm your diagnosis.	Nematodes	Soil solutions, page 248 Solarize the soil, page 252 Plant polycultures, page 258 Sanitize, page 263 *Paecilomyces lilacinus*, page 284
New shoots die back from the tip. Their leaves wilt, turn pale green, then turn brown and die. Cankers develop on shoots. Fruit becomes infected. Fuzzy, buff-colored mold grows on infected areas.	Botrytis blight	Manage water, page 253 Plant polycultures, page 258 Sanitize, page 263 Move the air, page 264 *Bacillus amyloliquefaciens*, page 288 *Bacillus subtilis*, page 289 *Reynoutria sachalinensis*, page 289 *Streptomyces lydicus*, page 290 Baking soda, page 290 Neem, page 290 Sulfur, page 291 Copper, page 291

Small brown bumps form on the undersides of leaves in summer. Small yellow spots appear on the upper surface of leaves in early summer. These bumps make golden yellow powdery spores that rub off like dust on your fingertips.

Rust

Manage water, page 253
Plant polycultures, page 258
Sanitize, page 263
Move the air, page 264
Bacillus subtilis, page 289
Reynoutria sachalinensis, page 289
Baking soda, page 290
Neem, page 290
Sulfur, page 291
Copper, page 291

Leaves are mottled with distinct yellow markings. Fruit also develops yellow mottling but it's more faint than on the foliage. Plants are stunted and produce fewer and smaller fruit. These viruses are spread by mites, which must be controlled to prevent this incurable disease.

Mosaic viruses

Plant polycultures, page 258
Encourage beneficial organisms, page 260
Sanitize, page 263
Sterilize tools, page 263
Blast with hose, page 278
Sticky bands, page 278
Beneficial predators, page 280
Insecticidal soap, page 285
Neem, page 286
Horticultural oil, page 286
Sulfur, page 287
Pyrethrin, page 287

Grape Problem-Solving Guide

Symptom	Diagnosis	Solution
 Tiny, green, woolly-gray, black, or brown, soft-bodied, pear-shaped insects (look for two tubes on their rear ends) cluster on the undersides of leaves. Tips of branches have curled, cupped, or deformed leaves. These insects coat the upper surfaces of leaves and fruit with clear, sticky, varnish-like honeydew. A gray-black coating that easily rubs off (sooty mold) forms on the honeydew.	Aphids	Plant polycultures, page 258 Encourage beneficial organisms, page 260 Blast with hose, page 278 Sticky bands, page 278 Beneficial predators, page 280 Insecticidal soap, page 285 Neem, page 286 Horticultural oil, page 286 Sulfur, page 287 Pyrethrin, page 287
 Small, gray-white, reddish brown, yellow, or black lumps stick to upper and lower leaf surfaces, or stems. You can easily remove them with your thumbnail. These insects coat the upper surfaces of leaves and fruit with clear, sticky, varnish-like honeydew. A gray-black coating that easily rubs off (sooty mold) forms on the honeydew.	Scale insects	Plant polycultures, page 258 Encourage beneficial organisms, page 260 Hand-pick pests, page 277 Sticky bands, page 278 Beneficial predators, page 280 Insecticidal soap, page 285 Horticultural oil, page 286 Sulfur, page 287 Pyrethrin, page 287
 Fluffy grayish white lumps cluster where leaves attach to stems and on the undersides of leaves. These insects do not fly. They coat the upper surfaces of leaves and fruit with clear, sticky, varnish-like honeydew. A gray-black coating that easily rubs off (sooty mold) forms on the honeydew.	Mealybugs	Plant polycultures, page 258 Encourage beneficial organisms, page 260 Blast with hose, page 278 Sticky bands, page 278 Beneficial predators, page 280 Insecticidal soap, page 285 Neem, page 286 Horticultural oil, page 286 Sulfur, page 287 Pyrethrin, page 287

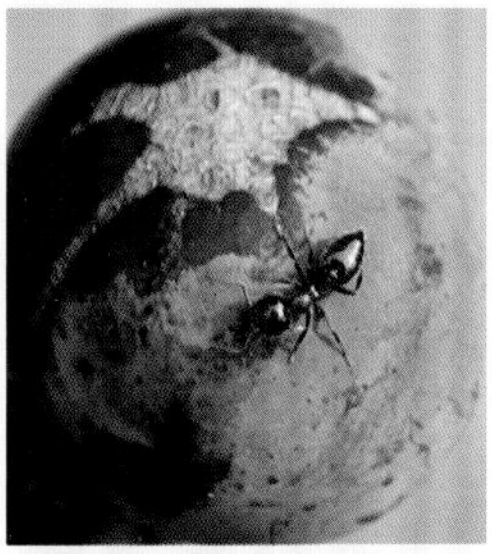

You watch ants scurry over deformed leaves and march up and down the stems. They are tending the aphids, scale insects, or mealybugs they bring to your vine. Ants feed on the sweet, sticky honeydew produced by these insects.

Ants and aphids, mealybugs, or scale

Plant polycultures, page 258
Sticky bands, page 278
Diatomaceous earth, page 285

You find scars on the fruit with patches and streaks of raised, rough, corky yellow-brown or silvery tissue. Leaves look silvery. Some damaged leaves roll up and drop off. Tiny (1/20 inch long) yellow to orangish insects congregate on flower petals, leaves, and young fruit.

Thrips

Plant polycultures, page 258
Encourage beneficial organisms, page 260
Weed, page 262
Sanitize, page 263
Kaolin spray, page 277
Blast with hose, page 278
Beneficial predators, page 280
Insecticidal soap, page 285
Spinosad, page 286
Neem, page 286
Horticultural oil, page 286
Pyrethrin, page 287

Berries are webbed together with silk and become mushy and wrinkled. Yellowish to grayish green to purplish worms (caterpillars) tunnel through the fruit. Through the skin of light-colored grapes you can see dark tunnels winding through the berries.

Grape berry moth

Plant polycultures, page 258
Encourage beneficial organisms, page 260
Hand-pick pests, page 277
Beneficial predators, page 280
BTK, page 283
Insecticidal soap, page 285
Spinosad, page 286
Neem, page 286
Horticultural oil, page 286
Pyrethrin, page 287

Symptom	Diagnosis	Solution
You notice large irregular holes on the edges and sometimes in the middle of leaves. You may find that the soft green tissue of the leaves is eaten away. You may also find blackish green pellets of caterpillar poop. The caterpillars eat flower buds and bore holes into the fruit. Look for caterpillars on your plants to confirm your diagnosis.	Caterpillars	Plant polycultures, page 258 Encourage beneficial organisms, page 260 Hand-pick pests, page 277 Beneficial predators, page 280 BTK, page 283 Insecticidal soap, page 285 Spinosad, page 286 Neem, page 286 Horticultural oil, page 286 Pyrethrin, page 287

Symptom	Diagnosis	Solution
Leaves have large patches of soft green tissue eaten away and the tough lace-like network of veins is left behind (the leaves are skeletonized).	Grapeleaf skeletonizers	Plant polycultures, page 258 Encourage beneficial organisms, page 260 Hand-pick pests, page 277 Beneficial predators, page 280 BTK, page 283 Insecticidal soap, page 285 Spinosad, page 286 Neem, page 286 Horticultural oil, page 286 Pyrethrin, page 287

Symptom	Diagnosis	Solution
You spot leaves with their edges rolled into tubes and sewn together with silk. Look inside to find a caterpillar hiding and eating the leaf tissue. Young leafrollers skeletonize leaves because they can only eat the soft green tissue and leave the tough veins behind. Older, stronger leafrollers eat large holes in the leaves.	Leafrollers	Plant polycultures, page 258 Encourage beneficial organisms, page 260 Hand-pick pests, page 277 Beneficial predators, page 280 BTK, page 283 Insecticidal soap, page 285 Spinosad, page 286 Neem, page 286 Horticultural oil, page 286 Pyrethrin, page 287

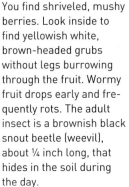

You find shriveled, mushy berries. Look inside to find yellowish white, brown-headed grubs without legs burrowing through the fruit. Wormy fruit drops early and frequently rots. The adult insect is a brownish black snout beetle (weevil), about ¼ inch long, that hides in the soil during the day.

Grape curculios

Soil solutions, page 248
Plant polycultures, page 258
Encourage beneficial organisms, page 260
Sanitize, page 263
Bags, page 277
Kaolin spray, page 277
Hand-pick pests, page 277
Traps, page 278
Beneficial predators, page 280
Chickens and ducks, page 282
Beneficial nematodes, page 282
Beauveria bassiana, page 285
Diatomaceous earth, page 285
Spinosad, page 286
Neem, page 286
Horticultural oil, page 286
Sulfur, page 287
Pyrethrin, page 287

Large (to 1 inch long) metallic green and copper-colored beetles eat holes in fruit. Larvae are whitish grubs (to 2 inches long) that live in the soil and eat plant roots. The grubs have three pairs of jointed legs and a brown head. They curl into a C shape when disturbed.

Green June beetles

Soil solutions, page 248
Plant polycultures, page 258
Encourage beneficial organisms, page 260
Hand-pick pests, page 277
Jug traps, page 279
Beneficial predators, page 280
Chickens and ducks, page 282
Beneficial nematodes, page 282
BTSD, page 284
Beauveria bassiana, page 285
Insecticidal soap, page 285
Spinosad, page 286
Neem, page 286
Horticultural oil, page 286
Pyrethrin, page 287

Symptom	Diagnosis	Solution

You spot holes in leaves. Upon closer inspection, you find metallic green and copper-colored beetles (to ½ inch long) with black legs chewing holes in leaves, flowers, and fruit. Larvae are whitish grubs (to 1 inch long) that live in the soil and eat plant roots. The grubs have three pairs of jointed legs and a brown head. They curl into a C shape when disturbed.

Japanese beetles

Soil solutions, page 248
Plant polycultures, page 258
Encourage beneficial organisms, page 260
Hand-pick pests, page 277
Jug traps, page 279
Beneficial predators, page 280
Chickens and ducks, page 282
Beneficial nematodes, page 282
BTSD, page 284
Milky spore, page 284
Beauveria bassiana, page 285
Insecticidal soap, page 285
Spinosad, page 286
Neem, page 286
Horticultural oil, page 286
Pyrethrin, page 287

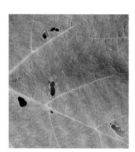

Small holes appear in the middle of leaves. Flowers and fruit may also be damaged. Swelling buds in spring are eaten. You see small, metallic, blue-green beetles on the plants. Larvae of this beetle feed on grape leaves.

Grape flea beetles

Soil solutions, page 248
Plant polycultures, page 258
Encourage beneficial organisms, page 260
Hand-pick pests, page 277
Jug traps, page 279
Beneficial predators, page 280
Chickens and ducks, page 282
Beneficial nematodes, page 282
BTSD, page 284
Beauveria bassiana, page 285
Insecticidal soap, page 285
Spinosad, page 286
Neem, page 286
Horticultural oil, page 286
Sulfur, page 287
Pyrethrin, page 287

Vines wilt and leaves turn brown. Beetle grubs inside the canes eat the tissue and kill the canes. Holes in the bark are created when the adult borer burrows its way out of the vine.

Borers

Plant polycultures, page 258
Encourage beneficial organisms, page 260
Sanitize, page 263
Hand-pick pests, page 277
Beneficial predators, page 280
Beauveria bassiana, page 285
Spinosad, page 286
Neem, page 286
Pyrethrin, page 287

You find shield-shaped insects sucking sap out of flower buds and fruit. These insects are true bugs and have mouthparts like hypodermic needles. Fruit becomes blemished, discolored, or deformed (cat-faced). Pits or pustules may develop on the fruit. Leaves become twisted, wilt, and turn brown.

Stink bugs, false chinch bugs, lygus bugs, tarnished plant bugs, boxelder bugs

Plant polycultures, page 258
Encourage beneficial organisms, page 260
Bags, page 277
Kaolin spray, page 277
Hand-pick pests, page 277
Beneficial predators, page 280
Chickens and ducks, page 282
Garlic spray, page 283
Pepper spray, page 283
Beauveria bassiana, page 285
Insecticidal soap, page 285
Spinosad, page 286
Neem, page 286
Horticultural oil, page 286
Pyrethrin, page 287

Tiny white specks stipple the leaves. Leaf edges may yellow and turn brown. Tiny wedge-shaped nymphs lurk on the undersides of leaves and scoot sideways when disturbed. Wedge-shaped insects (to ½ inch long) hide on the undersides of leaves. Fast fliers, they fly away when disturbed. These insects transmit serious bacterial and viral diseases to your plants.

Leafhoppers, sharpshooters, psyllids

Plant polycultures, page 258
Encourage beneficial organisms, page 260
Weed, page 262
Kaolin spray, page 277
Beneficial predators, page 280
Beauveria bassiana, page 285
Insecticidal soap, page 285
Neem, page 286
Horticultural oil, page 286
Pyrethrin, page 287

Symptom	Diagnosis	Solution

Stunted vines with yellow leaves produce little fruit. Examine the root systems to find hardened yellowish swellings on rootlets, dead roots, and tiny aphid-like insects infesting the root system. Replace infested vines with plants grafted to resistant rootstocks.

Root phylloxera

Soil solutions, page 248
Plant polycultures, page 258
Encourage beneficial organisms, page 260
Weed, page 262
Sanitize, page 263
Beneficial nematodes, page 282

Matchhead-sized pale yellow-green swellings occur on the undersides of leaves. Leaf edges curl upward, becoming quill-like. Plants are stunted and produce little fruit.

Leaf phylloxera

Plant polycultures, page 258
Encourage beneficial organisms, page 260
Weed, page 262
Kaolin spray, page 277
Beneficial predators, page 280
Beauveria bassiana, page 285
Insecticidal soap, page 285
Neem, page 286
Horticultural oil, page 286
Pyrethrin, page 287

You notice leaves stippled with tiny pale dots that sometimes turn the whole leaf bronze-colored. Fine webbing, like spider silk, covers leaves and twigs. Badly infested leaves turn yellow or red and drop off.

Spider mites

Plant polycultures, page 258
Encourage beneficial organisms, page 260
Sanitize, page 263
Kaolin spray, page 277
Blast with hose, page 278
Beneficial predators, page 280
Garlic spray, page 283
Pepper spray, page 283
Beauveria bassiana, page 285
Insecticidal soap, page 285
Spinosad, page 286
Neem, page 286
Horticultural oil, page 286
Sulfur, page 287
Pyrethrin, page 287

Symptom	Diagnosis	Solution
 Robbers strike in the middle of the night. You wake to find ripe grapes stripped off your vines and partially eaten or carried off. Canes are broken, berries smashed, and debris litters the ground.	**Raccoons, opossums**	Nets, page 277 Fright tactics, page 278 Garlic spray, page 283 Pepper spray, page 283
 Fruit hanging on the vine is half-eaten. Triangular holes are pecked into the edges of the damaged area. Pointed holes poke into the flesh. Whole berries are missing.	**Birds**	Nets, page 277 Bags, page 277 Fright tactics, page 278 Garlic spray, page 283 Pepper spray, page 283
 Slime trails criss-cross canes, leaves, and fruit. You find large irregular holes in leaves or fruit. Look for snails or slugs on your vines or hiding nearby.	**Slugs and snails**	Plant polycultures, page 258 Encourage beneficial organisms, page 260 Weed, page 262 Mulch, page 262 Hand-pick pests, page 277 Copper tape, page 278 Slug and snail traps, page 279 Beneficial predators, page 280 Chickens and ducks, page 282 Iron phosphate, page 285 Diatomaceous earth, page 285
 Leaves turn yellow. Vines wilt in the heat of the day even when adequate moisture is available. They lack vigor and grow slowly. Examine the roots for lumps (galls) that are firmly attached and cannot be rubbed off. Nematodes are microscopic. Send samples to a lab to confirm your diagnosis.	**Nematodes**	Soil solutions, page 248 Solarize the soil, page 252 Plant polycultures, page 258 Sanitize, page 263 *Paecilomyces lilacinus*, page 284

Symptom	Diagnosis	Solution
 Angular brown spots appear on leaves, and then leaves turn yellow. The spots become dry and may fall out of the leaf. Leaves wilt, dry, and drop off.	**Phomopsis cane- and leaf-spot**	Manage water, page 253 Plant polycultures, page 258 Sanitize, page 263 Move the air, page 264 *Bacillus subtilis*, page 289 *Reynoutria sachalinensis*, page 289 Baking soda, page 290 Neem, page 290 Sulfur, page 291 Copper, page 291
 Small yellow spots on new leaves and shoots grow larger and turn reddish brown. The spots are confined by major veins of the leaf and become angular rather than round. Infected leaves turn yellow and drop off.	**Angular leaf scorch**	Manage water, page 253 Plant polycultures, page 258 Sanitize, page 263 Move the air, page 264 *Bacillus subtilis*, page 289 *Reynoutria sachalinensis*, page 289 Baking soda, page 290 Neem, page 290 Sulfur, page 291 Copper, page 291
New leaves turn brown and mushy and may develop gray-brown mold. Ripening berries rot and become covered with gray-brown mold. The rot spreads from grape to grape within a bunch, ruining the whole cluster.	**Botrytis bunch rot**	Manage water, page 253 Plant polycultures, page 258 Sanitize, page 263 Move the air, page 264 *Bacillus amyloliquefaciens*, page 288 *Bacillus subtilis*, page 289 *Pseudomonas fluorescens*, page 289 *Reynoutria sachalinensis*, page 289 *Streptomyces lydicus*, page 290 Baking soda, page 290 Neem, page 290 Sulfur, page 291 Copper, page 291

Symptom	Diagnosis	Solution
 Infected berries turn light brown and then dark brown. They soon shrivel into black raisin-like mummies that hang on the vine. Infected fruits have tiny black bumps on the surface. Small circular brown spots develop on leaves and these spots also have tiny black bumps in the dead brown tissue.	Black rot	Manage water, page 253 Plant polycultures, page 258 Sanitize, page 263 Move the air, page 264 Baking soda, page 290 Neem, page 290 Copper, page 291
 White or grayish white powdery patches develop on leaves, stems, and fruit. You can easily rub the fungus off the plant tissue. New growth becomes distorted. Fruit develops web-like scars of russetted corky tissue.	Powdery mildew	Manage water, page 253 Plant polycultures, page 258 Sanitize, page 263 Move the air, page 264 *Bacillus amyloliquefaciens*, page 288 *Bacillus pumilus*, page 289 *Bacillus subtilis*, page 289 *Reynoutria sachalinensis*, page 289 *Streptomyces lydicus*, page 290 Baking soda, page 290 Neem, page 290 Sulfur, page 291 Copper, page 291
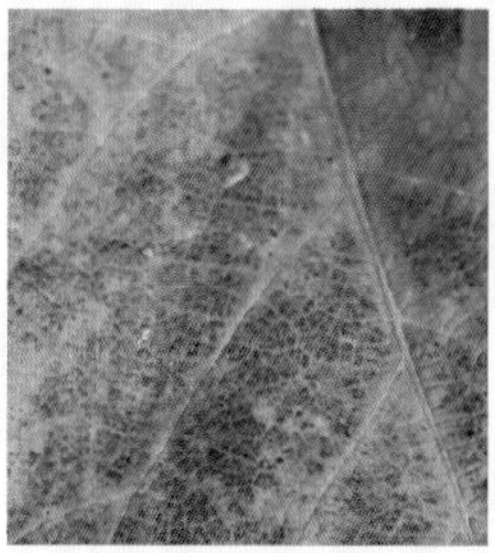 You discover yellow and/or reddish brown patches on the upper surface of leaves. Flip the leaf over to find cottony white mold. Downy mildew appears only on the undersurface of the leaves, unlike powdery mildew which shows up on both surfaces.	Downy mildew	Manage water, page 253 Plant polycultures, page 258 Sanitize, page 263 Move the air, page 264 *Bacillus amyloliquefaciens*, page 288 *Bacillus pumilus*, page 289 *Bacillus subtilis*, page 289 *Reynoutria sachalinensis*, page 289 *Streptomyces lydicus*, page 290 Baking soda, page 290 Neem, page 290 Sulfur, page 291 Copper, page 291

Symptom	Diagnosis	Solution

Honey-colored mushrooms sprout at the base of your vine. They are the fruiting bodies of a destructive fungus. Leaves are small and yellowish, and growth is slow. Shoots die back from the tips. Vines may develop autumn color early. Peel back the bark just below the soil line to find leathery white patches that smell like fresh mushrooms. Look at the roots to find blackish, root-like structures (rhizomorphs) adjacent to them.

Armillaria root rot

Soil solutions, page 248
Manage water, page 253
Plant polycultures, page 258
Sanitize, page 263
Bacillus subtilis, page 289
Reynoutria sachalinensis, page 289
Streptomyces lydicus, page 290
Trichoderma harzianum, page 290

Leaf edges turn brown and dry with a golden yellow band between the infected brown and the healthy green leaf tissue. After several years the entire crown is involved. Infected vines are late to bloom and leaf out, stunted, and less productive. This incurable disease is transmitted by leafhoppers, which must be controlled to prevent infection.

Pierce's disease

Plant polycultures, page 258
Encourage beneficial organisms, page 260
Weed, page 262
Kaolin spray, page 277
Beneficial predators, page 280
Beauveria bassiana, page 285
Insecticidal soap, page 285
Neem, page 286
Horticultural oil, page 286
Pyrethrin, page 287

Rough, warty tumors occur on larger roots near the base of the crown. Tumors may also develop on smaller roots underground.

Crown gall, root gall, hairy root

Soil solutions, page 248
Manage water, page 253
Plant polycultures, page 258
Sanitize, page 263
Reynoutria sachalinensis, page 289
Trichoderma harzianum, page 290
Baking soda, page 290
Copper, page 291

Leaves become cupped with the edges rolled downward. White grape varieties show yellowing of the leaves in addition to cupping. In red cultivars the cupped leaves become brownish red with green veins. Vines are stunted and yields reduced. These incurable viruses are spread by mealybugs, soft scales, pruning, and grafting. Control insects to prevent infection.

Grape leafroll virus

Plant polycultures, page 258
Encourage beneficial organisms, page 260
Sanitize, page 263
Sterilize tools, page 263
Blast with hose, page 278
Sticky bands, page 278
Beneficial predators, page 280
Insecticidal soap, page 285
Neem, page 286
Horticultural oil, page 286
Sulfur, page 287
Pyrethrin, page 287

Young leaves are distorted and mottled yellow. Veins turn yellow. Shoots develop with short internodes and branch abnormally. This incurable virus is spread by dagger nematodes, which must be controlled to prevent infection.

Fan leaf decline virus

Soil solutions, page 248
Solarize the soil, page 252
Plant polycultures, page 258
Sanitize, page 263
Sterilize tools, page 263
Paecilomyces lilacinus, page 284

Guava Problem-Solving Guide

Symptom	Diagnosis	Solution
 Small, gray-white, reddish brown, yellow, or black lumps stick to upper and lower leaf surfaces, or stems. You can easily remove them with your thumbnail. These insects coat the upper surfaces of leaves and fruit with clear, sticky, varnish-like honeydew. A gray-black coating that easily rubs off (sooty mold) forms on the honeydew.	Scale insects	Plant polycultures, page 258 Encourage beneficial organisms, page 260 Hand-pick pests, page 277 Sticky bands, page 278 Beneficial predators, page 280 Insecticidal soap, page 285 Horticultural oil, page 286 Sulfur, page 287 Pyrethrin, page 287
 You see small, bright white insects fly away when you disturb your plant. Large colonies on the undersides of leaves deposit patches of white residue. These insects coat the upper surfaces of leaves and fruit with clear, sticky, varnish-like honeydew. A gray-black coating that easily rubs off (sooty mold) forms on the honeydew.	Whitefly	Encourage beneficial organisms, page 260 Move the air, page 264 Blast with hose, page 278 Vacuum, page 278 Sticky cards, page 279 Beneficial predators, page 280 Insecticidal soap, page 285 Neem, page 286 Horticultural oil, page 286 Sulfur, page 287 Pyrethrin, page 287
 You find scars on the fruit with patches and streaks of raised, rough, corky yellow-brown or silvery tissue. Leaves look silvery. Some damaged leaves roll up and drop off. Tiny (1/20 inch long) yellow to orangish insects congregate on flower petals, leaves, and young fruit.	Thrips	Plant polycultures, page 258 Encourage beneficial organisms, page 260 Weed, page 262 Sanitize, page 263 Kaolin spray, page 277 Blast with hose, page 278 Beneficial predators, page 280 Insecticidal soap, page 285 Spinosad, page 286 Neem, page 286 Horticultural oil, page 286 Pyrethrin, page 287

Symptom	Diagnosis	Solution
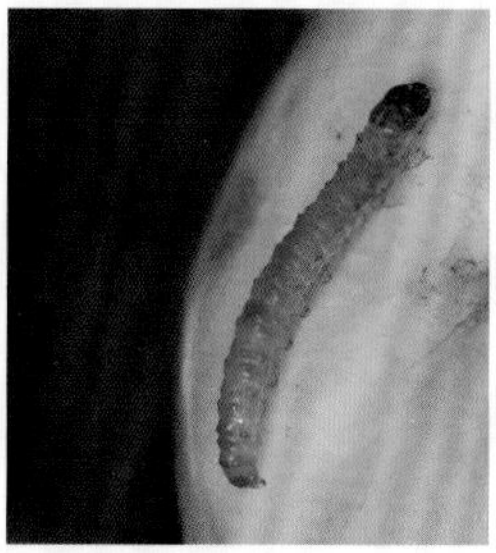 You find a pinkish brown caterpillar inside the fruit creating large, brown or black areas that ruin the fruit. The adult insect is a black and white moth.	Guava moth	Soil solutions, page 248 Plant polycultures, page 258 Encourage beneficial organisms, page 260 Sanitize, page 263 Bags, page 277 Kaolin spray, page 277 Beneficial predators, page 280 Chickens and ducks, page 282 BTK, page 283 *Beauveria bassiana*, page 285 Spinosad, page 286 Neem, page 286 Horticultural oil, page 286 Pyrethrin, page 287
 You find yellowish white, brown-headed, worm-like grubs without legs burrowing through fruit. Adult weevils lay their eggs inside young fruit. The grubs grow as the fruit develops. Wormy fruit drops early and frequently rots. The adult insect is a brownish black snout beetle (weevil), about ¼ inch long, that hides in the soil during the day.	Weevils	Soil solutions, page 248 Plant polycultures, page 258 Encourage beneficial organisms, page 260 Chickens and ducks, page 282 Beneficial nematodes, page 282 *Beauveria bassiana*, page 285 Insecticidal soap, page 285 Diatomaceous earth, page 285 Spinosad, page 286 Neem, page 286 Horticultural oil, page 286 Sulfur, page 287 Pyrethrin, page 287
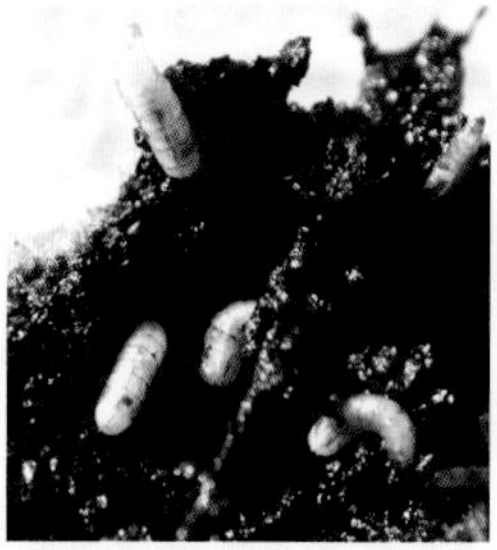 Tiny, white, headless and legless worms (maggots) tunnel through the flesh of the fruit. You see withering fruit that turns soft and leaks juice from sunken areas. When mature the maggots drop to the soil to pupate.	Fruit flies and maggots	Soil solutions, page 248 Plant polycultures, page 258 Encourage beneficial organisms, page 260 Sanitize, page 263 Bags, page 277 Kaolin spray, page 277 Traps, page 278 Beneficial predators, page 280 Chickens and ducks, page 282 Beneficial nematodes, page 282 BTI, page 283

Symptom	Diagnosis	Solution
 Large, irregular, brown spots appear on leaves. Spots develop masses of pinkish spores when the weather is moist. Shoots die back from the tips. Green fruits develop circular brown or black spots.	Anthracnose	Manage water, page 253 Plant polycultures, page 258 Sanitize, page 263 Move the air, page 264 *Bacillus subtilis*, page 289 *Reynoutria sachalinensis*, page 289 Baking soda, page 290 Neem, page 290 Sulfur, page 291 Copper, page 291
 Purplish brown, raised, circular spots develop on leaves. Spots develop yellowish centers as they mature. Infection may spread to branches and to fruit.	Algal spot	Manage water, page 253 Plant polycultures, page 258 Sanitize, page 263 Move the air, page 264 *Bacillus subtilis*, page 289 *Reynoutria sachalinensis*, page 289 *Trichoderma harzianum*, page 290 Sulfur, page 291 Copper, page 291
Small, irregular-shaped, smoky brown patches develop on leaves, stems, and fruit. The middle of the spot develops darker brown, concentric rings.	Leaf-spot	Manage water, page 253 Plant polycultures, page 258 Sanitize, page 263 Move the air, page 264 *Bacillus amyloliquefaciens*, page 288 *Bacillus subtilis*, page 289 *Reynoutria sachalinensis*, page 289 Baking soda, page 290 Neem, page 290 Sulfur, page 291 Copper, page 291

Kiwi Problem-Solving Guide

Symptom	Diagnosis	Solution
 Small, gray-white, reddish brown, yellow, or black lumps stick to upper and lower leaf surfaces, or stems. You can easily remove them with your thumbnail. These insects coat the upper surfaces of leaves and fruit with clear, sticky, varnish-like honeydew. A gray-black coating that easily rubs off (sooty mold) forms on the honeydew.	Scale insects	Plant polycultures, page 258 Encourage beneficial organisms, page 260 Hand-pick pests, page 277 Sticky bands, page 278 Beneficial predators, page 280 Insecticidal soap, page 285 Horticultural oil, page 286 Sulfur, page 287 Pyrethrin, page 287
 You spot large holes in leaves, then find their edges rolled into tubes and sewn together with silk. Look inside to find a caterpillar hiding and eating the leaf tissue. Young leafrollers skeletonize leaves because they can only eat the soft green tissue and leave the tough veins behind. Older, stronger leafrollers eat the holes.	Leafrollers	Plant polycultures, page 258 Encourage beneficial organisms, page 260 Hand-pick pests, page 277 Beneficial predators, page 280 BTK, page 283 Insecticidal soap, page 285 Spinosad, page 286 Neem, page 286 Horticultural oil, page 286 Pyrethrin, page 287

Symptom	Diagnosis	Solution

You spot holes in leaves, and then find metallic green and copper-colored beetles (to ½ inch long) with black legs munching on the leaves, flowers, and fruit. Larvae are whitish grubs (to 1 inch long) that live in the soil and eat plant roots. The grubs have three pairs of jointed legs and a brown head. They curl into a C shape when disturbed.

Japanese beetles

Soil solutions, page 248
Plant polycultures, page 258
Encourage beneficial organisms, page 260
Hand-pick pests, page 277
Jug traps, page 279
Beneficial predators, page 280
Chickens and ducks, page 282
Beneficial nematodes, page 282
BTSD, page 284
Milky spore, page 284
Beauveria bassiana, page 285
Insecticidal soap, page 285
Spinosad, page 286
Neem, page 286
Horticultural oil, page 286
Pyrethrin, page 287

Fruit hanging on the vine is half-eaten. Triangular holes are pecked into the edges of the damaged area. Pointed holes poke into the flesh. Whole berries are missing.

Birds

Nets, page 277
Bags, page 277
Fright tactics, page 278
Garlic spray, page 283
Pepper spray, page 283

Slime trails criss-cross canes, leaves, and fruit. You find large irregular holes in leaves or fruit. Look for snails or slugs on your vines or hiding nearby.

Slugs and snails

Plant polycultures, page 258
Encourage beneficial organisms, page 260
Weed, page 262
Mulch, page 262
Hand-pick pests, page 277
Copper tape, page 278
Slug and snail traps, page 279
Beneficial predators, page 280
Chickens and ducks, page 282
Iron phosphate, page 285
Diatomaceous earth, page 285

Symptom	Diagnosis	Solution
 Leaves turn yellow. Vines wilt in the heat of the day even when adequate moisture is available. They lack vigor and grow slowly. Examine the roots for lumps (galls) that are firmly attached and cannot be rubbed off. Nematodes are microscopic. Send samples to a lab to confirm your diagnosis.	Nematodes	Soil solutions, page 248 Solarize the soil, page 252 Plant polycultures, page 258 Sanitize, page 263 *Paecilomyces lilacinus*, page 284
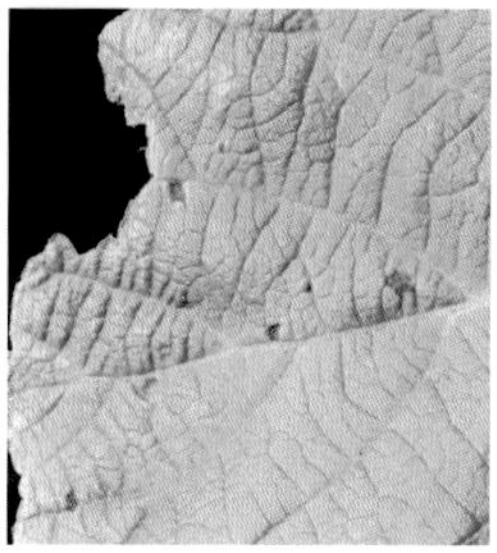 Leaves develop dry brown spots. You see leaves of new shoots wilt, turn pale green, and then turn brown and die. The shoot dies back from the tip. Cankers develop on shoots. Fruit becomes infected. Fuzzy, buff-colored mold grows on infected areas.	Botrytis blight	Manage water, page 253 Plant polycultures, page 258 Sanitize, page 263 Move the air, page 264 *Bacillus amyloliquefaciens*, page 288 *Bacillus subtilis*, page 289 *Reynoutria sachalinensis*, page 289 *Streptomyces lydicus*, page 290 Baking soda, page 290 Neem, page 290 Sulfur, page 291 Copper, page 291
 Dark patches develop at the base of the trunk. Leaves drop off and vines wilt and die. Reddish brown streaks occur in the inner bark and outer layers of wood.	Phytophthora root rot, crown rot	Soil solutions, page 248 Manage water, page 253 Plant polycultures, page 258 Sanitize, page 263 *Bacillus subtilis*, page 289 *Reynoutria sachalinensis*, page 289 *Streptomyces lydicus*, page 290

Symptom	Diagnosis	Solution
Leaves are small and yellowish, and growth is slow. Shoots die back from the tips. Vines may develop autumn color early. Honey-colored mushrooms sprout at the base of your vine. They are the fruiting bodies of a destructive fungus. Peel back the bark just below the soil line to find leathery white patches that smell like fresh mushrooms. Look at the roots to find blackish, root-like structures (rhizomorphs) adjacent to them.	**Armillaria root rot**	Soil solutions, page 248 Manage water, page 253 Plant polycultures, page 258 Sanitize, page 263 *Bacillus subtilis*, page 289 *Reynoutria sachalinensis*, page 289 *Streptomyces lydicus*, page 290
Rough, warty tumors occur on larger roots near the base of the trunk. Tumors may also develop on smaller roots underground.	**Crown gall, root gall, hairy root**	Soil solutions, page 248 Manage water, page 253 Plant polycultures, page 258 Sanitize, page 263 *Reynoutria sachalinensis*, page 289 Baking soda, page 290 Copper, page 291

Melon Problem-Solving Guide

Symptom	Diagnosis	Solution
 Tiny, green, woolly-gray, black, or brown, soft-bodied, pear-shaped insects (look for two tubes on their rear ends) cluster on the undersides of leaves. Tips of branches have curled, cupped, or deformed leaves. These insects coat the upper surfaces of leaves and fruit with clear, sticky, varnish-like honeydew. A gray-black coating that easily rubs off (sooty mold) forms on the honeydew.	Aphids	Plant polycultures, page 258 Encourage beneficial organisms, page 260 Row covers, page 274 Blast with hose, page 278 Sticky bands, page 278 Beneficial predators, page 280 Insecticidal soap, page 285 Neem, page 286 Horticultural oil, page 286 Sulfur, page 287 Pyrethrin, page 287
 You see small, bright white insects fly away when you disturb your plant. Large colonies on the undersides of leaves deposit patches of white residue. These insects coat the upper surfaces of leaves and fruit with a clear, sticky, varnish-like honeydew. A gray-black coating that easily rubs off (sooty mold) forms on the honeydew.	Whitefly	Encourage beneficial organisms, page 260 Move the air, page 264 Row covers, page 274 Blast with hose, page 278 Vacuum, page 278 Sticky cards, page 279 Beneficial predators, page 280 Insecticidal soap, page 285 Neem, page 286 Horticultural oil, page 286 Sulfur, page 287 Pyrethrin, page 287
 Caterpillars eat large irregular holes on the edges and sometimes in the middle of leaves. You may find black pellets of caterpillar poop. The soft tissue on the undersides of leaves may be eaten away. Caterpillars also eat flower buds and bore holes into the fruit.	Caterpillars	Plant polycultures, page 258 Encourage beneficial organisms, page 260 Row covers, page 274 Hand-pick pests, page 277 Beneficial predators, page 280 BTK, page 283 Insecticidal soap, page 285 Spinosad, page 286 Neem, page 286 Horticultural oil, page 286 Pyrethrin, page 287

Brown or green cater-pillars that roll into a C shape hide in the soil. They come out at night to munch on your plants. Seedlings are mowed down just above the soil line.

Cutworms

Plant polycultures, page 258
Encourage beneficial organisms, page 260
Row covers, page 274
Cutworm collars, page 274
Hand-pick pests, page 277
Beneficial predators, page 280
BTK, page 283
Insecticidal soap, page 285
Spinosad, page 286
Neem, page 286
Horticultural oil, page 286
Pyrethrin, page 287

Tiny, shiny beetles that jump like fleas rasp away tender leaf tissue, and eat small holes in leaves. Their larvae are very small grubs that live in the soil and eat the roots of your plants.

Flea beetles

Soil solutions, page 248
Plant polycultures, page 258
Encourage beneficial organisms, page 260
Hand-pick pests, page 277
Jug traps, page 279
Beneficial predators, page 280
Chickens and ducks, page 282
Beneficial nematodes, page 282
BTSD, page 284
Beauveria bassiana, page 285
Insecticidal soap, page 285
Spinosad, page 286
Neem, page 286
Horticultural oil, page 286
Pyrethrin, page 287

You see small, yellow bee-tles with black stripes on the plants. Large holes appear in the middle of leaves. Flowers and fruit may also be damaged. Larvae of this beetle live in the soil and eat plant roots.

Cucumber beetles

Soil solutions, page 248
Plant polycultures, page 258
Encourage beneficial organisms, page 260
Hand-pick pests, page 277
Jug traps, page 279
Beneficial predators, page 280
Chickens and ducks, page 282
Beneficial nematodes, page 282
BTSD, page 284
Beauveria bassiana, page 285
Insecticidal soap, page 285
Spinosad, page 286
Neem, page 286
Horticultural oil, page 286
Pyrethrin, page 287

Symptom	Diagnosis	Solution

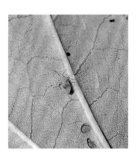

You find shield-shaped insects sucking sap out of stems, flower buds, and fruit. These insects are true bugs and have mouthparts like hypodermic needles. Fruit becomes blemished, discolored, or deformed (cat-faced). Pits or pustules may develop on the fruit. Leaves become twisted, wilt, and turn brown.

Stink bugs, boxelder bugs, squash bugs

Plant polycultures, page 258
Encourage beneficial organisms, page 260
Row covers, page 274
Kaolin spray, page 277
Hand-pick pests, page 277
Beneficial predators, page 280
Chickens and ducks, page 282
Garlic spray, page 283
Pepper spray, page 283
Beauveria bassiana, page 285
Insecticidal soap, page 285
Spinosad, page 286
Neem, page 286
Horticultural oil, page 286
Pyrethrin, page 287

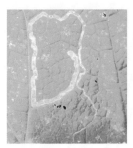

Tiny green nymphs lurk on the undersides of leaves and scoot sideways when disturbed. White specks stipple the leaves. Leaf edges may yellow and turn brown. Wedge-shaped, greenish blue or brownish gray insects (to ½ inch long) hide on the undersides of leaves. Fast fliers, they fly away when disturbed. These insects transmit serious bacterial and viral diseases to your plants.

Leafhoppers, sharpshooters, psyllids

Plant polycultures, page 258
Encourage beneficial organisms, page 260
Weed, page 262
Row covers, page 274
Kaolin spray, page 277
Beneficial predators, page 280
Beauveria bassiana, page 285
Insecticidal soap, page 285
Neem, page 286
Horticultural oil, page 286
Pyrethrin, page 287

Silvery gray trails loop through the leaves. The trails start small and get bigger toward the end. Maggots inside the leaf create the tunnels as they eat the interior tissue. The adult insect is a fly.

Leafminers

Soil solutions, page 248
Plant polycultures, page 258
Encourage beneficial organisms, page 260
Sanitize, page 263
Row covers, page 274
Kaolin spray, page 277
Beneficial predators, page 280
Chickens and ducks, page 282
Beneficial nematodes, page 282
BTI, page 283

Symptom	Diagnosis	Solution
 Small brown and black insects with two pincers on their rear ends hide during the day and come out at night to eat holes in the middle of tender new foliage and flower petals.	Earwigs	Row covers, page 274 Hand-pick pests, page 277 Traps, page 278 Chickens and ducks, page 282 Diatomaceous earth, page 285 Spinosad, page 286
 You see large holes on the edges and in the middle of leaves. Grasshoppers and katydids hop and fly about the garden during the day. Crickets hide during the day and do their damage at night.	Grasshoppers, katydids, crickets	Soil solutions, page 248 Plant polycultures, page 258 Encourage beneficial organisms, page 260 Row covers, page 274 Beneficial predators, page 280 Chickens and ducks, page 282 Nosema spore, page 283 *Beauveria bassiana*, page 285 Insecticidal soap, page 285 Spinosad, page 286 Neem, page 286 Horticultural oil, page 286 Pyrethrin, page 287
You notice leaves stippled with tiny pale dots that sometimes turn the whole leaf bronze-colored. Fine webbing, like spider silk, covers leaves and twigs. Badly infested leaves turn yellow or red and drop off.	Spider mites	Plant polycultures, page 258 Encourage beneficial organisms, page 260 Sanitize, page 263 Row covers, page 274 Kaolin spray, page 277 Blast with hose, page 278 Beneficial predators, page 280 Garlic spray, page 283 Pepper spray, page 283 *Beauveria bassiana*, page 285 Insecticidal soap, page 285 Spinosad, page 286 Neem, page 286 Horticultural oil, page 286 Sulfur, page 287 Pyrethrin, page 287

Symptom	Diagnosis	Solution
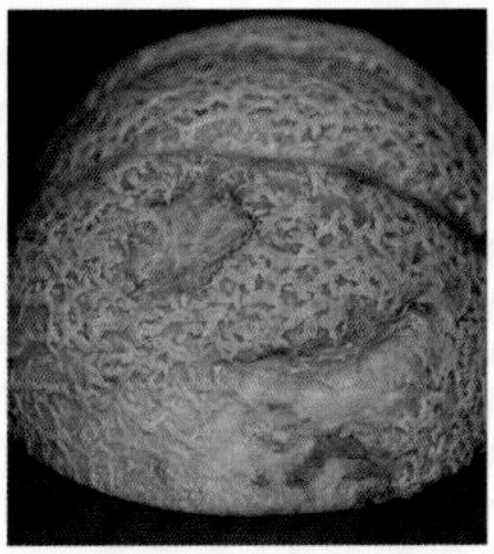 Melons are gnawed leaving open wounds. You can see the parallel grooves made by chisel-like teeth. Roots may be missing or seriously damaged.	**Squirrels, gophers, voles, rabbits**	Weed, page 262 Mulch, page 262 Wire mesh, page 274 Fence, page 276 Rodent traps, page 279 Garlic spray, page 283 Pepper spray, page 283
 Large irregular holes appear in leaves or fruit. Slime trails are present. You find snails or slugs hiding nearby.	**Slugs and snails**	Plant polycultures, page 258 Encourage beneficial organisms, page 260 Weed, page 262 Mulch, page 262 Row covers, page 274 Hand-pick pests, page 277 Copper tape, page 278 Slug and snail traps, page 279 Beneficial predators, page 280 Chickens and ducks, page 282 Iron phosphate, page 285 Diatomaceous earth, page 285
 Plants wilt in the heat of the day even when adequate moisture is available. They lack vigor and grow slowly. Leaves turn yellow. Examine the roots for lumps (galls) that are firmly attached and cannot be rubbed off. Nematodes are microscopic. Send samples to a lab to confirm your diagnosis.	**Nematodes**	Soil solutions, page 248 Solarize the soil, page 252 Plant polycultures, page 258 Sanitize, page 263 *Paecilomyces lilacinus*, page 284

Symptom	Diagnosis	Solution
 You see large brown blotches with yellow haloes that are confined by the veins on leaves. The brown tissue becomes crisp, and falls away to leave holes in leaves. White spots appear on fruits, and the fruit may rot.	Angular leaf-spot	Manage water, page 253 Plant polycultures, page 258 Sanitize, page 263 Move the air, page 264 *Bacillus amyloliquefaciens*, page 288 *Bacillus subtilis*, page 289 *Reynoutria sachalinensis*, page 289 Baking soda, page 290 Neem, page 290 Sulfur, page 291 Copper, page 291
 You discover yellow and/or reddish brown patches on the upper surface of leaves. Flip the leaf over to find cottony white mold. Downy mildew appears only on the undersurface of the leaves, unlike powdery mildew which shows up on both surfaces.	Downy mildew	Manage water, page 253 Plant polycultures, page 258 Sanitize, page 263 Move the air, page 264 *Bacillus amyloliquefaciens*, page 288 *Bacillus pumilus*, page 289 *Bacillus subtilis*, page 289 *Reynoutria sachalinensis*, page 289 *Streptomyces lydicus*, page 290 Baking soda, page 290 Neem, page 290 Sulfur, page 291 Copper, page 291
White or grayish white powdery patches develop on leaves, stems, and fruit. You can easily rub the fungus off the plant tissue. New growth becomes distorted. Fruit develops web-like scars of russetted corky tissue.	Powdery mildew	Manage water, page 253 Plant polycultures, page 258 Sanitize, page 263 Move the air, page 264 *Bacillus amyloliquefaciens*, page 288 *Bacillus pumilus*, page 289 *Bacillus subtilis*, page 289 *Reynoutria sachalinensis*, page 289 *Streptomyces lydicus*, page 290 Baking soda, page 290 Neem, page 290 Sulfur, page 291 Copper, page 291

Symptom	Diagnosis	Solution
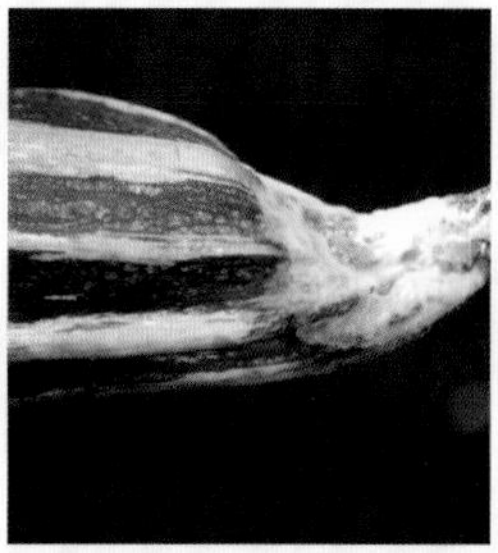 Fluffy, white mold develops on the fruit or on the stems at the soil line. Sometimes black seed-like pellets appear within the mold.	**Southern blight, white mold, stem canker, soft rot, crown rot**	Soil solutions, page 248 Solarize the soil, page 252 Manage water, page 253 Check and improve drainage, page 256 Plant polycultures, page 258 Weed, page 262 Mulch, page 262 Sanitize, page 263 Move the air, page 264 *Bacillus amyloliquefaciens*, page 288 *Bacillus subtilis*, page 289 *Reynoutria sachalinensis*, page 289
 Leaves drop off and vines wilt and die quickly. Dark patches oozing gum or dark sap develop at the base of the plant. Reddish brown streaks occur in the inner tissue of the stems.	**Phytophthora root rot, crown rot**	Soil solutions, page 248 Manage water, page 253 Plant polycultures, page 258 Sanitize, page 263 *Bacillus subtilis*, page 289 *Reynoutria sachalinensis*, page 289 *Streptomyces lydicus*, page 290 *Trichoderma harzianum*, page 290
 The lower leaves turn yellow and develop brown blotches on their tips. Often, this symptom appears on only one side of the plant. The leaves curl and die. The plant's growth slows. Look for black spots on the stems near the soil line. To confirm your diagnosis, cut stems in half lengthwise to see dark streaks inside.	**Fusarium wilt, verticillium wilt**	Soil solutions, page 248 Manage water, page 253 Plant polycultures, page 258 Sanitize, page 263 *Reynoutria sachalinensis*, page 289 *Streptomyces lydicus*, page 290 *Trichoderma harzianum*, page 290

Symptom	Diagnosis	Solution
Leaves are mottled with white markings. Plants are stunted. These incurable viruses are spread by aphids, which must be controlled to prevent infection.	Mosaic viruses	Plant polycultures, page 258 Encourage beneficial organisms, page 260 Sanitize, page 263 Sterilize tools, page 263 Blast with hose, page 278 Sticky bands, page 278 Beneficial predators, page 280 Insecticidal soap, page 285 Neem, page 286 Horticultural oil, page 286 Sulfur, page 287 Pyrethrin, page 287

Mulberry Problem-Solving Guide

Symptom	Diagnosis	Solution
Small, gray-white, reddish brown, yellow, or black lumps stick to upper and lower leaf surfaces, or stems. You can easily remove them with your thumbnail. These insects coat the upper surfaces of leaves and fruit with clear, sticky, varnish-like honeydew. A gray-black coating that easily rubs off (sooty mold) forms on the honeydew.	Scale insects	Plant polycultures, page 258 Encourage beneficial organisms, page 260 Hand-pick pests, page 277 Sticky bands, page 278 Beneficial predators, page 280 Insecticidal soap, page 285 Horticultural oil, page 286 Sulfur, page 287 Pyrethrin, page 287
You see small, bright white insects fly away when you disturb your plant. Large colonies on the undersides of leaves deposit patches of white residue. These insects coat the upper surfaces of leaves and fruit with clear, sticky, varnish-like honeydew. A gray-black coating that easily rubs off (sooty mold) forms on the honeydew.	Whitefly	Encourage beneficial organisms, page 260 Move the air, page 264 Row covers, page 274 Blast with hose, page 278 Vacuum, page 278 Sticky cards, page 279 Beneficial predators, page 280 Insecticidal soap, page 285 Neem, page 286 Horticultural oil, page 286 Sulfur, page 287 Pyrethrin, page 287
Webs in the branches house large colonies of caterpillars that devour every leaf in sight. Tent caterpillars occur in spring. Watch for fall webworms in mid to late summer.	Tent caterpillars, fall webworms	Plant polycultures, page 258 Encourage beneficial organisms, page 260 Hand-pick pests, page 277 Beneficial predators, page 280 BTK, page 283 Insecticidal soap, page 285 Spinosad, page 286 Neem, page 286 Horticultural oil, page 286 Pyrethrin, page 287

Symptom	Diagnosis	Solution
 Leaf edges yellow and turn brown. Wedge-shaped, greenish blue or brownish gray insects (to ½ inch long) suck sap out of stems and leaves. Fast fliers, they fly away when disturbed. These insects transmit mulberry leaf scorch disease to your plants.	Glassy-winged sharpshooters	Plant polycultures, page 258 Encourage beneficial organisms, page 260 Weed, page 262 Kaolin spray, page 277 Beneficial predators, page 280 *Beauveria bassiana*, page 285 Insecticidal soap, page 285 Neem, page 286 Horticultural oil, page 286 Pyrethrin, page 287
 Birds devour all the berries before you get a chance to harvest any for yourself.	Birds	Nets, page 277 Bags, page 277 Fright tactics, page 278 Garlic spray, page 283 Pepper spray, page 283
 Brown spots appear on leaves, and then leaves turn yellow. The spots become dry and may fall out of the leaf. Leaves wilt, dry, and drop off.	Leaf-spot	Manage water, page 253 Plant polycultures, page 258 Sanitize, page 263 Move the air, page 264 *Bacillus subtilis*, page 289 *Reynoutria sachalinensis*, page 289 Baking soda, page 290 Neem, page 290 Sulfur, page 291 Copper, page 291
You find branches dying back or weakened above brown, sunken patches of dead bark, known as cankers, on stems. Dark amber-colored gum oozes from the cankers and dries white.	Canker	Manage water, page 253 Plant polycultures, page 258 Sanitize, page 263 Move the air, page 264 Prune properly, page 264 *Bacillus subtilis*, page 289 Baking soda, page 290 Neem, page 290 Copper, page 291

Symptom	Diagnosis	Solution

Honey-colored mushrooms sprout at the base of your tree. They are the fruiting bodies of a destructive fungus. You notice leaves are small and yellowish, and growth is slow. Shoots die back from the tips. Trees may develop autumn color early. Peel back the bark from the trunk just below the soil line to find leathery white patches that smell like fresh mushrooms. Look at the roots to find blackish, root-like structures (rhizomorphs) adjacent to them.

Armillaria root rot

Soil solutions, page 248
Manage water, page 253
Plant polycultures, page 258
Sanitize, page 263
Bacillus subtilis, page 289
Reynoutria sachalinensis, page 289
Streptomyces lydicus, page 290
Trichoderma harzianum, page 290

Mushrooms or bracket fungi sprouting from the trunk of a tree sound its death knell. These fungi eat your tree from the inside out. By the time you see the mushrooms your tree is doomed. Remove this tree and protect your new or remaining trees.

Wood decay

Soil solutions, page 248
Manage water, page 253
Plant polycultures, page 258
Sanitize, page 263
Prune properly, page 264
Bacillus subtilis, page 289
Reynoutria sachalinensis, page 289
Streptomyces lydicus, page 290
Trichoderma harzianum, page 290

Trees ooze fluid that stains the bark dark brown or ochre. Foliage of severely infected trees wilts and branches die back. Bacteria and yeasts invade the wood through wounds such as large improper pruning cuts.

Slime flux or wetwood

Soil solutions, page 248
Manage water, page 253
Plant polycultures, page 258
Sanitize, page 263
Prune properly, page 264
Bacillus subtilis, page 289
Reynoutria sachalinensis, page 289
Streptomyces lydicus, page 290
Trichoderma harzianum, page 290

Leaves become brown or black and crispy dry as if burned by fire. Fruit withers. Young stems blacken and die back.	Bacterial blight	Manage water, page 253 Plant polycultures, page 258 Encourage beneficial organisms, page 260 Sanitize, page 263 Sterilize tools, page 263 Move the air, page 264 Prune properly, page 264 *Bacillus amyloliquefaciens*, page 288 *Bacillus subtilis*, page 289 *Pseudomonas fluorescens*, page 289 *Reynoutria sachalinensis*, page 289 *Streptomyces lydicus*, page 290 Copper, page 291

Nut Problem-Solving Guide

Symptom	Diagnosis	Solution
 Tiny, black or yellow, soft-bodied, pear-shaped insects (look for two tubes on their rear ends) cluster on the undersides of leaves. Tips of branches have curled, cupped, or deformed leaves. These insects coat the upper surfaces of leaves and fruit with clear, sticky, varnish-like honeydew. A gray-black coating that easily rubs off (sooty mold) forms on the honeydew.	Aphids	Plant polycultures, page 258 Encourage beneficial organisms, page 260 Blast with hose, page 278 Sticky bands, page 278 Beneficial predators, page 280 Insecticidal soap, page 285 Neem, page 286 Horticultural oil, page 286 Sulfur, page 287 Pyrethrin, page 287
 Small, gray-white, reddish brown, yellow, or black lumps stick to upper and lower leaf surfaces, or stems. You can easily remove them with your thumbnail. These insects coat the upper surfaces of leaves and fruit with clear, sticky, varnish-like honeydew. A gray-black coating that easily rubs off (sooty mold) forms on the honeydew.	Scale insects	Plant polycultures, page 258 Encourage beneficial organisms, page 260 Hand-pick pests, page 277 Sticky bands, page 278 Beneficial predators, page 280 Insecticidal soap, page 285 Horticultural oil, page 286 Sulfur, page 287 Pyrethrin, page 287
 Matchhead-sized yellow galls on the leaflets contain tiny aphid-like insects. Galls also occur on fruits and shoots. Severe infestations cause shoots to become distorted and die back.	Pecan phylloxera	Plant polycultures, page 258 Encourage beneficial organisms, page 260 Weed, page 262 Kaolin spray, page 277 Beneficial predators, page 280 *Beauveria bassiana*, page 285 Insecticidal soap, page 285 Neem, page 286 Horticultural oil, page 286 Pyrethrin, page 287

Symptom	Diagnosis	Solution
A pinkish brown worm inside the fruit creates sawdust-like material in its large, brown or black tunnel.	**Codling moth, pecan nut casebearer, hickory shuckworm, filbertworm**	Soil solutions, page 248 Plant polycultures, page 258 Encourage beneficial organisms, page 260 Sanitize, page 263 Bags, page 277 Kaolin spray, page 277 Beneficial predators, page 280 Chickens and ducks, page 282 BTK, page 283 Granulosis virus, page 284 *Beauveria bassiana*, page 285 Spinosad, page 286 Neem, page 286 Horticultural oil, page 286 Pyrethrin, page 287
You notice large irregular holes on the edges and sometimes in the middle of leaves. You may find that the soft green tissue of the leaves is eaten away. You may also find blackish green pellets of caterpillar poop. The caterpillars eat flower buds and bore holes into the fruit. Look for caterpillars on your plants to confirm your diagnosis.	**Caterpillars**	Plant polycultures, page 258 Encourage beneficial organisms, page 260 Hand-pick pests, page 277 Beneficial predators, page 280 BTK, page 283 Insecticidal soap, page 285 Spinosad, page 286 Neem, page 286 Horticultural oil, page 286 Pyrethrin, page 287
Caterpillars hide inside leaves with their edges rolled into tubes and sewn together with silk. They eat leaf tissue. Young leafrollers skeletonize leaves because they can only eat the soft green tissue and leave the tough veins behind. Older, stronger leafrollers eat large holes in the leaves.	**Leafrollers**	Plant polycultures, page 258 Encourage beneficial organisms, page 260 Hand-pick pests, page 277 Beneficial predators, page 280 BTK, page 283 Insecticidal soap, page 285 Spinosad, page 286 Neem, page 286 Horticultural oil, page 286 Pyrethrin, page 287

Symptom	Diagnosis	Solution
Webs in the branches house large colonies of caterpillars that devour every leaf in sight. Tent caterpillars occur in spring. Watch for fall webworms in mid to late summer.	**Tent caterpillars, fall webworms**	Plant polycultures, page 258 Encourage beneficial organisms, page 260 Hand-pick pests, page 277 Beneficial predators, page 280 BTK, page 283 Insecticidal soap, page 285 Spinosad, page 286 Neem, page 286 Horticultural oil, page 286 Pyrethrin, page 287
Yellowish white, brown-headed grubs without legs burrow through fruit. Wormy fruit drops early and frequently rots. Fruit may become cat-faced due to feeding by the adult insects. The adult insect is a brownish black snout beetle (weevil), about ¼ inch long, that hides in the soil during the day.	**Chestnut weevils, nut curculios, pecan weevil, filbert weevil**	Soil solutions, page 248 Plant polycultures, page 258 Encourage beneficial organisms, page 260 Sanitize, page 263 Bags, page 277 Kaolin spray, page 277 Hand-pick pests, page 277 Traps, page 278 Beneficial predators, page 280 Chickens and ducks, page 282 Beneficial nematodes, page 282 *Beauveria bassiana*, page 285 Diatomaceous earth, page 285 Spinosad, page 286 Neem, page 286 Horticultural oil, page 286 Sulfur, page 287 Pyrethrin, page 287

Symptom	Diagnosis	Solution
You spot metallic green and copper-colored beetles (to ½ inch long) with black legs chewing holes in leaves, flowers, and fruit. Larvae are whitish grubs (to 1 inch long) that live in the soil and eat plant roots. The grubs have three pairs of jointed legs and a brown head. They curl into a C shape when disturbed.	Japanese beetles	Soil solutions, page 248 Plant polycultures, page 258 Encourage beneficial organisms, page 260 Hand-pick pests, page 277 Jug traps, page 279 Beneficial predators, page 280 Chickens and ducks, page 282 Beneficial nematodes, page 282 BTSD, page 284 Milky spore, page 284 *Beauveria bassiana*, page 285 Insecticidal soap, page 285 Spinosad, page 286 Neem, page 286 Horticultural oil, page 286 Pyrethrin, page 287
Holes in the bark (just under ¼ inch wide) are created when the adult flatheaded borer beetle burrows its way out of the tree. Female shothole borers create numerous tiny holes in the bark when they lay their eggs. Borer larvae excavate tunnels under the damaged bark. The bark sometimes cracks open.	Flatheaded borer, shothole borer	Plant polycultures, page 258 Encourage beneficial organisms, page 260 Sanitize, page 263 Hand-pick pests, page 277 Beneficial predators, page 280 *Beauveria bassiana*, page 285 Spinosad, page 286 Neem, page 286 Pyrethrin, page 287
Tiny white specks stipple the leaves. Leaf edges may yellow and turn brown. Wedge-shaped, greenish blue or brownish gray insects (to ½ inch long) hide on the undersides of leaves. Fast fliers, they fly away when disturbed. These insects transmit serious bacterial and viral diseases to your plants.	Leafhoppers	Plant polycultures, page 258 Encourage beneficial organisms, page 260 Weed, page 262 Kaolin spray, page 277 Beneficial predators, page 280 *Beauveria bassiana*, page 285 Insecticidal soap, page 285 Neem, page 286 Horticultural oil, page 286 Pyrethrin, page 287

Symptom	Diagnosis	Solution
The husk of the nut turns brown and soft with sunken areas that leak juice. Tiny, white, head-less and legless worms (maggots) tunnel through the flesh of the husk sur-rounding the nut. When mature the maggots drop to the soil to pupate.	Husk flies and maggots	Soil solutions, page 248 Plant polycultures, page 258 Encourage beneficial organisms, page 260 Sanitize, page 263 Bags, page 277 Kaolin spray, page 277 Traps, page 278 Beneficial predators, page 280 Chickens and ducks, page 282 Beneficial nematodes, page 282 BTI, page 283
Leaves develop blisters, nipple-like or finger-like extensions. Mites live inside these struc-tures. These four-legged mites are very tiny and difficult to see without a hand lens. They transmit viruses.	Gall mites, blister mites	Plant polycultures, page 258 Encourage beneficial organisms, page 260 Sanitize, page 263 Kaolin spray, page 277 Beneficial predators, page 280 Garlic spray, page 283 Pepper spray, page 283 *Beauveria bassiana*, page 285 Insecticidal soap, page 285 Spinosad, page 286 Neem, page 286 Horticultural oil, page 286 Sulfur, page 287 Pyrethrin, page 287
You notice leaves stippled with tiny pale dots that sometimes turn the whole leaf bronze-colored. Fine webbing, like spider silk, covers leaves and twigs. Badly infested leaves turn yellow or red and drop off.	Spider mites	Plant polycultures, page 258 Encourage beneficial organisms, page 260 Sanitize, page 263 Kaolin spray, page 277 Blast with hose, page 278 Beneficial predators, page 280 Garlic spray, page 283 Pepper spray, page 283 *Beauveria bassiana*, page 285 Insecticidal soap, page 285 Spinosad, page 286 Neem, page 286 Horticultural oil, page 286 Sulfur, page 287 Pyrethrin, page 287

Symptom	Diagnosis	Solution
Leaves, flowers, and fruit are bitten off and completely missing. Trees lack leaves or branches within 4 feet of the ground.	**Deer**	Plant polycultures, page 258 Trunk guards, page 276 Fence, page 276 Nets, page 277 Fright tactics, page 278 Garlic spray, page 283 Pepper spray, page 283 Deer repellent spray, page 283
Mature nuts nipped off the tree and thrown on the ground are partially eaten. Fruit can be half-eaten while still hanging on the tree. Or you might find the nuts completely missing because they've been carried off and hidden somewhere.	**Squirrels**	Metal collars, page 276 Bags, page 277 Fright tactics, page 278 Rodent traps, page 279 Garlic spray, page 283 Pepper spray, page 283
You think thieves have stolen your nuts. You could be right. Jays often harvest ripe nuts and fly away to bury them for winter snacks. Other birds just peck them open and eat them.	**Birds**	Nets, page 277 Bags, page 277 Fright tactics, page 278 Garlic spray, page 283 Pepper spray, page 283
Plants wilt in the heat of the day even when adequate moisture is available. They lack vigor and grow slowly. Leaves turn yellow. Examine the roots for lumps (galls) that are firmly attached and cannot be rubbed off. Nematodes are microscopic. Send samples to a lab to confirm your diagnosis.	**Nematodes**	Soil solutions, page 248 Solarize the soil, page 252 Plant polycultures, page 258 Sanitize, page 263 *Paecilomyces lilacinus*, page 284

Symptom	Diagnosis	Solution
Black spots appear on leaves and leaves turn yellow. The spots become dry and may fall out of the leaf. Leaves wilt, dry, and drop off.	Anthracnose	Manage water, page 253 Plant polycultures, page 258 Sanitize, page 263 Move the air, page 264 *Bacillus subtilis*, page 289 *Reynoutria sachalinensis*, page 289 Baking soda, page 290 Neem, page 290 Sulfur, page 291 Copper, page 291
You see leaves of new shoots wilt, turn pale green, and then turn brown and die. The shoot dies back from the tip. Cankers develop on shoots. Fruit becomes infected. Fuzzy, buff-colored mold grows on infected areas.	Botrytis blight	Manage water, page 253 Plant polycultures, page 258 Sanitize, page 263 Move the air, page 264 *Bacillus amyloliquefaciens*, page 288 *Bacillus subtilis*, page 289 *Reynoutria sachalinensis*, page 289 *Streptomyces lydicus*, page 290 Baking soda, page 290 Neem, page 290 Sulfur, page 291 Copper, page 291
White or grayish white powdery patches develop on leaves, stems, and fruit. You can easily rub the fungus off the plant tissue. New growth becomes distorted. Fruit develops web-like scars of russetted corky tissue.	Powdery mildew	Manage water, page 253 Plant polycultures, page 258 Sanitize, page 263 Move the air, page 264 *Bacillus amyloliquefaciens*, page 288 *Bacillus pumilus*, page 289 *Bacillus subtilis*, page 289 *Reynoutria sachalinensis*, page 289 *Streptomyces lydicus*, page 290 Baking soda, page 290 Neem, page 290 Sulfur, page 291 Copper, page 291

Symptom	Diagnosis	Solution
Small, circular black spots occur on leaves, fruit, and stems. Spots on leaves dry and drop out of the leaf, producing a shothole effect. Fruit may become deformed.	**Pecan scab, walnut blight**	Manage water, page 253 Plant polycultures, page 258 Encourage beneficial organisms, page 260 Sanitize, page 263 Sterilize tools, page 263 Move the air, page 264 Prune properly, page 264 *Bacillus amyloliquefaciens*, page 288 *Bacillus subtilis*, page 289 *Pseudomonas fluorescens*, page 289 *Reynoutria sachalinensis*, page 289 *Streptomyces lydicus*, page 290 Copper, page 291
Brown, sunken patches of dead bark on stems and branches crack and fall off the tree. Usually the remainder of the branch dies or is weakened. Amber-colored gum oozes from the cankers.	**Canker**	Manage water, page 253 Plant polycultures, page 258 Sanitize, page 263 Move the air, page 264 Prune properly, page 264 *Bacillus subtilis*, page 289 Baking soda, page 290 Neem, page 290 Copper, page 291
Leaves drop off, and trees wilt and die. Dark patches develop at the base of the trunk. Reddish brown streaks occur in the inner bark and outer layers of wood.	**Phytophthora root rot, crown rot**	Soil solutions, page 248 Manage water, page 253 Plant polycultures, page 258 Sanitize, page 263 *Bacillus subtilis*, page 289 *Reynoutria sachalinensis*, page 289 *Streptomyces lydicus*, page 290 *Trichoderma harzianum*, page 290

Symptom	Diagnosis	Solution
 Pale mushrooms sprout at the base of your tree. They are the fruiting bodies of a destructive fungus. Leaves are small and yellowish, and growth is slow. Shoots die back from the tips. Trees may develop autumn color early. Peel back the bark from the trunk just below the soil line to find leathery white patches that smell like fresh mushrooms. Look at the roots to find blackish, root-like structures (rhizomorphs) adjacent to them.	**Armillaria root rot**	Soil solutions, page 248 Manage water, page 253 Plant polycultures, page 258 Sanitize, page 263 *Bacillus subtilis*, page 289 *Reynoutria sachalinensis*, page 289 *Streptomyces lydicus*, page 290 *Trichoderma harzianum*, page 290
 Fruit develops black spots at the blossom end that enlarge and spread over the fruit. Leaves develop black spots.	**Bacterial blight**	Manage water, page 253 Plant polycultures, page 258 Encourage beneficial organisms, page 260 Sanitize, page 263 Sterilize tools, page 263 Move the air, page 264 Prune properly, page 264 *Bacillus amyloliquefaciens*, page 288 *Bacillus subtilis*, page 289 *Pseudomonas fluorescens*, page 289 *Reynoutria sachalinensis*, page 289 *Streptomyces lydicus*, page 290 Copper, page 291
 Rough, warty tumors occur on larger roots near the base of the trunk. Tumors may also develop on smaller roots underground.	**Crown gall, root gall, hairy root**	Soil solutions, page 248 Manage water, page 253 Plant polycultures, page 258 Sanitize, page 263 *Reynoutria sachalinensis*, page 289 *Trichoderma harzianum*, page 290 Baking soda, page 290 Copper, page 291

Olive Problem-Solving Guide

Symptom	Diagnosis	Solution
Small, gray-white, reddish brown, yellow, or black lumps stick to upper and lower leaf surfaces, or stems. You can easily remove them with your thumbnail. These insects coat the upper surfaces of leaves and fruit with clear, sticky, varnish-like honeydew. A gray-black coating that easily rubs off (sooty mold) forms on the honeydew.	Scale insects	Plant polycultures, page 258 Encourage beneficial organisms, page 260 Hand-pick pests, page 277 Sticky bands, page 278 Beneficial predators, page 280 Insecticidal soap, page 285 Horticultural oil, page 286 Sulfur, page 287 Pyrethrin, page 287
You find scars on the fruit with patches and streaks of raised, rough, corky yellow-brown or silvery tissue. Leaves look silvery. Some damaged leaves roll up and drop off. Tiny (1/20 inch long) yellow to orangish insects congregate on flower petals, leaves, and young fruit.	Thrips	Plant polycultures, page 258 Encourage beneficial organisms, page 260 Weed, page 262 Sanitize, page 263 Kaolin spray, page 277 Blast with hose, page 278 Beneficial predators, page 280 Insecticidal soap, page 285 Spinosad, page 286 Neem, page 286 Horticultural oil, page 286 Pyrethrin, page 287
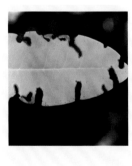You discover notches on edges of leaves nearest the ground. This is your main clue that gray-brown snout beetles (weevils) have crawled up the trunk and branches to eat the edges of the lower leaves on the trees. Their larvae are white grubs with brown heads that live in the soil and eat plant roots.	Weevils	Soil solutions, page 248 Plant polycultures, page 258 Encourage beneficial organisms, page 260 Chickens and ducks, page 282 Beneficial nematodes, page 282 *Beauveria bassiana*, page 285 Insecticidal soap, page 285 Diatomaceous earth, page 285 Spinosad, page 286 Neem, page 286 Horticultural oil, page 286 Sulfur, page 287 Pyrethrin, page 287

Symptom	Diagnosis	Solution
 Holes in the trunk and base of branches exude gum and/or sawdust-like material (frass). A caterpillar lives inside the tree and tunnels under the bark. Weakened trees break in wind or with a heavy load of fruit.	Borers	Plant polycultures, page 258 Encourage beneficial organisms, page 260 Sanitize, page 263 Hand-pick pests, page 277 Beneficial predators, page 280 Beneficial nematodes, page 282 *Beauveria bassiana*, page 285 Spinosad, page 286 Neem, page 286 Pyrethrin, page 287
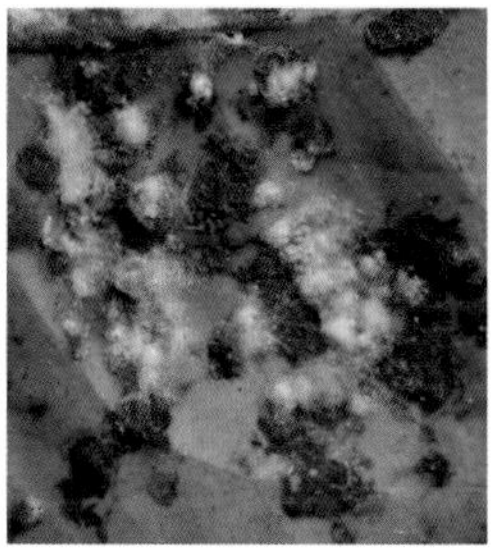 You find sticky white wax on your olive trees. Wedge-shaped, light green and tan insects (to $1/10$ inch long) hide on the undersides of leaves, flower clusters, and young shoots. Strong jumpers and fast fliers, they fly away when disturbed. These insects coat the upper surfaces of leaves and fruit with clear, sticky, varnish-like honeydew. A gray-black coating that easily rubs off (sooty mold) forms on the honeydew.	Psyllids	Plant polycultures, page 258 Encourage beneficial organisms, page 260 Weed, page 262 Kaolin spray, page 277 Beneficial predators, page 280 *Beauveria bassiana*, page 285 Insecticidal soap, page 285 Neem, page 286 Horticultural oil, page 286 Pyrethrin, page 287
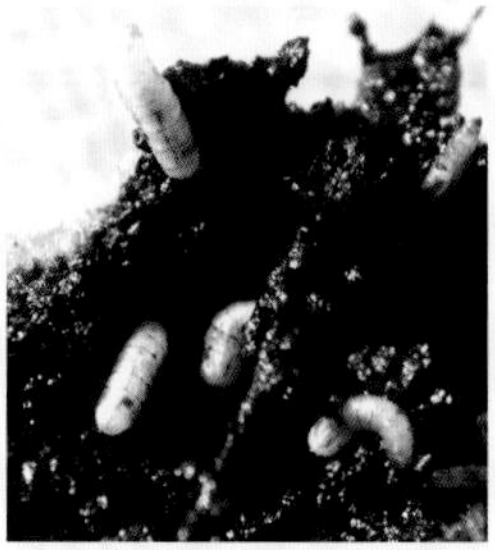 Fruit turns brown and soft with sunken areas that leak juice. Tiny, white, headless and legless worms (maggots) tunnel through the flesh of the fruit. When mature the maggots drop to the soil to pupate.	Fruit flies and maggots	Soil solutions, page 248 Plant polycultures, page 258 Encourage beneficial organisms, page 260 Sanitize, page 263 Bags, page 277 Kaolin spray, page 277 Traps, page 278 Beneficial predators, page 280 Chickens and ducks, page 282 Beneficial nematodes, page 282 BTI, page 283

Symptom	Diagnosis	Solution
 Plants wilt in the heat of the day even when adequate moisture is available. They lack vigor and grow slowly. Leaves turn yellow. Examine the roots for lumps (galls) that are firmly attached and cannot be rubbed off. Nematodes are micro-scopic. Send samples to a lab to confirm your diagnosis.	Nematodes	Soil solutions, page 248 Solarize the soil, page 252 Plant polycultures, page 258 Sanitize, page 263 *Paecilomyces lilacinus*, page 284
 Brown spots appear on leaves, and then leaves turn yellow. The under-sides of infected leaves become covered with black dust (fungal spores). Most of the infected leaves are shed but some remain on the tree and develop a white crusty appearance.	Olive leaf-spot	Manage water, page 253 Plant polycultures, page 258 Sanitize, page 263 Move the air, page 264 *Bacillus subtilis*, page 289 *Reynoutria sachalinensis*, page 289 Baking soda, page 290 Neem, page 290 Sulfur, page 291 Copper, page 291
The lower leaves turn yel-low and develop brown blotches on their tips. Often, this symptom appears on only one side of the tree. The leaves curl and die. The plant's growth slows. Look for black spots on the stems near the soil line. To con-firm your diagnosis, cut stems in half lengthwise to see dark streaks inside.	Fusarium wilt, verticillium wilt	Soil solutions, page 248 Manage water, page 253 Plant polycultures, page 258 Sanitize, page 263 *Reynoutria sachalinensis*, page 289 *Streptomyces lydicus*, page 290 *Trichoderma harzianum*, page 290

Symptom	Diagnosis	Solution
Rough irregular-shaped swellings or galls up to 2 inches in diameter occur on twigs, leaves, roots, or trunk. Young trees can be girdled and killed.	**Olive knot**	Manage water, page 253 Plant polycultures, page 258 Encourage beneficial organisms, page 260 Sanitize, page 263 Sterilize tools, page 263 Move the air, page 264 Prune properly, page 264 *Bacillus amyloliquefaciens*, page 288 *Bacillus subtilis*, page 289 *Pseudomonas fluorescens*, page 289 *Reynoutria sachalinensis*, page 289 *Streptomyces lydicus*, page 290 Copper, page 291

Passionfruit Problem-Solving Guide

Symptom	Diagnosis	Solution
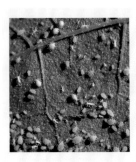 Tiny, green, woolly-gray, black, or brown, soft-bodied, pear-shaped insects (look for two tubes on their rear ends) cluster on the undersides of leaves. Tips of branches have curled, cupped, or deformed leaves. These insects coat the upper surfaces of leaves and fruit with clear, sticky, varnish-like honeydew. A gray-black coating that easily rubs off (sooty mold) forms on the honeydew.	Aphids	Plant polycultures, page 258 Encourage beneficial organisms, page 260 Blast with hose, page 278 Sticky bands, page 278 Beneficial predators, page 280 Insecticidal soap, page 285 Neem, page 286 Horticultural oil, page 286 Sulfur, page 287 Pyrethrin, page 287
 You notice large irregular holes on the edges and sometimes in the middle of leaves. You may find that the soft green tissue of the leaves is eaten away. You may also find blackish green pellets of caterpillar poop. The caterpillars eat flower buds and bore holes into the fruit. Look for caterpillars on your plants to confirm your diagnosis.	Caterpillars	Plant polycultures, page 258 Encourage beneficial organisms, page 260 Hand-pick pests, page 277 Beneficial predators, page 280 BTK, page 283 Insecticidal soap, page 285 Spinosad, page 286 Neem, page 286 Horticultural oil, page 286 Pyrethrin, page 287

Symptom	Diagnosis	Solution
 You find shield-shaped insects sucking sap out of developing fruit. These insects are true bugs and have mouthparts like hypodermic needles. Fruit becomes blemished with discolored spots.	Stink bugs	Plant polycultures, page 258 Encourage beneficial organisms, page 260 Bags, page 277 Kaolin spray, page 277 Hand-pick pests, page 277 Beneficial predators, page 280 Chickens and ducks, page 282 Garlic spray, page 283 Pepper spray, page 283 *Beauveria bassiana*, page 285 Insecticidal soap, page 285 Spinosad, page 286 Neem, page 286 Horticultural oil, page 286 Pyrethrin, page 287
 Large irregular holes appear in leaves. Slime trails are present. Plants can be defoliated. Look for snails or slugs hiding nearby.	Slugs and snails	Plant polycultures, page 258 Encourage beneficial organisms, page 260 Weed, page 262 Mulch, page 262 Hand-pick pests, page 277 Copper tape, page 278 Slug and snail traps, page 279 Beneficial predators, page 280 Chickens and ducks, page 282 Iron phosphate, page 285 Diatomaceous earth, page 285
 Vines wilt in the heat of the day even when adequate moisture is available. They lack vigor and grow slowly. Leaves turn yellow. Examine the roots for lumps (pictured) that are firmly attached and cannot be rubbed off. Nematodes are microscopic. Send samples to a lab to confirm your diagnosis.	Nematodes	Soil solutions, page 248 Solarize the soil, page 252 Plant polycultures, page 258 Sanitize, page 263 *Paecilomyces lilacinus*, page 284

Symptom	Diagnosis	Solution
 Vines wilt, leaves drop off, and plants die. Dark patches oozing gum or dark sap develop at their base. Reddish brown streaks occur in the inner bark and outer layers of wood.	**Phytophthora root rot, crown rot**	Soil solutions, page 248 Manage water, page 253 Plant polycultures, page 258 Sanitize, page 263 *Bacillus subtilis*, page 289 *Reynoutria sachalinensis*, page 289 *Streptomyces lydicus*, page 290 *Trichoderma harzianum*, page 290
 The lower leaves turn yellow and develop brown blotches on their tips. Often, this symptom appears on only one side of the plant. The leaves curl and die. The plant's growth slows. Look for black spots on the stems near the soil line. To confirm your diagnosis, cut stems in half lengthwise to see dark streaks inside.	**Fusarium wilt**	Soil solutions, page 248 Manage water, page 253 Plant polycultures, page 258 Sanitize, page 263 *Reynoutria sachalinensis*, page 289 *Streptomyces lydicus*, page 290 *Trichoderma harzianum*, page 290
Leaves are mottled with yellow. Plants are stunted and yields are poor. These incurable viruses are spread by aphids, which must be controlled to prevent infection.	**Mosaic viruses**	Plant polycultures, page 258 Encourage beneficial organisms, page 260 Sanitize, page 263 Sterilize tools, page 263 Blast with hose, page 278 Sticky bands, page 278 Beneficial predators, page 280 Insecticidal soap, page 285 Neem, page 286 Horticultural oil, page 286 Sulfur, page 287 Pyrethrin, page 287

Persimmon Problem-Solving Guide

Symptom	Diagnosis	Solution
 Small, gray-white, reddish brown, yellow, or black lumps stick to upper and lower leaf surfaces, or stems. You can easily remove them with your thumbnail. These insects coat the upper surfaces of leaves and fruit with clear, sticky, varnish-like honeydew. A gray-black coating that easily rubs off (sooty mold) forms on the honeydew.	Scale insects	Plant polycultures, page 258 Encourage beneficial organisms, page 260 Hand-pick pests, page 277 Sticky bands, page 278 Beneficial predators, page 280 Insecticidal soap, page 285 Horticultural oil, page 286 Sulfur, page 287 Pyrethrin, page 287
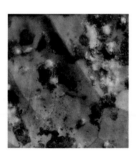 You discover fluffy grayish white lumps clustered where leaves attach to stems and on the undersides of leaves. These insects do not fly. They coat the upper surfaces of leaves and fruit with clear, sticky, varnish-like honeydew. A gray-black coating that easily rubs off (sooty mold) forms on the honeydew.	Mealybugs	Plant polycultures, page 258 Encourage beneficial organisms, page 260 Blast with hose, page 278 Sticky bands, page 278 Beneficial predators, page 280 Insecticidal soap, page 285 Neem, page 286 Horticultural oil, page 286 Sulfur, page 287 Pyrethrin, page 287
 You notice large irregular holes on the edges and sometimes in the middle of leaves. You may find that the soft green tissue of the leaves is eaten away. You may also find blackish green pellets of caterpillar poop. The caterpillars eat flower buds and bore holes into the fruit. Look for caterpillars on your plants to confirm your diagnosis.	Caterpillars	Plant polycultures, page 258 Encourage beneficial organisms, page 260 Hand-pick pests, page 277 Beneficial predators, page 280 BTK, page 283 Insecticidal soap, page 285 Spinosad, page 286 Neem, page 286 Horticultural oil, page 286 Pyrethrin, page 287

Symptom	Diagnosis	Solution
 Webs in the branches house large colonies of caterpillars that devour every leaf in sight. Tent caterpillars occur in spring. Watch for fall webworms in mid to late summer.	**Tent caterpillars, fall webworms**	Plant polycultures, page 258 Encourage beneficial organisms, page 260 Hand-pick pests, page 277 Beneficial predators, page 280 BTK, page 283 Insecticidal soap, page 285 Spinosad, page 286 Neem, page 286 Horticultural oil, page 286 Pyrethrin, page 287
 Numerous tiny holes in the bark and wood indicate borer beetles are active in your tree. Borer larvae excavate tunnels under damaged bark. The bark sometimes cracks open.	**Borers**	Plant polycultures, page 258 Encourage beneficial organisms, page 260 Sanitize, page 263 Hand-pick pests, page 277 Beneficial predators, page 280 *Beauveria bassiana*, page 285 Spinosad, page 286 Neem, page 286 Pyrethrin, page 287
 Leaves become badly distorted. Tiny, white, fuzzy insect nymphs lurk on the undersides of leaves. Wedge-shaped, shiny black adult insects (to ¼ inch long) hide on the undersides of leaves. Fast fliers, they fly away when disturbed. These insects transmit serious bacterial and viral diseases to your plants.	**Psyllids**	Plant polycultures, page 258 Encourage beneficial organisms, page 260 Weed, page 262 Kaolin spray, page 277 Beneficial predators, page 280 *Beauveria bassiana*, page 285 Insecticidal soap, page 285 Neem, page 286 Horticultural oil, page 286 Pyrethrin, page 287

Symptom	Diagnosis	Solution
 Brown spots appear on leaves and leaves become distorted. The spots dry up and may fall out of the leaf. Leaves wilt, dry, and drop off.	Anthracnose	Manage water, page 253 Plant polycultures, page 258 Sanitize, page 263 Move the air, page 264 *Bacillus subtilis*, page 289 *Reynoutria sachalinensis*, page 289 Baking soda, page 290 Neem, page 290 Sulfur, page 291 Copper, page 291
 You see leaves of new shoots wilt, turn pale green, and then turn brown and die. The shoot dies back from the tip. Cankers develop on shoots. Fruit becomes infected. Fuzzy, buff-colored mold grows on infected areas.	Botrytis blight	Manage water, page 253 Plant polycultures, page 258 Sanitize, page 263 Move the air, page 264 *Bacillus amyloliquefaciens*, page 288 *Bacillus subtilis*, page 289 *Reynoutria sachalinensis*, page 289 *Streptomyces lydicus*, page 290 Baking soda, page 290 Neem, page 290 Sulfur, page 291 Copper, page 291
 Leaves wilt and turn yellow. The whole tree is affected. Dark patches oozing gum or dark sap develop at the base of the trunk. Reddish brown streaks occur in the inner bark and outer layers of wood.	Phytophthora root rot, crown rot	Soil solutions, page 248 Manage water, page 253 Plant polycultures, page 258 Sanitize, page 263 *Bacillus subtilis*, page 289 *Reynoutria sachalinensis*, page 289 *Streptomyces lydicus*, page 290 *Trichoderma harzianum*, page 290

Pome Fruit Problem-Solving Guide

Symptom	Diagnosis	Solution
 Tiny, green, woolly-gray, black, or brown, soft-bodied, pear-shaped insects (look for two tubes on their rear ends) cluster on the undersides of leaves. Tips of branches have curled, cupped, or deformed leaves. These insects coat the upper surfaces of leaves and fruit with clear, sticky, varnish-like honeydew. A gray-black coating that easily rubs off (sooty mold) forms on the honeydew.	Aphids	Plant polycultures, page 258 Encourage beneficial organisms, page 260 Blast with hose, page 278 Sticky bands, page 278 Beneficial predators, page 280 Insecticidal soap, page 285 Neem, page 286 Horticultural oil, page 286 Sulfur, page 287 Pyrethrin, page 287
 Small, gray-white, reddish brown, yellow, or black lumps stick to upper and lower leaf surfaces, or stems. You can easily remove them with your thumbnail. These insects coat the upper surfaces of leaves and fruit with clear, sticky, varnish-like honeydew. A gray-black coating that easily rubs off (sooty mold) forms on the honeydew.	Scale insects	Plant polycultures, page 258 Encourage beneficial organisms, page 260 Hand-pick pests, page 277 Sticky bands, page 278 Beneficial predators, page 280 Insecticidal soap, page 285 Horticultural oil, page 286 Sulfur, page 287 Pyrethrin, page 287
 You watch ants scurry over deformed leaves and march up and down the trunk. They are tending the aphids or scale insects they bring to your tree. Ants feed on the sweet, sticky honeydew produced by these insects.	**Ants and aphids or scale**	Plant polycultures, page 258 Sticky bands, page 278 Diatomaceous earth, page 285

Symptom	Diagnosis	Solution
You find scars on the fruit with patches and streaks of raised, rough, corky yellow-brown or silvery tissue. Leaves look silvery. Some damaged leaves roll up and drop off. Tiny (1/20 inch long) yellow to orangish insects congregate on flower petals, leaves, and young fruit.	Thrips	Plant polycultures, page 258 Encourage beneficial organisms, page 260 Weed, page 262 Sanitize, page 263 Kaolin spray, page 277 Blast with hose, page 278 Beneficial predators, page 280 Insecticidal soap, page 285 Spinosad, page 286 Neem, page 286 Horticultural oil, page 286 Pyrethrin, page 287
Tiny white specks stipple the leaves. Leaf edges may yellow and turn brown. Wedge-shaped, greenish blue or brownish gray insects (to 1/2 inch long) hide on the undersides of leaves. Fast fliers, they fly away when disturbed. These insects transmit serious bacterial and viral diseases to your plants.	Leafhoppers, sharpshooters	Plant polycultures, page 258 Encourage beneficial organisms, page 260 Weed, page 262 Kaolin spray, page 277 Beneficial predators, page 280 *Beauveria bassiana*, page 285 Insecticidal soap, page 285 Neem, page 286 Horticultural oil, page 286 Pyrethrin, page 287
A large, brown or black tunnel in the core the fruit houses a pinkish brown worm. This caterpillar creates a quantity of blackish sawdust-like material inside the fruit as it feasts. It burrows out and crawls or drops to the soil to pupate.	Codling moth	Soil solutions, page 248 Plant polycultures, page 258 Encourage beneficial organisms, page 260 Sanitize, page 263 Bags, page 277 Kaolin spray, page 277 Beneficial predators, page 280 Chickens and ducks, page 282 BTK, page 283 Granulosis virus, page 284 *Beauveria bassiana*, page 285 Spinosad, page 286 Neem, page 286 Horticultural oil, page 286 Pyrethrin, page 287

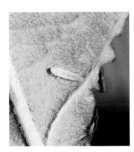
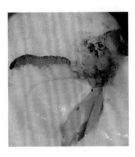

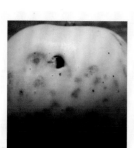

Fruits are punctured by D-shaped holes. Yellowish white, brown-headed grubs without legs burrow through fruit. Wormy fruit drops early and frequently rots. Fruit may become cat-faced due to feeding by the adult insect, which is a brownish black snout beetle (weevil) about ¼ inch long. They hide in the soil during the day.

Plum curculios

Soil solutions, page 248
Plant polycultures, page 258
Encourage beneficial organisms, page 260
Sanitize, page 263
Bags, page 277
Kaolin spray, page 277
Hand-pick pests, page 277
Traps, page 278
Beneficial predators, page 280
Chickens and ducks, page 282
Beneficial nematodes, page 282
Beauveria bassiana, page 285
Diatomaceous earth, page 285
Spinosad, page 286
Neem, page 286
Horticultural oil, page 286
Sulfur, page 287
Pyrethrin, page 287

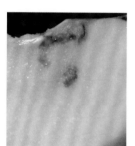

Tiny, rusty brown tunnels wander through mushy fruit. Small, yellowish white maggots are present inside the tunnels.

Apple maggot

Soil solutions, page 248
Plant polycultures, page 258
Encourage beneficial organisms, page 260
Sanitize, page 263
Bags, page 277
Kaolin spray, page 277
Apple maggot Traps, page 279
Beneficial predators, page 280
Chickens and ducks, page 282
Beneficial nematodes, page 282
BTI, page 283

Symptom	Diagnosis	Solution

You see large (to 1 inch long) metallic green beetles and/or large (to 1½ inches long) brown and white striped beetles eating holes in leaves or fruit. Larvae of these beetles are whitish grubs (to 2 inches long) that live in the soil and eat plant roots. The grubs have three pairs of jointed legs and a brown head. They curl into a C shape when disturbed.

Ten-lined and green June beetles, figeater beetles

Soil solutions, page 248
Plant polycultures, page 258
Encourage beneficial organisms, page 260
Hand-pick pests, page 277
Jug traps, page 279
Beneficial predators, page 280
Chickens and ducks, page 282
Beneficial nematodes, page 282
BTSD, page 284
Beauveria bassiana, page 285
Insecticidal soap, page 285
Spinosad, page 286
Neem, page 286
Horticultural oil, page 286
Pyrethrin, page 287

You spot metallic green and copper-colored beetles (to ½ inch long) with black legs chewing holes in leaves, flowers, and fruit. Larvae are whitish grubs (to 1 inch long) that live in the soil and eat plant roots. The grubs have three pairs of jointed legs and a brown head. They curl into a C shape when disturbed.

Japanese beetles

Soil solutions, page 248
Plant polycultures, page 258
Encourage beneficial organisms, page 260
Hand-pick pests, page 277
Jug traps, page 279
Beneficial predators, page 280
Chickens and ducks, page 282
Beneficial nematodes, page 282
BTSD, page 284
Milky spore, page 284
Beauveria bassiana, page 285
Insecticidal soap, page 285
Spinosad, page 286
Neem, page 286
Horticultural oil, page 286
Pyrethrin, page 287

Symptom	Diagnosis	Solution
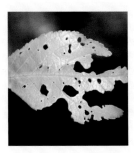You notice large irregular holes on the edges and sometimes in the middle of leaves. You may find that the soft green tissue of the leaves is eaten away. You may also find blackish green pellets of caterpillar poop. The caterpillars eat flower buds and bore holes into the fruit. Look for caterpillars on your plants to confirm your diagnosis.	Caterpillars	Plant polycultures, page 258 Encourage beneficial organisms, page 260 Hand-pick pests, page 277 Beneficial predators, page 280 BTK, page 283 Insecticidal soap, page 285 Spinosad, page 286 Neem, page 286 Horticultural oil, page 286 Pyrethrin, page 287
You spot leaves with their edges rolled into tubes and sewn together with silk. Look inside to find a caterpillar hiding and eating the leaf tissue. Young leafrollers skeletonize leaves because they can only eat the soft green tissue and leave the tough veins behind. Older, stronger leafrollers eat large holes in the leaves.	Leafrollers	Plant polycultures, page 258 Encourage beneficial organisms, page 260 Hand-pick pests, page 277 Beneficial predators, page 280 BTK, page 283 Insecticidal soap, page 285 Spinosad, page 286 Neem, page 286 Horticultural oil, page 286 Pyrethrin, page 287
Green caterpillars chew holes in young fruit. The holes become large and lined with rough, corky tissue. Straw-colored caterpillars leave shallow, irregular scars on the surface of the fruit.	Green fruit-worms, orange tortrix	Plant polycultures, page 258 Encourage beneficial organisms, page 260 Hand-pick pests, page 277 Beneficial predators, page 280 BTK, page 283 Insecticidal soap, page 285 Spinosad, page 286 Neem, page 286 Horticultural oil, page 286 Pyrethrin, page 287

Symptom	Diagnosis	Solution
Caterpillar-like larvae feed inside developing fruitlets, causing many of them to abort and fall to the ground. Some fruit will reach maturity despite the attack and will bear an unsightly spiral scar around the blossom end. The larvae pupate in the soil.	European apple sawfly	Plant polycultures, page 258 Encourage beneficial organisms, page 260 Sanitize, page 263 Kaolin spray, page 277 Hand-pick pests, page 277 Blast with hose, page 278 Beneficial predators, page 280 Chickens and ducks, page 282 Benefical nematodes, page 282 Garlic spray, page 283 Pepper spray, page 283 *Beauveria bassiana*, page 285 Insecticidal soap, page 285 Spinosad, page 286 Neem, page 286 Horticultural oil, page 286 Sulfur, page 287 Pyrethrin, page 287
Webs in the branches house large colonies of caterpillars. When young they devour the soft tissue between the veins of the leaves. Older, larger caterpillars eat the entire leaf. Tent caterpillars occur in spring. Fall webworms show up in mid to late summer.	Tent caterpillars, fall webworms	Plant polycultures, page 258 Encourage beneficial organisms, page 260 Hand-pick pests, page 277 Beneficial predators, page 280 BTK, page 283 Insecticidal soap, page 285 Spinosad, page 286 Neem, page 286 Horticultural oil, page 286 Pyrethrin, page 287
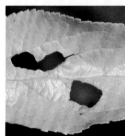Small brown and black insects with two pincers on their rear ends hide during the day and come out at night to eat holes in the middle of tender new foliage and flower petals.	Earwigs	Hand-pick pests, page 277 Traps, page 278 Chickens and ducks, page 282 Diatomaceous earth, page 285 Spinosad, page 286

Symptom	Diagnosis	Solution
 Grasshoppers and katydids hop and fly about the garden during the day. You see large holes on the edges and in the middle of leaves. Crickets hide during the day and do their damage at night.	Grasshoppers, katydids, crickets	Soil solutions, page 248 Plant polycultures, page 258 Encourage beneficial organisms, page 260 Beneficial predators, page 280 Chickens and ducks, page 282 Nosema spore, page 283 *Beauveria bassiana*, page 285 Insecticidal soap, page 285 Spinosad, page 286 Neem, page 286 Horticultural oil, page 286 Pyrethrin, page 287
 You find holes in the trunk and branches. Holes fill with fine sawdust-like material (frass) and may exude sap. A beetle grub or a caterpillar lives inside the tree and tunnels under the bark. Trees grow poorly. Weakened trees break in wind or with a heavy load of fruit.	Flatheaded borer, dogwood borer	Plant polycultures, page 258 Encourage beneficial organisms, page 260 Sanitize, page 263 Hand-pick pests, page 277 Beneficial predators, page 280 *Beauveria bassiana*, page 285 Spinosad, page 286 Neem, page 286 Pyrethrin, page 287
You find shield-shaped insects sucking sap out of stems, flower buds, and fruit. These insects are true bugs and have mouthparts like hypodermic needles. Fruit becomes blemished, discolored, or deformed (cat-faced). Pits or pustules may develop on the fruit. Leaves become twisted, wilt, and turn brown.	Stink bugs, lygus bugs, tarnished plant bugs, boxelder bugs	Plant polycultures, page 258 Encourage beneficial organisms, page 260 Bags, page 277 Kaolin spray, page 277 Hand-pick pests, page 277 Beneficial predators, page 280 Chickens and ducks, page 282 Garlic spray, page 283 Pepper spray, page 283 *Beauveria bassiana*, page 285 Insecticidal soap, page 285 Spinosad, page 286 Neem, page 286 Horticultural oil, page 286 Pyrethrin, page 287

Symptom	Diagnosis	Solution

Small, greenish black, slimy, slug-like creatures crawl over the surfaces of leaves and skeletonize them. Not a slug at all, this is the larva of a sawfly, an insect.

Pear slug

Plant polycultures, page 258
Encourage beneficial organisms, page 260
Sanitize, page 263
Kaolin spray, page 277
Hand-pick pests, page 277
Blast with hose, page 278
Beneficial predators, page 280
Chickens and ducks, page 282
Garlic spray, page 283
Pepper spray, page 283
Beauveria bassiana, page 285
Insecticidal soap, page 285
Spinosad, page 286
Neem, page 286
Horticultural oil, page 286
Sulfur, page 287
Pyrethrin, page 287

Pink bumps or blisters on new leaves turn red, then brown. Mites live inside the blisters.

Blister mites

Plant polycultures, page 258
Encourage beneficial organisms, page 260
Sanitize, page 263
Kaolin spray, page 277
Beneficial predators, page 280
Garlic spray, page 283
Pepper spray, page 283
Beauveria bassiana, page 285
Insecticidal soap, page 285
Spinosad, page 286
Neem, page 286
Horticultural oil, page 286
Sulfur, page 287
Pyrethrin, page 287

| You notice leaves stippled with tiny pale dots that sometimes turn the whole leaf bronze-colored. Fine webbing, like spider silk, covers leaves and twigs. Badly infested leaves turn yellow or red and drop off. | Spider mites | Plant polycultures, page 258
Encourage beneficial organisms, page 260
Sanitize, page 263
Kaolin spray, page 277
Blast with hose, page 278
Beneficial predators, page 280
Garlic spray, page 283
Pepper spray, page 283
Beauveria bassiana, page 285
Insecticidal soap, page 285
Spinosad, page 286
Neem, page 286
Horticultural oil, page 286
Sulfur, page 287
Pyrethrin, page 287 |

| Leaves, flowers, and fruit are bitten off and completely missing. Trees lack leaves or branches lower than 4 feet off the ground. | Deer | Plant polycultures, page 258
Trunk guards, page 276
Fence, page 276
Nets, page 277
Fright tactics, page 278
Garlic spray, page 283
Pepper spray, page 283
Deer repellent spray, page 283 |

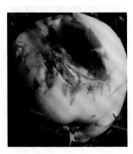

| You find half-eaten fruit hanging on the tree. Triangular holes are pecked into the edges of the damaged area. Pointed holes poke into the flesh. | Birds | Nets, page 277
Bags, page 277
Fright tactics, page 278
Garlic spray, page 283
Pepper spray, page 283 |

Symptom	Diagnosis	Solution
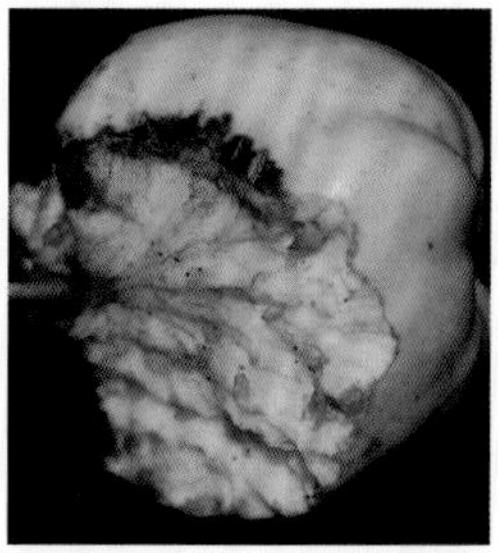 Fruit is gnawed open and either thrown on the ground or left hanging in the tree. The flesh is gouged out with parallel grooves like little chisel marks.	Squirrels, rats	Metal collars, page 276 Bags, page 277 Fright tactics, page 278 Rodent traps, page 279 Garlic spray, page 283 Pepper spray, page 283
 Suspect voles or rabbits if the bark is missing from the trunks of your trees near the soil line. Holes in the ground near trees indicate gophers are present. If the gophers have eaten or seriously damaged the roots, your trees may be wilting and dying.	Gophers, voles, rabbits	Weed, page 262 Mulch, page 262 Wire mesh, page 274 Trunk guards, page 276 Fence, page 276 Rodent traps, page 279 Garlic spray, page 283 Pepper spray, page 283
 You realize thieves have come in the night when you wake to find fruit stripped off your trees and partially eaten. Ruined fruit litters the ground. Branches are broken.	Raccoons, opossums, black bears	Metal collars, page 276 Nets, page 277 Fright tactics, page 278 Garlic spray, page 283 Pepper spray, page 283
 You find large irregular holes in leaves or fruit. Look for slime trails crisscrossing trunks, leaves, and fruit to confirm your diagnosis. Look for snails or slugs on your plants or hiding nearby.	Slugs and snails	Plant polycultures, page 258 Encourage beneficial organisms, page 260 Weed, page 262 Mulch, page 262 Hand-pick pests, page 277 Copper tape, page 278 Slug and snail traps, page 279 Beneficial predators, page 280 Chickens and ducks, page 282 Iron phosphate, page 285 Diatomaceous earth, page 285

Symptom	Diagnosis	Solution
White or grayish white powdery patches develop on leaves, stems, and fruit. You can easily rub the fungus off the plant tissue. New growth becomes distorted. Fruit develops web-like scars of russetted corky tissue.	**Powdery mildew**	Manage water, page 253 Plant polycultures, page 258 Sanitize, page 263 Move the air, page 264 *Bacillus amyloliquefaciens*, page 288 *Bacillus pumilus*, page 289 *Bacillus subtilis*, page 289 *Reynoutria sachalinensis*, page 289 *Streptomyces lydicus*, page 290 Baking soda, page 290 Neem, page 290 Sulfur, page 291 Copper, page 291
Brown corky spots occur on fruit and brown spots develop on leaves. Fruit may become deformed or even ruined. Trees may defoliate.	**Apple scab**	Manage water, page 253 Plant polycultures, page 258 Mulch, page 262 Sanitize, page 263 Move the air, page 264 *Bacillus pumilus*, page 289 *Bacillus subtilis*, page 289 *Reynoutria sachalinensis*, page 289 Baking soda, page 290 Neem, page 290 Copper, page 291
Fruit becomes infected at the blossom end with red-dish spots which enlarge and turn black and brown. The infected flesh is firm and leathery, not soft and mushy. Foliage develops small brown spots with lighter centers. Cankers develop at wound sites on branches and trunk and can kill your tree.	**Black rot**	Manage water, page 253 Plant polycultures, page 258 Mulch, page 262 Sanitize, page 263 Move the air, page 264 *Bacillus pumilus*, page 289 *Bacillus subtilis*, page 289 *Reynoutria sachalinensis*, page 289 Baking soda, page 290 Neem, page 290 Copper, page 291

Symptom	Diagnosis	Solution
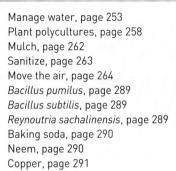 Dark brown to blackish lesions form on pome fruits. The flesh underneath these dark patches develops cone-shaped, brown tissue that penetrates deep within the fruit. Infected fruit is inedible.	**Bitter rot**	Manage water, page 253 Plant polycultures, page 258 Mulch, page 262 Sanitize, page 263 Move the air, page 264 *Bacillus pumilus*, page 289 *Bacillus subtilis*, page 289 *Reynoutria sachalinensis*, page 289 Baking soda, page 290 Neem, page 290 Copper, page 291
 Dark smudges blemish the surface of fruits. This fungus infection is a cosmetic problem, not life-threatening to your tree, and often occurs with flyspeck.	**Sooty blotch**	Manage water, page 253 Plant polycultures, page 258 Mulch, page 262 Sanitize, page 263 Move the air, page 264 *Bacillus pumilus*, page 289 *Bacillus subtilis*, page 289 *Reynoutria sachalinensis*, page 289 Baking soda, page 290 Neem, page 290 Copper, page 291
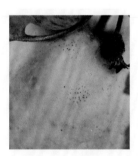 Clusters of tiny black specks in irregular circles blemish the surface of fruits. This fungus infection is a cosmetic problem, not life-threatening to your tree, and often occurs with sooty blotch.	**Flyspeck**	Manage water, page 253 Plant polycultures, page 258 Mulch, page 262 Sanitize, page 263 Move the air, page 264 *Bacillus pumilus*, page 289 *Bacillus subtilis*, page 289 *Reynoutria sachalinensis*, page 289 Baking soda, page 290 Neem, page 290 Copper, page 291

Symptom	Diagnosis	Solution
Small yellow-orange spots appear on leaves in early summer. The spots grow larger and turn orange. Small black bumps form in the middle of the spots.	**Cedar-apple rust, trellis rust, hawthorn rust**	Manage water, page 253 Plant polycultures, page 258 Mulch, page 262 Sanitize, page 263 Move the air, page 264 *Bacillus pumilus*, page 289 *Bacillus subtilis*, page 289 *Reynoutria sachalinensis*, page 289 *Streptomyces lydicus*, page 290 Baking soda, page 290 Neem, page 290 Sulfur, page 291 Copper, page 291

| Sunken patches of dead bark on stems and branches crack and fall off the tree. Usually the remainder of the branch dies or is weakened. | **European canker** | Manage water, page 253
Plant polycultures, page 258
Sanitize, page 263
Move the air, page 264
Prune properly, page 264
Bacillus subtilis, page 289
Baking soda, page 290
Neem, page 290
Copper, page 291 |

| The bark at the base of the trunk at the soil line sloughs off. Reddish brown streaks occur in the inner bark and outer layers of wood. Trees have been stunted and growing poorly for years and now the tree is dying. | **Phytophthora root rot, crown rot** | Soil solutions, page 248
Manage water, page 253
Plant polycultures, page 258
Sanitize, page 263
Bacillus subtilis, page 289
Reynoutria sachalinensis, page 289
Streptomyces lydicus, page 290
Trichoderma harzianum, page 290 |

Symptom	Diagnosis	Solution

Honey-colored mush-rooms sprout at the base of your tree. They are the fruiting bodies of a destructive fungus. Leaves are small and yellowish, and growth is slow. Shoots die back from the tips. Trees may develop autumn color early. Peel back the bark from the trunk just below the soil line to find leathery white patches that smell like fresh mush-rooms. Look at the roots to find blackish, root-like structures (rhizomorphs) adjacent to them.

Armillaria root rot

Soil solutions, page 248
Manage water, page 253
Plant polycultures, page 258
Sanitize, page 263
Bacillus subtilis, page 289
Reynoutria sachalinensis, page 289
Streptomyces lydicus, page 290
Trichoderma harzianum, page 290

Leaves become brown or black and crispy dry as if burned by fire. Stems leak gooey bacterial ooze. Fruit withers. Young stem tips may curl into a "shepherd's crook." Whole trees blacken and die.

Fire blight

Manage water, page 253
Plant polycultures, page 258
Encourage beneficial organisms, page 260
Sanitize, page 263
Sterilize tools, page 263
Move the air, page 264
Prune properly, page 264
Bacillus amyloliquefaciens, page 288
Bacillus subtilis, page 289
Pseudomonas fluorescens, page 289
Reynoutria sachalinensis, page 289
Streptomyces lydicus, page 290
Copper, page 291

Symptom	Diagnosis	Solution

Flower buds fail to open. They turn brown and papery and might drop off. Older flower petals, stalks, and fruit clusters turn brown or black. Leaves are not affected and gooey bacterial ooze is not present.

Blossom blast

Manage water, page 253
Plant polycultures, page 258
Encourage beneficial organisms, page 260
Sanitize, page 263
Sterilize tools, page 263
Move the air, page 264
Prune properly, page 264
Bacillus amyloliquefaciens, page 288
Bacillus subtilis, page 289
Pseudomonas fluorescens, page 289
Reynoutria sachalinensis, page 289
Streptomyces lydicus, page 290
Copper, page 291

Rough, warty tumors occur on larger roots near the base of the trunk. Tumors may also develop on smaller roots underground.

Crown gall, root gall, hairy root

Soil solutions, page 248
Manage water, page 253
Plant polycultures, page 258
Sanitize, page 263
Reynoutria sachalinensis, page 289
Trichoderma harzianum, page 290
Baking soda, page 290
Copper, page 291

Leaves are mottled with yellow. Plants are stunted. These incurable viruses are spread by aphids, pruning, and grafting. Control aphids to prevent infection.

Mosaic viruses

Plant polycultures, page 258
Encourage beneficial organisms, page 260
Sanitize, page 263
Sterilize tools, page 263
Blast with hose, page 278
Sticky bands, page 278
Beneficial predators, page 280
Insecticidal soap, page 285
Neem, page 286
Horticultural oil, page 286
Sulfur, page 287
Pyrethrin, page 287

Pomegranate Problem-Solving Guide

Symptom	Diagnosis	Solution
 Tiny, yellowish green, soft-bodied, pear-shaped insects (look for two tubes on their rear ends) cluster on the undersides of leaves, flowers, and sometimes the fruit. Tips of branches have curled, cupped, or deformed leaves. These insects coat the upper surfaces of leaves and fruit with clear, sticky, varnish-like honeydew. A gray-black coating that easily rubs off (sooty mold) forms on the honeydew.	Aphids	Plant polycultures, page 258 Encourage beneficial organisms, page 260 Blast with hose, page 278 Sticky bands, page 278 Beneficial predators, page 280 Insecticidal soap, page 285 Neem, page 286 Horticultural oil, page 286 Sulfur, page 287 Pyrethrin, page 287
 Small, gray-white, reddish brown, yellow, or black lumps stick to upper and lower leaf surfaces, or stems. You can easily remove them with your thumbnail. These insects coat the upper surfaces of leaves and fruit with clear, sticky, varnish-like honeydew. A gray-black coating that easily rubs off (sooty mold) forms on the honeydew.	Scale insects	Plant polycultures, page 258 Encourage beneficial organisms, page 260 Hand-pick pests, page 277 Sticky bands, page 278 Beneficial predators, page 280 Insecticidal soap, page 285 Horticultural oil, page 286 Sulfur, page 287 Pyrethrin, page 287

Symptom	Diagnosis	Solution
You discover fluffy gray-ish white lumps clustered where leaves attach to stems and on the under-sides of leaves. These insects do not fly. They coat the upper surfaces of leaves and fruit with clear, sticky, varnish-like honeydew. A gray-black coating that easily rubs off (sooty mold) forms on the honeydew.	**Mealybugs**	Plant polycultures, page 258 Encourage beneficial organisms, page 260 Blast with hose, page 278 Sticky bands, page 278 Beneficial predators, page 280 Insecticidal soap, page 285 Neem, page 286 Horticultural oil, page 286 Sulfur, page 287 Pyrethrin, page 287

You watch ants scurry over deformed leaves and march up and down the trunk. They are tending the aphids, scale insects, or mealybugs they bring to your tree. Ants feed on the sweet, sticky honey-dew produced by these insects.	**Ants and aphids, mealy-bugs, or scale**	Plant polycultures, page 258 Sticky bands, page 278 Diatomaceous earth, page 285

You see small, bright white insects fly away when you disturb your plant. Large colonies on the undersides of leaves deposit patches of white residue. These insects coat the upper surfaces of leaves and fruit with a clear, sticky, varnish-like honeydew. A gray-black coating that easily rubs off (sooty mold) forms on the honeydew.	**Whitefly**	Encourage beneficial organisms, page 260 Move the air, page 264 Blast with hose, page 278 Vacuum, page 278 Sticky cards, page 279 Beneficial predators, page 280 Insecticidal soap, page 285 Neem, page 286 Horticultural oil, page 286 Sulfur, page 287 Pyrethrin, page 287

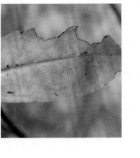

You notice large irregular holes on the edges and sometimes in the middle of leaves. You may find that the soft green tissue of the leaves is eaten away. You may also find blackish green pellets of caterpillar poop. The caterpillars eat flower buds and bore holes into the fruit. Look for caterpillars on your plants to confirm your diagnosis.

Caterpillars

Plant polycultures, page 258
Encourage beneficial organisms, page 260
Hand-pick pests, page 277
Beneficial predators, page 280
BTK, page 283
Insecticidal soap, page 285
Spinosad, page 286
Neem, page 286
Horticultural oil, page 286
Pyrethrin, page 287

You spot leaves with their edges rolled into tubes and sewn together with silk. Look inside to find a caterpillar hiding and eating the leaf tissue. Young leafrollers skeletonize leaves because they can only eat the soft green tissue and leave the tough veins behind. Older, stronger leafrollers eat large holes in the leaves.

Leafrollers

Plant polycultures, page 258
Encourage beneficial organisms, page 260
Hand-pick pests, page 277
Beneficial predators, page 280
BTK, page 283
Insecticidal soap, page 285
Spinosad, page 286
Neem, page 286
Horticultural oil, page 286
Pyrethrin, page 287

You find shield-shaped insects sucking sap out of stems, flower buds, and fruit. These insects are true bugs and have mouthparts like hypodermic needles. Fruit becomes blemished, discolored, or deformed (cat-faced). Pits or pustules may develop on the fruit. Leaves become twisted, wilt, and turn brown.

Leaffooted bugs, false chinch bugs, boxelder bugs

Plant polycultures, page 258
Encourage beneficial organisms, page 260
Bags, page 277
Kaolin spray, page 277
Hand-pick pests, page 277
Beneficial predators, page 280
Chickens and ducks, page 282
Garlic spray, page 283
Pepper spray, page 283
Beauveria bassiana, page 285
Insecticidal soap, page 285
Spinosad, page 286
Neem, page 286
Horticultural oil, page 286
Pyrethrin, page 287

Symptom	Diagnosis	Solution
 Brown spots appear on leaves, and then leaves turn yellow. The spots become dry and may fall out of the leaf. Leaves wilt, dry, and drop off.	Anthracnose	Manage water, page 253 Plant polycultures, page 258 Sanitize, page 263 Move the air, page 264 *Bacillus subtilis*, page 289 *Reynoutria sachalinensis*, page 289 Baking soda, page 290 Neem, page 290 Sulfur, page 291 Copper, page 291
 White or grayish white powdery patches develop on leaves, stems, and fruit. You can easily rub the fungus off the plant tissue. New growth becomes distorted. Fruit develops web-like scars of russetted corky tissue.	Powdery mildew	Manage water, page 253 Plant polycultures, page 258 Sanitize, page 263 Move the air, page 264 *Bacillus amyloliquefaciens*, page 288 *Bacillus pumilus*, page 289 *Bacillus subtilis*, page 289 *Reynoutria sachalinensis*, page 289 *Streptomyces lydicus*, page 290 Baking soda, page 290 Neem, page 290 Sulfur, page 291 Copper, page 291
Limbs or twigs suddenly wilt and die in late spring or summer. The leaves do not fall off. Dark, rough-textured cankers develop at pruning wounds and exude amber-colored gum.	Twig dieback	Manage water, page 253 Plant polycultures, page 258 Sanitize, page 263 Move the air, page 264 Prune properly, page 264 *Bacillus subtilis*, page 289 Baking soda, page 290 Neem, page 290 Sulfur, page 291 Copper, page 291

Stone Fruit Problem-Solving Guide

Symptom	Diagnosis	Solution
 Tiny, green, woolly-gray, black, or brown, soft-bodied, pear-shaped insects (look for two tubes on their rear ends) cluster on the undersides of leaves. Tips of branches have curled, cupped, or deformed leaves. These insects coat the upper surfaces of leaves and fruit with clear, sticky, varnish-like honeydew. A gray-black coating that easily rubs off (sooty mold) forms on the honeydew.	Aphids	Plant polycultures, page 258 Encourage beneficial organisms, page 260 Blast with hose, page 278 Sticky bands, page 278 Beneficial predators, page 280 Insecticidal soap, page 285 Neem, page 286 Horticultural oil, page 286 Sulfur, page 287 Pyrethrin, page 287
 Small, gray-white, reddish brown, yellow, or black lumps stick to upper and lower leaf surfaces, or stems. You can easily remove them with your thumbnail. These insects coat the upper surfaces of leaves and fruit with clear, sticky, varnish-like honeydew. A gray-black coating that easily rubs off (sooty mold) forms on the honeydew.	Scale insects	Plant polycultures, page 258 Encourage beneficial organisms, page 260 Hand-pick pests, page 277 Sticky bands, page 278 Beneficial predators, page 280 Insecticidal soap, page 285 Horticultural oil, page 286 Sulfur, page 287 Pyrethrin, page 287
 You watch ants scurry over deformed leaves and march up and down the trunk. They are tending the aphids or scale insects they bring to your tree. Ants feed on the sweet, sticky honeydew produced by these insects.	Ants and aphids or scale	Plant polycultures, page 258 Sticky bands, page 278 Diatomaceous earth, page 285

Symptom	Diagnosis	Solution

You find scars on the fruit with patches and streaks of raised, rough, corky yellow-brown or silvery tissue. Leaves look silvery. Some damaged leaves roll up and drop off. Tiny (1/20 inch long) yellow to orangish insects congregate on flower petals, leaves, and young fruit.

Thrips

Plant polycultures, page 258
Encourage beneficial organisms, page 260
Weed, page 262
Sanitize, page 263
Kaolin spray, page 277
Blast with hose, page 278
Beneficial predators, page 280
Insecticidal soap, page 285
Spinosad, page 286
Neem, page 286
Horticultural oil, page 286
Pyrethrin, page 287

Tiny white specks stipple the leaves. Leaf edges may yellow and turn brown. Wedge-shaped, greenish blue or brownish gray insects (to ½ inch long) hide on the undersides of leaves. Fast fliers, they fly away when disturbed. These insects transmit serious bacterial and viral diseases to your plants.

Leafhoppers, sharpshooters

Plant polycultures, page 258
Encourage beneficial organisms, page 260
Weed, page 262
Kaolin spray, page 277
Beneficial predators, page 280
Beauveria bassiana, page 285
Insecticidal soap, page 285
Neem, page 286
Horticultural oil, page 286
Pyrethrin, page 287

A large, brown or black tunnel in your stone fruit houses a pinkish brown worm. This caterpillar creates a quantity of blackish sawdust-like material inside the fruit as it feasts. It burrows out and crawls or drops to the soil to pupate.

Codling moth

Soil solutions, page 248
Plant polycultures, page 258
Encourage beneficial organisms, page 260
Sanitize, page 263
Bags, page 277
Kaolin spray, page 277
Beneficial predators, page 280
Chickens and ducks, page 282
BTK, page 283
Granulosis virus, page 284
Beauveria bassiana, page 285
Spinosad, page 286
Neem, page 286
Horticultural oil, page 286
Pyrethrin, page 287

You notice gum oozing out of holes in young fruit. Cut open the fruit to find yellowish white, brown-headed grubs without legs burrowing through the fruit. Wormy fruit drops early and frequently rots. Fruit may become cat-faced due to feeding by the adult insect, which is a brownish black snout beetle (weevil) about ¼ inch long. The adult hides in the soil during the day.	**Plum curculios**	Soil solutions, page 248 Plant polycultures, page 258 Encourage beneficial organisms, page 260 Sanitize, page 263 Bags, page 277 Kaolin spray, page 277 Hand-pick pests, page 277 Traps, page 278 Beneficial predators, page 280 Chickens and ducks, page 282 Beneficial nematodes, page 282 *Beauveria bassiana*, page 285 Diatomaceous earth, page 285 Spinosad, page 286 Neem, page 286 Horticultural oil, page 286 Sulfur, page 287 Pyrethrin, page 287

You see withering fruit that turns soft and leaks juice from sunken areas. Tiny, white, headless and legless worms (maggots) tunnel through the flesh of the fruit. When mature the maggots drop to the soil to pupate.	**Fruit flies and maggots**	Soil solutions, page 248 Plant polycultures, page 258 Encourage beneficial organisms, page 260 Sanitize, page 263 Bags, page 277 Kaolin spray, page 277 Traps, page 278 Beneficial predators, page 280 Chickens and ducks, page 282 Beneficial nematodes, page 282 BTI, page 283

Symptom	Diagnosis	Solution
 You see large (to 1 inch long) metallic green beetles and/or large (to 1½ inches long) brown and white striped beetles eating holes in leaves or fruit. Larvae are whitish grubs (to 2 inches long) that live in the soil and eat plant roots. The grubs have three pairs of jointed legs and a brown head. They curl into a C shape when disturbed.	**Ten-lined and green June beetles, figeater beetles**	Soil solutions, page 248 Plant polycultures, page 258 Encourage beneficial organisms, page 260 Hand-pick pests, page 277 Jug traps, page 279 Beneficial predators, page 280 Chickens and ducks, page 282 Beneficial nematodes, page 282 BTSD, page 284 *Beauveria bassiana*, page 285 Insecticidal soap, page 285 Spinosad, page 286 Neem, page 286 Horticultural oil, page 286 Pyrethrin, page 287
 You spot metallic green and copper-colored beetles (to ½ inch long) with black legs chewing holes in leaves, flowers, and fruit. Larvae are whitish grubs (to 1 inch long) that live in the soil and eat plant roots. The grubs have three pairs of jointed legs and a brown head. They curl into a C shape when disturbed.	**Japanese beetles**	Soil solutions, page 248 Plant polycultures, page 258 Encourage beneficial organisms, page 260 Hand-pick pests, page 277 Jug traps, page 279 Beneficial predators, page 280 Chickens and ducks, page 282 Beneficial nematodes, page 282 BTSD, page 284 Milky spore, page 284 *Beauveria bassiana*, page 285 Insecticidal soap, page 285 Spinosad, page 286 Neem, page 286 Horticultural oil, page 286 Pyrethrin, page 287
 Caterpillars eat large irregular holes on the edges and sometimes in the middle of leaves. You may find that the soft green tissue of the leaves is eaten away. You may also find blackish green pellets of caterpillar poop. The caterpillars eat flower buds and bore holes into the fruit.	**Caterpillars**	Plant polycultures, page 258 Encourage beneficial organisms, page 260 Hand-pick pests, page 277 Beneficial predators, page 280 BTK, page 283 Insecticidal soap, page 285 Spinosad, page 286 Neem, page 286 Horticultural oil, page 286 Pyrethrin, page 287

Leaves are skeletonized. Large patches of soft green tissue have been eaten away and the tough lace-like network of veins is left behind.

Cankerworms, young redhumped caterpillars

Plant polycultures, page 258
Encourage beneficial organisms, page 260
Hand-pick pests, page 277
Beneficial predators, page 280
BTK, page 283
Insecticidal soap, page 285
Spinosad, page 286
Neem, page 286
Horticultural oil, page 286
Pyrethrin, page 287

You spot leaves with their edges rolled into tubes and sewn together with silk. Look inside to find a caterpillar hiding and eating the leaf tissue. Young leafrollers skeletonize leaves because they can only eat the soft green tissue and leave the tough veins behind. Older, stronger leafrollers eat large holes in the leaves.

Leafrollers

Plant polycultures, page 258
Encourage beneficial organisms, page 260
Hand-pick pests, page 277
Beneficial predators, page 280
BTK, page 283
Insecticidal soap, page 285
Spinosad, page 286
Neem, page 286
Horticultural oil, page 286
Pyrethrin, page 287

You observe new shoots wilt and die back 1 to 2 inches or more from the tip and ooze gum. Cut the twigs open to find pinkish or banded caterpillars inside the twig eating the center of the stem. Oriental fruit moth larvae also bore into fruit and eat the flesh around the pit creating mushy, brown tunnels. Peach twig borer damage to fruit is usually superficial.

Oriental fruit moth, peach twig borer

Plant polycultures, page 258
Encourage beneficial organisms, page 260
Sanitize, page 263
Hand-pick pests, page 277
Beneficial predators, page 280
BTK, page 283
Insecticidal soap, page 285
Spinosad, page 286
Neem, page 286
Horticultural oil, page 286
Pyrethrin, page 287

Symptom	Diagnosis	Solution

Webs in the branches house large colonies of caterpillars. When young they devour the soft tissue between the veins of the leaves. Older, larger caterpillars eat the entire leaf. Tent caterpillars occur in spring. Fall webworms show up in mid to late summer.

Tent caterpillars, fall webworms

Plant polycultures, page 258
Encourage beneficial organisms, page 260
Hand-pick pests, page 277
Beneficial predators, page 280
BTK, page 283
Insecticidal soap, page 285
Spinosad, page 286
Neem, page 286
Horticultural oil, page 286
Pyrethrin, page 287

You discover holes in the middle of tender new foliage and flower petals. Small brown and black insects with two pincers on their rear ends hide nearby during the day. They come out at night to eat.

Earwigs

Hand-pick pests, page 277
Traps, page 278
Chickens and ducks, page 282
Diatomaceous earth, page 285
Spinosad, page 286

You see large holes on the edges and in the middle of leaves. Grasshoppers and katydids hop and fly about the garden during the day. Crickets hide during the day and do their damage at night.

Grasshoppers, katydids, crickets

Soil solutions, page 248
Plant polycultures, page 258
Encourage beneficial organisms, page 260
Beneficial predators, page 280
Chickens and ducks, page 282
Nosema spore, page 283
Beauveria bassiana, page 285
Insecticidal soap, page 285
Spinosad, page 286
Neem, page 286
Horticultural oil, page 286
Pyrethrin, page 287

Holes in the trunk and base of branches exude gum and/or sawdust-like material (frass). A caterpillar lives inside the tree and tunnels under the bark. Weakened trees break in wind or with a heavy load of fruit.

American plum borer, peachtree borer, prune limb borer, carpenter worm

Plant polycultures, page 258
Encourage beneficial organisms, page 260
Sanitize, page 263
Hand-pick pests, page 277
Beneficial predators, page 280
Beneficial nematodes, page 282
Beauveria bassiana, page 285
Spinosad, page 286
Neem, page 286
Pyrethrin, page 287

Holes in the bark (just under ¼ inch wide) are created when the adult flatheaded borer beetle burrows its way out of the tree. Female shothole borers create numerous tiny holes in the bark when they lay their eggs. Borer larvae excavate tunnels under the damaged bark. The bark sometimes cracks open.

Flatheaded borer, shothole borer

Plant polycultures, page 258
Encourage beneficial organisms, page 260
Sanitize, page 263
Beneficial predators, page 280
Beauveria bassiana, page 285
Spinosad, page 286
Neem, page 286
Pyrethrin, page 287

Fruit becomes blemished or discolored. It may also become deformed and cat-faced. You may find shield-shaped insects sucking sap out of flower buds and fruit. These insects are true bugs and have mouthparts like hypodermic needles. Pits or pustules may develop on the fruit. Leaves become twisted, wilt, and turn brown.

Stink bugs, lygus bugs, tarnished plant bugs, boxelder bugs

Plant polycultures, page 258
Encourage beneficial organisms, page 260
Bags, page 277
Kaolin spray, page 277
Hand-pick pests, page 277
Beneficial predators, page 280
Chickens and ducks, page 282
Garlic spray, page 283
Pepper spray, page 283
Beauveria bassiana, page 285
Insecticidal soap, page 285
Spinosad, page 286
Neem, page 286
Horticultural oil, page 286
Pyrethrin, page 287

Symptom	Diagnosis	Solution
	Small, slimy, greenish black creatures crawl over the surfaces of leaves and eat the soft green tissue, leaving the lace-like network of tough veins behind, skeletonizing the leaf. Not a slug at all, this is the larva of a sawfly, an insect.	Cherry slug	Plant polycultures, page 258 Encourage beneficial organisms, page 260 Sanitize, page 263 Kaolin spray, page 277 Hand-pick pests, page 277 Blast with hose, page 278 Beneficial predators, page 280 Chickens and ducks, page 282 Garlic spray, page 283 Pepper spray, page 283 *Beauveria bassiana*, page 285 Insecticidal soap, page 285 Spinosad, page 286 Neem, page 286 Horticultural oil, page 286 Sulfur, page 287 Pyrethrin, page 287
	Leaves develop blisters, nipple-like or finger-like extensions. Four-legged mites live inside these structures. The mites are very tiny and difficult to see without a hand lens. They transmit viruses.	Gall mites, blister mites	Plant polycultures, page 258 Encourage beneficial organisms, page 260 Sanitize, page 263 Kaolin spray, page 277 Beneficial predators, page 280 Garlic spray, page 283 Pepper spray, page 283 *Beauveria bassiana*, page 285 Insecticidal soap, page 285 Spinosad, page 286 Neem, page 286 Horticultural oil, page 286 Sulfur, page 287 Pyrethrin, page 287

Symptom	Diagnosis	Solution
You notice leaves stippled with tiny pale dots that sometimes turn the whole leaf bronze-colored. Fine webbing, like spider silk, covers leaves and twigs. Badly infested leaves turn yellow or red and drop off.	Spider mites	Plant polycultures, page 258 Encourage beneficial organisms, page 260 Sanitize, page 263 Kaolin spray, page 277 Blast with hose, page 278 Beneficial predators, page 280 Garlic spray, page 283 Pepper spray, page 283 *Beauveria bassiana*, page 285 Insecticidal soap, page 285 Spinosad, page 286 Neem, page 286 Horticultural oil, page 286 Sulfur, page 287 Pyrethrin, page 287
Leaves, flowers, and fruit are bitten off and completely missing. Trees lack leaves or branches within 4 feet of the ground.	Deer	Plant polycultures, page 258 Trunk guards, page 276 Fence, page 276 Nets, page 277 Fright tactics, page 278 Garlic spray, page 283 Pepper spray, page 283 Deer repellent spray, page 283
You find half-eaten fruit hanging on the tree. Triangular holes are pecked into the edges of the damaged area. Pointed holes poke into the flesh.	Birds	Nets, page 277 Bags, page 277 Fright tactics, page 278 Garlic spray, page 283 Pepper spray, page 283

Symptom	Diagnosis	Solution
 You realize thieves have come in the night when you wake to find ripe fruit stripped off your trees and partially eaten. Ruined fruit litters the ground. Branches are broken.	**Raccoons, opossums, black bears**	Metal collars, page 276 Nets, page 277 Fright tactics, page 278 Garlic spray, page 283 Pepper spray, page 283
 Holes in the ground near trees indicate gophers are present. If the gophers have eaten or seriously damaged the roots, your trees may be wilting and dying. Suspect voles or rabbits if the bark is missing from the trunks of your trees near the soil line.	**Gophers, voles, rabbits**	Weed, page 262 Mulch, page 262 Wire mesh, page 274 Trunk guards, page 276 Fence, page 276 Rodent traps, page 279 Garlic spray, page 283 Pepper spray, page 283
 Fruit is gnawed open and either thrown on the ground or left hanging in the tree. The flesh is gouged out with parallel grooves like little chisel marks.	**Squirrels, rats**	Metal collars, page 276 Bags, page 277 Fright tactics, page 278 Rodent traps, page 279 Garlic spray, page 283 Pepper spray, page 283
 Slime trails criss-cross trunks, leaves, and fruit. You find large irregular holes in leaves or fruit. Look for snails or slugs on your plants or hiding nearby.	**Slugs and snails**	Plant polycultures, page 258 Encourage beneficial organisms, page 260 Weed, page 262 Mulch, page 262 Hand-pick pests, page 277 Copper tape, page 278 Slug and snail traps, page 279 Beneficial predators, page 280 Chickens and ducks, page 282 Iron phosphate, page 285 Diatomaceous earth, page 285

Leaves turn yellow. Plants lack vigor and grow slowly. They wilt in the heat of the day even when adequate moisture is available. Examine the roots for lumps (galls) that are firmly attached and cannot be rubbed off. Nematodes are microscopic. Send samples to a lab to confirm your diagnosis.

Nematodes

Soil solutions, page 248
Solarize the soil, page 252
Plant polycultures, page 258
Sanitize, page 263
Paecilomyces lilacinus, page 284

Brown spots appear on leaves and leaves turn yellow. The spots become dry and may fall out of the leaf. Leaves wilt, dry, and drop off.

Anthracnose

Manage water, page 253
Plant polycultures, page 258
Sanitize, page 263
Move the air, page 264
Bacillus subtilis, page 289
Reynoutria sachalinensis, page 289
Baking soda, page 290
Neem, page 290
Sulfur, page 291
Copper, page 291

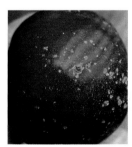

Reddish purple spots on new leaves and shoots grow larger and turn brown. A narrow, pale green to yellowish halo surrounds these spots. Spots develop dark specks in the center. The centers fall out of the leaf, leaving holes behind.

Shothole, coryneum blight

Manage water, page 253
Plant polycultures, page 258
Sanitize, page 263
Move the air, page 264
Bacillus subtilis, page 289
Baking soda, page 290
Neem, page 290
Sulfur, page 291
Copper, page 291

Brown corky spots occur on fruit and brown spots develop on leaves. Fruit may become deformed.

Scab

Manage water, page 253
Plant polycultures, page 258
Mulch, page 262
Sanitize, page 263
Move the air, page 264
Bacillus pumilus, page 289
Bacillus subtilis, page 289
Reynoutria sachalinensis, page 289
Baking soda, page 290
Neem, page 290
Copper, page 291

Symptom	Diagnosis	Solution
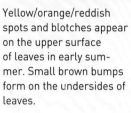 Yellow/orange/reddish spots and blotches appear on the upper surface of leaves in early summer. Small brown bumps form on the undersides of leaves.	Rust	Manage water, page 253 Plant polycultures, page 258 Mulch, page 262 Sanitize, page 263 Move the air, page 264 *Bacillus pumilus*, page 289 *Bacillus subtilis*, page 289 *Reynoutria sachalinensis*, page 289 *Streptomyces lydicus*, page 290 Baking soda, page 290 Neem, page 290 Sulfur, page 291 Copper, page 291
 White or grayish white powdery patches develop on leaves, stems, and fruit. The fungus is easily rubbed off the plant tissue. New growth becomes distorted. Fruit develops web-like scars of russetted corky tissue.	Powdery mildew	Manage water, page 253 Plant polycultures, page 258 Sanitize, page 263 Move the air, page 264 *Bacillus amyloliquefaciens*, page 288 *Bacillus pumilus*, page 289 *Bacillus subtilis*, page 289 *Reynoutria sachalinensis*, page 289 *Streptomyces lydicus*, page 290 Baking soda, page 290 Neem, page 290 Sulfur, page 291 Copper, page 291
 You watch brown spots on fruit enlarge rapidly and develop fuzzy gray masses of spores. Flowers turn brown, wither, and hang on the plant. Leaves at twig tips shrivel. Twigs exude brown, sticky gum. Fruit mummifies and hangs on the tree.	Brown rot blossom and twig blight	Manage water, page 253 Plant polycultures, page 258 Sanitize, page 263 Move the air, page 264 Prune properly, page 264 *Bacillus amyloliquefaciens*, page 288 *Bacillus subtilis*, page 289 *Reynoutria sachalinensis*, page 289 Baking soda, page 290 Neem, page 290 Sulfur, page 291 Copper, page 291

Symptom	Diagnosis	Solution
Leaves become grossly swollen, deformed, and turn brownish red. Badly infected leaves drop and shoots die. New infections continue to appear through the growing season.	**Peach leaf curl, plum pockets**	Manage water, page 253 Plant polycultures, page 258 Sanitize, page 263 Move the air, page 264 *Bacillus subtilis*, page 289 Baking soda, page 290 Neem, page 290 Sulfur, page 291 Copper, page 291
Twigs are swollen, black, and twisted.	**Black knot**	Manage water, page 253 Plant polycultures, page 258 Sanitize, page 263 Move the air, page 264 *Bacillus subtilis*, page 289 Baking soda, page 290 Neem, page 290 Sulfur, page 291 Copper, page 291
You find branches dying back or weakened above brown, sunken patches of dead bark, known as cankers, on stems. Dark amber-colored gum oozes from the cankers and dries white.	**Canker**	Manage water, page 253 Plant polycultures, page 258 Sanitize, page 263 Move the air, page 264 Prune properly, page 264 *Bacillus subtilis*, page 289 Baking soda, page 290 Neem, page 290 Copper, page 291
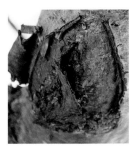You observe sunken, brown, irregular-shaped areas of the bark exuding amber-colored gum in spring. Blossoms turn brown, shrivel, and cling to the tree. Sunken spots develop on fruit.	**Bacterial canker and blast**	Manage water, page 253 Plant polycultures, page 258 Sanitize, page 263 Sterilize tools, page 263 Move the air, page 264 Prune properly, page 264 *Bacillus amyloliquefaciens*, page 288 *Bacillus subtilis*, page 289 *Reynoutria sachalinensis*, page 289 Copper, page 291

Symptom	Diagnosis	Solution
 Leaves drop off and trees wilt and die quickly when the weather turns warm in spring. Dark patches oozing gum or dark sap develop at the base of the trunk. Reddish brown streaks occur in the inner bark and outer layers of wood.	**Phytophthora root rot, crown rot**	Soil solutions, page 248 Manage water, page 253 Plant polycultures, page 258 Sanitize, page 263 *Bacillus subtilis*, page 289 *Reynoutria sachalinensis*, page 289 *Streptomyces lydicus*, page 290 *Trichoderma harzianum*, page 290
 Pale mushrooms sprout at the base of your tree. They are the fruiting bodies of a destructive fungus. Leaves are small and yellowish, and growth is slow. Shoots die back from the tips. Trees may develop autumn color early. Peel back the bark from the trunk just below the soil line to find leathery white patches that smell like fresh mushrooms. Look at the roots to find blackish, root-like structures (rhizomorphs) adjacent to them.	**Armillaria root rot**	Soil solutions, page 248 Manage water, page 253 Plant polycultures, page 258 Sanitize, page 263 *Bacillus subtilis*, page 289 *Reynoutria sachalinensis*, page 289 *Streptomyces lydicus*, page 290 *Trichoderma harzianum*, page 290
Limbs or twigs suddenly wilt and die in late spring or summer. The leaves do not fall off. Rough-textured, dark-colored cankers develop at pruning wounds and exude amber-colored gum.	**Eutypa dieback**	Manage water, page 253 Plant polycultures, page 258 Sanitize, page 263 Move the air, page 264 Prune properly, page 264 *Bacillus subtilis*, page 289 Baking soda, page 290 Neem, page 290 Sulfur, page 291 Copper, page 291

The lower leaves turn yellow and develop brown blotches on their tips. Often, this symptom appears on only one side of the tree. The leaves curl and die. The plant's growth slows. Look for black spots on the stems near the soil line. To confirm your diagnosis, cut stems in half lengthwise to see dark streaks inside.

Verticillium wilt

Soil solutions, page 248
Manage water, page 253
Plant polycultures, page 258
Sanitize, page 263
Reynoutria sachalinensis, page 289
Streptomyces lydicus, page 290
Trichoderma harzianum, page 290

You discover brown or black, crispy dry leaves and twigs that look as if burned by fire. Stems ooze gum. Fruit withers. Young stem tips may curl into a "shepherd's crook." Whole trees blacken and die.

Bacterial blight, fire blight

Manage water, page 253
Plant polycultures, page 258
Encourage beneficial organisms, page 260
Sanitize, page 263
Sterilize tools, page 263
Move the air, page 264
Prune properly, page 264
Bacillus amyloliquefaciens, page 288
Bacillus subtilis, page 289
Pseudomonas fluorescens, page 289
Reynoutria sachalinensis, page 289
Streptomyces lydicus, page 290
Copper, page 291

Rough, warty tumors occur on larger roots near the base of the trunk. Tumors may also develop on smaller roots underground.

Crown gall, root gall, hairy root

Soil solutions, page 248
Manage water, page 253
Plant polycultures, page 258
Sanitize, page 263
Reynoutria sachalinensis, page 289
Trichoderma harzianum, page 290
Baking soda, page 290
Copper, page 291

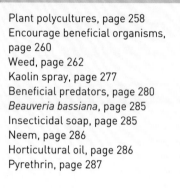

Dense tangles of twiggy growth (witches' brooms) are seen. Leaves are stippled with whitish dots and somewhat twisted. Trees are stunted and slow growing. Fruit ripens early and tastes bitter. These incurable diseases are spread by leafhoppers, sharpshooters, pruning, and grafting. Control insects to prevent infection.

European stone fruit yellows, X-disease, phony peach, plum leaf scald

Plant polycultures, page 258
Encourage beneficial organisms, page 260
Weed, page 262
Kaolin spray, page 277
Beneficial predators, page 280
Beauveria bassiana, page 285
Insecticidal soap, page 285
Neem, page 286
Horticultural oil, page 286
Pyrethrin, page 287

Leaves are mottled with yellow. Plants are stunted. These incurable viruses are spread by aphids, pruning, and grafting. Control aphids to prevent infection.

Mosaic viruses, yellow bud mosaic, ringspot viruses, mottles, stem pitting, prune dwarf, peach stunt

Plant polycultures, page 258
Encourage beneficial organisms, page 260
Sanitize, page 263
Sterilize tools, page 263
Blast with hose, page 278
Sticky bands, page 278
Beneficial predators, page 280
Insecticidal soap, page 285
Neem, page 286
Horticultural oil, page 286
Sulfur, page 287
Pyrethrin, page 287

Young leaves are distorted and badly puckered. A subtle yellowish mottling occurs. This incurable virus is spread by bud mites, pruning, and grafting. Control mites to prevent infection.

Cherry mottle leaf

Plant polycultures, page 258
Encourage beneficial organisms, page 260
Sanitize, page 263
Sterilize tools, page 263
Kaolin spray, page 277
Blast with hose, page 278
Beneficial predators, page 280
Garlic spray, page 283
Pepper spray, page 283
Beauveria bassiana, page 285
Insecticidal soap, page 285
Spinosad, page 286
Neem, page 286
Horticultural oil, page 286
Sulfur, page 287
Pyrethrin, page 287

Strawberry Problem-Solving Guide

Symptom	Diagnosis	Solution
 Tiny, green or yellowish, soft-bodied, pear-shaped insects (look for two tubes on their rear ends) cluster on the undersides of leaves. Tips of branches have curled, cupped, or deformed leaves. These insects coat the upper surfaces of leaves and fruit with clear, sticky, varnish-like honeydew. A gray-black coating that easily rubs off (sooty mold) forms on the honeydew.	Aphids	Plant polycultures, page 258 Encourage beneficial organisms, page 260 Row covers, page 274 Blast with hose, page 278 Beneficial predators, page 280 Insecticidal soap, page 285 Neem, page 286 Horticultural oil, page 286 Sulfur, page 287 Pyrethrin, page 287
 You see small, bright white insects fly away when you disturb your plant. Large colonies on the undersides of leaves deposit patches of white residue. These insects coat the upper surfaces of leaves and fruit with a clear, sticky, varnish-like honeydew. A gray-black coating that easily rubs off (sooty mold) forms on the honeydew.	Whitefly	Encourage beneficial organisms, page 260 Move the air, page 264 Row covers, page 274 Blast with hose, page 278 Vacuum, page 278 Sticky cards, page 279 Beneficial predators, page 280 Insecticidal soap, page 285 Neem, page 286 Horticultural oil, page 286 Sulfur, page 287 Pyrethrin, page 287
 You find scars on the fruit with patches and streaks of raised, rough, corky yellow-brown or silvery tissue. Leaves look silvery. Some damaged leaves roll up and drop off. Tiny (1/20 inch long) yellow to orangish insects congregate on flower petals, leaves, and young fruit.	Thrips	Plant polycultures, page 258 Encourage beneficial organisms, page 260 Weed, page 262 Sanitize, page 263 Row covers, page 274 Kaolin spray, page 277 Blast with hose, page 278 Beneficial predators, page 280 Insecticidal soap, page 285 Spinosad, page 286 Neem, page 286 Horticultural oil, page 286 Pyrethrin, page 287

Symptom	Diagnosis	Solution

Caterpillars eat large irregular holes on the edges and sometimes in the middle of leaves. You may find that the soft green tissue of the leaves is eaten away. You may also find blackish green pellets of caterpillar poop. The caterpillars eat flower buds and bore holes into the fruit.

Caterpillars

Plant polycultures, page 258
Encourage beneficial organisms, page 260
Row covers, page 274
Hand-pick pests, page 277
Beneficial predators, page 280
BTK, page 283
Insecticidal soap, page 285
Spinosad, page 286
Neem, page 286
Horticultural oil, page 286
Pyrethrin, page 287

You find brown or green caterpillars hiding in the soil. They curl into a C shape when disturbed. They come out at night to eat holes in your strawberry leaves.

Cutworms

Plant polycultures, page 258
Encourage beneficial organisms, page 260
Row covers, page 274
Cutworm collars, page 274
Hand-pick pests, page 277
Beneficial predators, page 280
BTK, page 283
Insecticidal soap, page 285
Spinosad, page 286
Neem, page 286
Horticultural oil, page 286
Pyrethrin, page 287

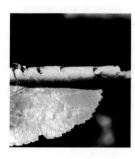

You spot leaves with their edges rolled into tubes and sewn together with silk. Look inside to find a caterpillar hiding and eating the leaf tissue. Young leafrollers skeletonize leaves because they can only eat the soft green tissue and leave the tough veins behind. Older, stronger leafrollers eat large holes in the leaves.

Leafrollers

Plant polycultures, page 258
Encourage beneficial organisms, page 260
Row covers, page 274
Hand-pick pests, page 277
Beneficial predators, page 280
BTK, page 283
Insecticidal soap, page 285
Spinosad, page 286
Neem, page 286
Horticultural oil, page 286
Pyrethrin, page 287

Symptom	Diagnosis	Solution

You find notched leaves. This is your main clue that gray-brown snout beetles (weevils) have been enjoying your strawberry leaves. Their larvae are white grubs with brown heads that live in the soil and eat plant roots.

Weevils

Soil solutions, page 248
Plant polycultures, page 258
Encourage beneficial organisms, page 260
Row covers, page 274
Chickens and ducks, page 282
Beneficial nematodes, page 282
Beauveria bassiana, page 285
Insecticidal soap, page 285
Diatomaceous earth, page 285
Spinosad, page 286
Neem, page 286
Horticultural oil, page 286
Sulfur, page 287
Pyrethrin, page 287

You spot metallic green and copper-colored beetles (to ½ inch long) with black legs chewing holes in leaves, flowers, and fruit. Larvae are whitish grubs (to 1 inch long) that live in the soil and eat plant roots. The grubs have three pairs of jointed legs and a brown head. They curl into a C shape when disturbed.

Japanese beetles

Soil solutions, page 248
Plant polycultures, page 258
Encourage beneficial organisms, page 260
Hand-pick pests, page 277
Jug traps, page 279
Beneficial predators, page 280
Chickens and ducks, page 282
Beneficial nematodes, page 282
BTSD, page 284
Milky spore, page 284
Beauveria bassiana, page 285
Insecticidal soap, page 285
Spinosad, page 286
Neem, page 286
Horticultural oil, page 286
Pyrethrin, page 287

Symptom	Diagnosis	Solution
Overripe berries left on the plant too long are eaten by tiny brown beetles to 1/16 inch long. These beetles damage ripe berries as well.	**Sap beetles**	Plant polycultures, page 258 Encourage beneficial organisms, page 260 Row covers, page 274 Hand-pick pests, page 277 Traps, page 278 Beneficial predators, page 280 Chickens and ducks, page 282 Beneficial nematodes, page 282 BTSD, page 284 *Beauveria bassiana*, page 285 Insecticidal soap, page 285 Spinosad, page 286 Neem, page 286 Horticultural oil, page 286 Sulfur, page 287 Pyrethrin, page 287
Fruit becomes blemished, discolored, or deformed (cat-faced). Pits or pustules may develop on the fruit. Leaves become twisted, wilt, and turn brown. You find shield-shaped insects sucking sap out of flower buds and fruit. These insects are true bugs and have mouthparts like hypodermic needles.	**Stink bugs, lygus bugs, tarnished plant bugs, boxelder bugs, leaf-footed bugs**	Plant polycultures, page 258 Encourage beneficial organisms, page 260 Row covers, page 274 Bags, page 277 Kaolin spray, page 277 Hand-pick pests, page 277 Beneficial predators, page 280 Chickens and ducks, page 282 Garlic spray, page 283 Pepper spray, page 283 *Beauveria bassiana*, page 285 Insecticidal soap, page 285 Spinosad, page 286 Neem, page 286 Horticultural oil, page 286 Pyrethrin, page 287

Symptom	Diagnosis	Solution

Small, green, soft-bodied insects hide inside wet globs of foamy white stuff that looks like spittle on the leaves of your plants.

Spittlebugs

Plant polycultures, page 258
Encourage beneficial organisms, page 260
Row covers, page 274
Blast with hose, page 278
Beneficial predators, page 280
Chickens and ducks, page 282

Fruit turns brown and soft with sunken areas that leak juice. Tiny, white, headless and legless worms (maggots) tunnel through the flesh of the fruit. When mature the maggots drop to the soil to pupate.

Fruit flies and maggots

Soil solutions, page 248
Plant polycultures, page 258
Encourage beneficial organisms, page 260
Sanitize, page 263
Row covers, page 274
Kaolin spray, page 277
Traps, page 278
Beneficial predators, page 280
Chickens and ducks, page 282
Beneficial nematodes, page 282
BTI, page 283

You find holes in the middle of tender new foliage and flower petals. Small brown and black insects with two pincers on their rear ends hide during the day and come out at night to ruin your plants.

Earwigs

Row covers, page 274
Hand-pick pests, page 277
Traps, page 278
Chickens and ducks, page 282
Diatomaceous earth, page 285
Spinosad, page 286

Symptom	Diagnosis	Solution

You notice leaves stippled with tiny pale dots that sometimes turn the whole leaf bronze-colored. Fine webbing, like spider silk, covers leaves and twigs. Badly infested leaves turn yellow or red and drop off.

Spider mites

Plant polycultures, page 258
Encourage beneficial organisms, page 260
Sanitize, page 263
Row covers, page 274
Kaolin spray, page 277
Blast with hose, page 278
Beneficial predators, page 280
Garlic spray, page 283
Pepper spray, page 283
Beauveria bassiana, page 285
Insecticidal soap, page 285
Spinosad, page 286
Neem, page 286
Horticultural oil, page 286
Sulfur, page 287
Pyrethrin, page 287

You find half-eaten fruit hanging on plants. Triangular holes are pecked into the edges of the damaged area. Pointed holes poke into the flesh.

Birds

Row covers, page 274
Nets, page 277
Fright tactics, page 278
Garlic spray, page 283
Pepper spray, page 283

Leaves, flowers, and fruit are bitten off and completely missing. Plants are mowed to the ground.

Deer, elk, livestock

Plant polycultures, page 258
Fence, page 276
Nets, page 277
Fright tactics, page 278
Garlic spray, page 283
Pepper spray, page 283
Deer repellent spray, page 283

Symptom	Diagnosis	Solution
 You find large irregular holes in leaves and fruit is half-eaten. Slime trails are present. The culprits hide during the day and come out at night or on cloudy, moist days to eat your plants.	**Slugs and snails**	Plant polycultures, page 258 Encourage beneficial organisms, page 260 Weed, page 262 Mulch, page 262 Row covers, page 274 Hand-pick pests, page 277 Copper tape, page 278 Slug and snail traps, page 279 Beneficial predators, page 280 Chickens and ducks, page 282 Iron phosphate, page 285 Diatomaceous earth, page 285
 Plants wilt in the heat of the day even when adequate moisture is available. They lack vigor and grow slowly. Leaves turn yellow. Examine the roots for lumps (galls) that are firmly attached and cannot be rubbed off. Nematodes are microscopic. Send samples to a lab to confirm your diagnosis.	**Nematodes**	Soil solutions, page 248 Solarize the soil, page 252 Plant polycultures, page 258 Sanitize, page 263 *Paecilomyces lilacinus*, page 284
 Black or brown spots appear on leaf edges and on fruit. Leaves and stems collapse. Plants may die.	**Anthracnose**	Manage water, page 253 Plant polycultures, page 258 Sanitize, page 263 Move the air, page 264 *Bacillus subtilis*, page 289 *Reynoutria sachalinensis*, page 289 Baking soda, page 290 Neem, page 290 Sulfur, page 291 Copper, page 291

Symptom	Diagnosis	Solution
Tender new leaves wilt, turn brown, and then die. Fruit becomes infected, turns brown, and rots. Fuzzy, grayish buff-colored mold grows on infected areas.	Botrytis blight	Manage water, page 253 Plant polycultures, page 258 Sanitize, page 263 Move the air, page 264 *Bacillus amyloliquefaciens*, page 288 *Bacillus subtilis*, page 289 *Reynoutria sachalinensis*, page 289 *Streptomyces lydicus*, page 290 Baking soda, page 290 Neem, page 290 Sulfur, page 291 Copper, page 291
 White or grayish white powdery patches develop on leaves, stems, and fruit. You can easily rub the fungus off the plant tissue. New growth becomes distorted. Fruit develops web-like scars of brown corky tissue.	Powdery mildew	Manage water, page 253 Plant polycultures, page 258 Sanitize, page 263 Move the air, page 264 *Bacillus amyloliquefaciens*, page 288 *Bacillus pumilus*, page 289 *Bacillus subtilis*, page 289 *Reynoutria sachalinensis*, page 289 *Streptomyces lydicus*, page 290 Baking soda, page 290 Neem, page 290 Sulfur, page 291 Copper, page 291
 Brown or purplish spots on fruit enlarge to cover the entire berry. Fruit becomes brown, tough, and leathery. Infected fruit tastes bitter and hangs on the plant.	Leather rot	Manage water, page 253 Plant polycultures, page 258 Sanitize, page 263 Move the air, page 264 *Bacillus amyloliquefaciens*, page 288 *Bacillus pumilus*, page 289 *Bacillus subtilis*, page 289 *Reynoutria sachalinensis*, page 289 *Streptomyces lydicus*, page 290 Baking soda, page 290 Neem, page 290 Sulfur, page 291 Copper, page 291

Plants become smaller and shorter than normal in the early stages of this disease. Later on the plants collapse and die. Cut the crown of infected plants in half to find brown discoloration.

Phytophthora root rot, crown rot

Soil solutions, page 248
Manage water, page 253
Plant polycultures, page 258
Sanitize, page 263
Bacillus subtilis, page 289
Reynoutria sachalinensis, page 289
Streptomyces lydicus, page 290
Trichoderma harzianum, page 290

Plants become stunted as older leaves get replaced by smaller and shorter new leaves. Roots die and rot starting from their tips. Split open affected roots to find the core of the root is red.

Red stele

Soil solutions, page 248
Manage water, page 253
Plant polycultures, page 258
Sanitize, page 263
Bacillus subtilis, page 289
Reynoutria sachalinensis, page 289
Streptomyces lydicus, page 290
Trichoderma harzianum, page 290

The lower leaves turn yellow and develop brown blotches on their tips. Often, this symptom appears on only one side of the plant. The leaves curl and die. The plant's growth slows. Look for black spots on the stems near the soil line. To confirm your diagnosis, cut stems in half lengthwise to see dark streaks inside.

Verticillium wilt

Soil solutions, page 248
Manage water, page 253
Plant polycultures, page 258
Sanitize, page 263
Reynoutria sachalinensis, page 289
Streptomyces lydicus, page 290
Trichoderma harzianum, page 290

Symptom	Diagnosis	Solution
 Reddish brown spots on the leaves have a dark edge. Sometimes a yellow halo surrounds them. The spots are confined by the veins of the leaf. Eventually the entire plant collapses and dies.	**Angular leaf-spot**	Manage water, page 253 Plant polycultures, page 258 Encourage beneficial organisms, page 260 Sanitize, page 263 Sterilize tools, page 263 Move the air, page 264 *Bacillus amyloliquefaciens*, page 288 *Bacillus subtilis*, page 289 *Pseudomonas fluorescens*, page 289 *Reynoutria sachalinensis*, page 289 *Streptomyces lydicus*, page 290 Copper, page 291
Leaves develop odd patches or streaks of yellowish to off-white tissue. Fruit production is greatly reduced. Roots become brittle. These incurable viruses are spread by sap-sucking insects like aphids or whitefly. Control insects to prevent infection.	**Strawberry mosaic viruses, mottles**	Plant polycultures, page 258 Encourage beneficial organisms, page 260 Sanitize, page 263 Sterilize tools, page 263 Blast with hose, page 278 Sticky bands, page 278 Beneficial predators, page 280 Insecticidal soap, page 285 Neem, page 286 Horticultural oil, page 286 Sulfur, page 287 Pyrethrin, page 287

Organic Solutions to Common Problems

To get a handle on plant problems, plant pathologists often use what they call the 80 percent rule: when something goes wrong in the garden, 80 percent of the time, the problem lies with the plant's growing conditions. This is called a disorder. If you eliminate disorders, and find that a pest is the problem, then 80 percent of the time, the pest is an insect. And finally, if you eliminate both causes, and determine that a disease is the problem, then 80 percent of the time that disease is a fungus infection.

For the gardener the rule boils down to this: 80 percent of the time, changing the growing conditions solves garden problems. Although all the solutions we offer in this book are safe to use in organic gardening, we hope that before you ever reach for a remedy, you will have reviewed the Introduction, the relevant problem-solving guide for an accurate diagnosis, and "Change the Growing Conditions" (page 247) to find preventative solutions.

SAFETY FIRST

We recommend many non-toxic solutions; several target specific pests without harming other creatures. But other products, even though they are approved for organic gardens, are both toxic and non-targeted. Take care using them. **We strongly encourage you to follow these five rules:**

1. Always use the least toxic product first.

2. Keep all products out of the reach of children and pets.

3. Read the label carefully. Use a product only on the plant or type of plant for which it is labeled.

4. Follow all the instructions on the label; dispose of the product properly after you are done using it.

5. Wear recommended protective gear and clothing: respirator mask, goggles, gloves, long-sleeved shirts, and long pants. Because some labels do not list inactive ingredients, safety gear is especially important. Avoid breathing dust or spray mist of all products, and be aware that any product can cause an allergic reaction in some people.

All pesticides, fungicides, and bactericides in the United States have undergone testing required by the Environmental Protection Agency (EPA), and manufacturers must follow EPA rules for labeling products. In addition, a product with an OMRI (Organic Materials Review Institute) label means that it has been certified for use on organically grown plants. Here's how to decipher the EPA product safety labels:

- The safest products, such as deterrents and barriers, need no safety labels.

- The next rung on the toxicity ladder requires a CAUTION label.

- Up one more rung, products require a WARNING label.

- On the highest rung, products require a DANGER label.

If you decide to use products to combat pests and diseases, again, try the least toxic product first. Use products labeled CAUTION and WARNING only after all other techniques have failed. Products labeled DANGER/POISON are available only to people who possess a Professional Applicators License: never use any of these dangerous products on food plants.

Change the Growing Conditions

Eighty percent of the time, sick plants are suffering from a disorder, all conditions caused by uncooperative weather and poor management. While we gardeners cannot control the weather, we can modify its impacts by providing the right nutrients, light, and water. Poor management might include pruning at the wrong time, or neglecting to thin a heavy crop of fruit. We can change the way we do things to keep our plants and their ecosystem healthy. Remember the old adage: prevention is the best medicine. We can all practice prevention by monitoring and changing the growing conditions in our gardens to help plants thrive.

TEMPERATURE SOLUTIONS

Temperature extremes, whether too hot or cold, affect your ability to grow fruit. You will want to know your climate and choose the right plants for it. You must make this key decision to achieve your goals. Once you have the right plant in the right place, you may need to take some further steps, such as those that follow, to keep it safe from the vagaries of weather.

Modify the effects of cold
Freeze damage. Provide winter protection for tender plants by planting them up against a south-facing wall. Reflected, stored heat from the wall can get them through the winter. Be aware that both cold winter and cool summer air flows downhill like water. It pools in depressions, and dams up against barriers, creating frost pockets. Don't put a plant in a low spot unless you're sure it can take the cooler temperature. If you already have a plant that dislikes the cool temperatures of its location, transplant it to warmer ground.

Winter desiccation. Broadleaf evergreens (avocado, banana, loquat, olive, guava, all citrus trees) keep their leaves all winter long. They may dry out in cold weather, especially if the sun is bright and it is windy. Give them extra water and plenty of mulch in winter. It will also help to dress your plants in an "overcoat," as needed. Like dressing kids in their snowsuits, wrap your plants in a blanket or other barrier during cold weather to help protect them from bright sun and wind. The fabrics made for floating row covers work well for this purpose.

Frost cracks. Stop feeding woody plants fertilizer in late summer so that they harden off before winter arrives. New stems may crack in severe winter weather. If this happens, the best thing to do is keep an eye on them. Trees can usually heal the crack, but you can encourage healthy callus development by making sure plants are well hydrated all winter. Then in early spring, give them an extra dose of organic fertilizer.

Modify the effects of heat
Too hot. If it is too hot for a plant to thrive, provide dappled shade with a small structure and a temporary covering of shade cloth, especially if you have young, newly planted berry bushes or trees. This prevents leaf scorch. Also take note of the direction of your summer prevailing winds. Sometimes a hot afternoon wind can scorch your plants. Protection from strong winds may be necessary. Create a windbreak with a fence or row of other trees. If you have not yet planted,

note the wind direction and intensity and site your new plants in a protected location, such as in the lee of your house or outbuilding.

Sulfur phytotoxicity. If you have treated your plants with sulfur, a hot day can cause the foliage to turn black. This is a phytotoxic reaction. It does no permanent harm, but does temporarily interfere with photosynthesis and limits productivity. Your plant will grow out of it in time. Do not use sulfur when high temperatures are expected.

Lack of winter chill. Many plants require a certain amount of winter chilling (hours below 45°F) or they are unable to flower. The exceptions are avocado, banana, loquat, passionfruit, melons, and citrus. Consult the Introduction and individual plant portraits for more guidance.

Everybody has their favorite way to make compost. This gardener has problems with raccoons who want to dine on kitchen scraps, so the compost pile is inside a bin that can be closed and latched at night.

SOIL SOLUTIONS

As you learned in the Introduction, creating biologically active soil is the easiest and most cost-effective solution to any disorder of the soil. You may also choose any of the following solutions that fit your circumstances.

Make and use compost. Compost is a simple and economical choice for all gardeners. It's the ultimate in recycling, returning to the earth many nutrients that plants use as they grow. You already have the material you need to make it. Dead plant tissue—kitchen scraps (minus animal products), grass clippings, leaves, prunings from trees and shrubs, paper—is the primary ingredient for sumptuous, loamy compost. Well-made compost is a biologically rich wonderland of beneficial fungi and bacteria that aggressively outcompete agents of disease, preventing them from gaining a toehold in your garden. If the

decomposer community works hard and everything goes well, the pile will get hot.

Composting made easy

1. Pile up kitchen (no animal products) and garden waste and let it decompose. Everything you put into your compost pile should be free of weed seeds, diseases, pests, and chemicals.

2. The pile should be made up of two-thirds "brown" material and one-third "green" material. The proportions can be measured by the handful, shovelful, or bucket. It is the 2:1 proportion that counts. Brown materials include straw, autumn leaves, shredded paper and cardboard, branches that have been run through a chipper, sawdust from untreated wood, and dry pine needles. Green materials include kitchen waste with no animal products, green leaves, and grass clippings.

3. Toss the brown and green material together randomly.

4. Once a week add one part healthy, weed-free soil from your garden or purchased from a vendor to three parts brown/green material mix, and turn the pile over with a shovel or pitch fork.

5. After you have a pile equal to about one wheelbarrow full, add a 40-pound bag of chicken manure.

6. If your climate is cold and wet, cover the pile with a tarp, and recognize that you may not have rich soil for up to a year. In a warm and moist climate you could have finished soil in a matter of weeks. In a very dry climate, water the pile to keep it moist.

Lay down sheet mulch. Use sheet mulch to prepare an area before you plant. The idea behind sheet mulching is to skip the backbreaking labor of tilling or removing weeds or sod by blocking light. The technique is simple. Lay cardboard on the ground to keep light from reaching plants you want to eliminate. Before you begin, remove any plastic from the cardboard, such as packing tape, which will never decompose. It is also wise to cut the vegetation you plan to cover to the ground. Leave it where it falls and lay the cardboard over it. When you spread the cardboard, make sure there are no gaps between the sheets. The goal: no light whatsoever should reach the plants you are trying to eliminate.

Cover the cardboard with 3 inches of mature organic compost or aged manure. Then spread 3 inches of mulch over that, and wait until the cardboard decomposes. Water frequently and thoroughly to speed decomposition. Then plant. In all honesty we don't have the patience to wait the year that decomposition can sometimes take. We leave it be for a couple of weeks, and then cut

Sheet mulching with flattened cardboard boxes easily eliminates weeds. Keep the cardboard covered with mulch and wet it down. As long as the weeds cannot get to the light they will die.

(top) Untreated lumber is the material of choice for the sides of these raised beds, which are planted with strawberries.

(bottom) Containers make excellent "raised beds" for fruit and nut trees, especially if you want to bring a tender evergreen like this Meyer lemon inside for the winter.

a hole in the cardboard where we want to plant and dig the planting hole. The mulch we spread around the plant discourages weeds that might peek up through the hole.

Make raised beds. Raised beds are easier to plant, and give you an almost trouble-free way to keep soil alive and healthy. It is far less effort to maintain good drainage. Raised beds warm up earlier in the spring than the surrounding ground, and that gives your plants a head start. They make installing water delivery systems simple and it's easy to water the soil, not the foliage. In addition, it is nearly painless to reach weeds and their seeds without excessive bending and pulling. Why not kill two birds with one stone, and lay cardboard down then build the raised beds on top? Use just about any material to make the sides of your raised beds: untreated lumber, rocks, cinder blocks, recycled concrete pavement that has been broken into chunks, slabs of stone, bender board, tree trunks, or branches. If you choose recycled material to make the sides, make sure it cannot leach pollutants into your garden or the ground water. You don't even have to build sides; piling soil up into a mound or berm also effectively creates a raised bed.

Use organic fertilizer. All fertilizers have three numbers on the label that stand for the percentages of nitrogen (N), phosphorus (P), and potassium (K). All three of these macronutrients are important for plant health. Keep in mind that high nitrogen fertilizers, in which the first number is larger than the other two, stimulate vegetative growth and can sometimes suppress flowering and fruiting. Good for lawns, bad for cherries. Fertilizers with higher phosphorus and potassium promote flowering and fruiting. In general, a balanced fertilizer, in which all three numbers are the same, meets the needs of most plants.

Nutrition Guidelines

Nutrient	Needed for . . .	Deficiency symptoms	Organic sources
Nitrogen	Vegetative growth, protein synthesis for new tissue	Lower leaves turn yellow but veins stay green. Plants stunted.	Blood meal, alfalfa meal, cottonseed meal, fish fertilizer
Phosphorus	Flower and fruit production	Leaves look purplish, veins turn purple.	Bonemeal, rock phosphate, guano, greensand
Potassium	Flower and fruit production	Leaves mottled yellow, leaf edges turn brown. Plants weak.	Greensand, seaweed (kelp), wood ashes, guano
Calcium	Numerous metabolic and physiological processes, cell elongation, and division	Water core. Bitter pit.	Lime, dolomite lime, gypsum, greensand
Magnesium	Plant growth and chlorophyll production	Lower leaves turn yellow but veins stay green.	Dolomite lime, Epsom salts, greensand
Sulfur	Plant growth, especially roots and seed production	New leaves turn yellow.	Epsom salts, gypsum, sulfur
Boron	Cell walls and membrane function	Edges of leaves curl under.	Seaweed (kelp), Borax (Fertibor, Granubor, Solubor)
Chloride	Reproductive growth, root metabolism, and protein utilization	Plants stunted, growth reduced.	Seaweed (kelp)
Copper	Photosynthesis and plant growth	Leaves are pale green, tips die back and twist.	Seaweed (kelp)
Iron	Photosynthesis	New leaves turn yellow but veins stay green.	Seaweed (kelp), iron chelate
Manganese	Carbohydrate and nitrogen metabolism	New leaves turn yellow but veins stay green.	Seaweed (kelp)
Molybdenum	Nitrogen metabolism	Lower leaves turn yellow but veins stay green. Plants stunted.	Seaweed (kelp)

Organic fertilizers are as effective as synthetic fertilizers and have many advantages over them. They feed the decomposer community in your soil. They release their nutrients slowly, making them available to your plants for a long time. Typically, this slow-release action means the fertilizer lasts for the entire growing season. Organic fertilizers do not contribute to water pollution, because their nutrients are fully absorbed by the plants. No fertilizer flees the garden into the water table.

The potential downside to this lack of speed is that the nutrients are not immediately available to your plants. In a nutritional emergency use a liquid foliar spray. Plants can absorb nutrients through their leaves very quickly. Organic foliar sprays include fish emulsion and liquid seaweed. Rock phosphate, guano, greensand, and borax, while allowed in organic gardening, are limited mined resources and are not sustainable.

Measure and modify pH. The pH of any growing media affects the plant's ability to absorb nutrients. Before changing the pH of your garden soil, especially for plants that like an acid soil, such as blueberries, you had best test it. You can take a soil sample to your local extension agent, master gardener group, or private lab; or you can buy a test kit at your local garden center. While not as accurate as the lab tests, the results will probably be close enough for your needs.

Almost all fruit needs a soil pH between 6.0 and 6.5. A measurement of 7.0 is considered neutral, but good garden soil lies within the 6.0 to 6.5 range and is slightly acid. If the number of your soil pH is higher than 6.0 to 6.5 then your soil may be too alkaline, and you will need to add a source of acid.

Be advised that blueberries need quite acid soil, which means a soil pH of 4.5 to 5.5. A handy source of acid for garden or container soil is coffee grounds. Add the grounds to growing media when you plant the blueberry bush. If the plant is already in the ground or container, clear mulch away and spread your morning coffee grounds over the surface of the soil. Don't worry that you might add too much; you can probably never add too many coffee grounds to upset a blueberry. Water the grounds in and replace the mulch.

Coffee grounds make the soil more acid, but if you do not reach your targeted pH, then add sulfur, following the directions on the product label. In addition, make sure to use an acid-based organic fertilizer on your blueberries. Labels on the product will indicate its acidity.

If your soil pH is below 6.0 for any soil where you are growing any fruit other than blueberries, you will need to adjust the soil to be more alkaline. Add dolomite lime, which also provides calcium and magnesium, to the soil. Follow directions on the product label.

Solarize the soil. This is a pretty extreme measure, but it is sometimes necessary. The goal is to get the soil very, very hot by laying plastic down over it, effectively making a solar cooker. This kills not only damaging nematodes and soilborne fungi but all your beneficial fungi and bacteria as well, so be sure it is necessary before doing it. The process takes four to six weeks. In the hottest, sunniest time of the year, remove the dead plant, its roots, and any soil that clings to the roots. Make sure the soil is not compacted by turning it over. Mound that soil slightly above the surface of the surrounding ground, and wet it thoroughly. Lay clear plastic, one to six millimeters thick, over the mound and hold it in place with rocks or bricks. After four to six weeks, remove the plastic. Before you garden here again, make sure the drainage is good. Spread 3 to 4 inches of mature, organic compost over the area to reintroduce beneficial microorganisms.

LIGHT SOLUTIONS

Too little or too much light poses some of the trickiest problems for fruit and nut growers. Most of the time, if insufficient light is the diagnosis, it is a case of right plant, wrong place. It may sound drastic, but move the plant to a new location. Prune surrounding plants, or prune away overhanging limbs of nearby plants. If possible, remove any structures that block sunlight.

For too much light (transplant shock, sunburn, leaf scorch), provide shade, especially on hot days. This seems like a simple solution, doesn't it? But implementing it will depend on your situation. A temporary solution is to throw a lightweight piece of 50-percent shade cloth over the plant on hot, sunny days, or until it adapts to its site. If your troubled plant is small enough, plant a small deciduous tree that will cast dappled shade onto it, especially during the hottest part of the day. A structure such as an overhead trellis can also provide adequate protection from intense sunlight.

And don't forget that you can always grow certain plants in pots and place them in the best locations for their needs, full sun or temporarily shady, as needed.

WATER SOLUTIONS

On this marvelous blue planet we do not have life without water. Too little water and your plant will die of drought, so no matter where you live, if Mother Nature doesn't provide adequate water for your fruits and nuts (about 1 inch a week), you'll have to give them more. Oddly enough, occasionally plants can get too much water, causing roots to suffocate and die, or be subject to invasion by root rot fungi. Even the way you choose to deliver supplemental water can affect the incidence of disorders, pests, or diseases in your garden.

A shade structure of 50-percent shade cloth gives plants a leg up to recover from transplant shock, sunburn, or leaf scorch from excessive light.

Manage water. Consistent moisture is crucial for fruits and nuts. This means that you do not allow the soil to dry out completely between watering. Nor do you let soil become saturated and waterlogged. Reliable moisture of 1 inch per week is just the ticket. If your plants are not receiving enough water, increase the watering time or amount. Revisit the Introduction for tips on how to measure the amount of water that reaches your plant. In addition, try rerouting runoff from your rain gutter downspouts and direct it toward plants that need supplemental water. A constructed dry streambed can reroute water in an effective and aesthetically pleasing way.

Harvest and store water. Harvest water runoff from impervious surfaces (roofs, driveways, sidewalks, and patios). Use catchment devices such as rain barrels or cisterns to store water for

(left) The dry streambed is a landscape feature designed to look like the gravelly bed of a creek in dry season. When there is no rainwater, the dry bed itself can suggest the presence of water, creating a lovely design element, as here. When it rains, runoff follows your streambed and the flow is directed into the garden.

(below) Rain barrels placed under rain gutter downspouts can store hundreds of gallons of water for future use. More rain barrels equals more water, water that costs you nothing. The rain barrels themselves cost money but will last for many years.

later use in your garden. Runoff water can also be harvested and stored in pools and fish ponds that enhance the landscape and provide irrigation in an emergency. Keep in mind that still water can harbor mosquito larvae. Be vigilant, and use mosquito dunks as necessary. These release BTI, which kills the larvae of mosquitoes and flies.

Ground water is diminishing because more is pumped all the time. Consequently municipalities charge more for it, making it a major garden expense in some locations. Save money while "going green" by storing water to enhance natural rainfall. Before you spend time and money on this effort, please check your local or state regulations regarding the capture of precipitation. In some places it is illegal to interrupt the flow of water from your property.

Retain water. This is different from water harvesting. In this case, the land itself is a water catchment system. Sunken gardens, retention ponds, or depressions hold water and allow it to percolate down to recharge groundwater. But the water can also be pumped out to irrigate your fruit garden whenever necessary. Swales are useful on sloping land. Dig a ditch across the land on the contour. Pile the soil excavated from the ditch on the downslope side to create a berm along the length of the ditch. The swale captures and retains the rainfall or runoff from the slope above. Plant the berm with a variety of fruits, nuts, herbs, and flowers that will thrive on water from the swale.

(opposite, left) Cisterns, either above or below ground, also store rainwater captured from roofs through downspouts. They are common in the western United States where drought conditions are the norm.

(opposite, right) This attractive sunken garden retains water in significant rainfall events, helping to recharge the groundwater.

Use effective watering techniques

Water soil, not foliage. Fungi often, and bacteria and foliar nematodes always, need a film of surface moisture to infect the plant host. Drip-trickle systems use tiny emitters placed next to a plant's root system to deliver water directly to the soil; place these systems on top of the ground, so that when they need repair they are easy to get at. Soaker hoses are permeable and allow the water to soak deeply into the soil below. Whichever method you choose, be sure to drain all water from the system before freezing temperatures strike. Alternatively, incorporate shallow trenches into your fruit garden. Plant the tops of the furrows and fill the trenches with water at watering time. The plant roots will reach under the furrows for the water they need. For container plants, use a watering can with a narrow spout or a hose with a narrow tip and water the growing media at the base of the plant directly, avoiding the foliage and fruit.

Allow the soil to dry out. This applies to plants in the ground as well as those in containers. Some root rot fungi, called water molds, thrive in soggy soil. Overly wet soil stresses plants, making them susceptible to invasion by deadly pathogens. Most plants cannot tolerate these conditions, and fruits and nuts are no exception. All root rot fungi can be lethal. They are well able to kill fully mature trees as well as tiny seedlings.

Do not work with wet plants. Wet plants are most susceptible to invasion by fungi, bacteria, and foliar nematodes. Most pathogens require moisture to stay alive. Many move from plant to plant in flowing water, driving rain, or splash-up from the soil. Others are carried on the wet hands, clothes, shoes, or tools of gardeners. Do not walk through your garden while it is wet. Do not handle your houseplants after watering them, if the foliage is wet.

Check and improve drainage. You must make sure you have good drainage. This phrase means two things. Water must be able to drain away from plant roots quickly enough that they do not rot. On the other hand, soil must retain water long enough for plant roots to draw it up and hydrate the foliage. A delicate balance must be struck, but corrective measures are pretty easy.

To check drainage where you want to plant, dig a hole at least 1 foot deep. Fill the hole with water and wait. If the water drains away within five minutes, that's too fast. In this case, you do not need to improve drainage. Rather, you need to increase the organic content in the soil to hold adequate moisture. If the hole still has water in it after one hour, drainage is not adequate, and needs improvement. Revisit the Introduction for tips on creating healthy, biologically active soil.

Our favorite solution for dealing with poor drainage is to go up. Create a raised bed in which to plant. Alternatively, create a drainage hole. Dig into the low-lying wet area, making sure you do not cut the roots of your plants. See if a layer of clay, rock, or other hard material prevents water from draining away. If so, dig through the layer to create a drainage hole. If that is not possible, you may need to dig a drainage ditch to allow the water to drain away. If you need a series of ditches, drains, or sump pumps, consult an engineer or landscape architect. Local and state governments regulate how you treat wetlands and surface runoff.

Watering the container plant. Overwatering is the number one killer of all potted plants. Allow the soil to drain before watering the plant again, and make sure the soil dries out between watering. Making sure drainage is adequate is equally important. Every pot should have a drainage hole. Look to see if it is clogged and open it up if it is. Do not allow the pot to sit in a water-filled saucer. Put supports under the pot to lift it at least 1 inch above standing water. To water containers effectively, use a watering can with a narrow spout or a hose with a narrow tip. By watering the growing media at the base of the plant, you will avoid wetting the foliage, keeping fungi and bacteria at bay.

Berms, containers, constructed beds, and terraces stand above the natural soil level and all effectively constitute raised beds. Because raised beds are on top of the wet soil they drain better and help to prevent the problems resulting from saturated soil.

(opposite) This nest box for mason bees will contribute to a bumper fruit crop.

OTHER ENVIRONMENTAL DISORDERS

In addition to disorders caused by unsettling circumstances of temperature, soil, light, and water, fruit and nut growers occasionally make a mistake that can lead to difficulties. We touched on these problems in the Introduction. Note especially its sections on planting and pollination.

Too much fruit. An abundance of fruit results in stunted fruit that is smaller than expected, or in branches broken by the weight of the fruit. Thin the fruit while the fruitlets are still quite small, about the size of the end of your finger. Pull most fruitlets off the plant leaving only a few on each branch.

Poor pollination. This results in distorted fruit. It may be shaped normally at one end, where seeds are developing, and be shriveled at the other end, where no seeds are developing. This problem is often weather-related because bees are most active on sunny, warm days and less active on cool, wet days. It is also true that many bee species are in trouble, and may not be

visiting your plants in sufficient numbers. Too few bees can cause poor pollination. Honeybee colonies are dying due to colony collapse disorder (CCD). For insurance, create habitat for native solitary bees like the blue orchard mason bee. They are extremely efficient pollinators of numerous crops. Nest boxes for these and other native bees are available at most garden centers and on the Internet. The upcoming section on encouraging beneficial organisms will help you learn how to lure pollinators into your garden.

Mechanical damage. Keep string trimmers, lawnmowers, and other equipment at a healthy distance. They can harm your plants, especially trunks and main stems, leaving wounds that are open invitations to pathogenic fungi and bacteria. Create barriers to protect your plants from equipment mishaps. Compaction of the soil during construction projects, or digging around your plants can harm roots. The plant may die many months after the project is completed. If only a portion of the root system has been damaged, however, the plant may recover and grow a new root system to replace the damaged one. If you have recently completed a construction project and your plant is looking sickly but isn't dead yet, give it extra fertilizer and water to help it grow new roots.

Chemical damage. Both herbicides and pesticides, even organic ones, can harm plants. A variety of symptoms may show up, on leaves, flowers, or stems. Once the damage has occurred, the affected tissue will not recover. The plant may grow out of it, however, and be back to normal the next growing season. We do not recommend herbicides, apart from using pre-emergent herbicides against weeds. Pesticides, like sulfur and copper, while organic solutions, cause phytotoxic reactions. Read product labels and follow directions to avoid damaging plants.

Rootbound. Plants that have outgrown their pots become rootbound. One remedy is to up-pot the plant to a larger container to give it a larger volume of soil to plumb for water. Alternatively, pull the plant out of its pot; shave off 1 inch of roots and soil around the sides and bottom of the root ball. Then put the plant back in its pot and pack it with fresh new potting soil. Use this second technique to keep a fruit or nut tree or shrub in the same container for many years.

PLANT POLYCULTURES

In a polyculture garden unrelated plants grow next to each other. Think of it as the opposite of a field of corn, the classic example of a monoculture. As in an abundant English cottage garden, a polyculture approach means there will be flowers, herbs, ornamental grasses, and vegetables throughout your fruit garden. One polyculture that has stood the test of time is "The Three Sisters"— corn, beans, and squash. These three vegetables were extensively interplanted by native peoples of North America.

In nature all plants live in communities, and all these communities are polycultures. In a polyculture garden you construct an artificial plant community that emulates a natural one. As in nature, plants fulfill many functions while they interact with each other, wildlife, and you. As you plan and tend the fruit garden, be mindful of the interactive and multi-tasking nature of your creation.

Start by paying attention to what these trees and shrubs do in addition to providing us with fruit. The canopy, with its leaves, flowers, and fruit, makes oxygen, filters and cleans the air, captures sunlight and converts it to food, diffuses raindrops, and provides habitat for microorganisms, insects, bees, and birds. Stems and trunks, in addition to transporting water and nutrients from the roots, and sugar from the leaves, provide support for the plant as well as other plants around it. Roots take up water and nutrients from the soil, contribute to the healthy soil ecosystem, provide habitat for thousands of soil organisms, and control erosion. These are just a few of the jobs our trees and shrubs take on.

The practice of polyculture may be the oldest garden and farming technique in the world. It has many names: interplanting, companion planting, creating plant guilds, and agroforestry. These techniques all amount to the same thing, and they all mimic natural plant communities, a distinct advantage in creating a healthy garden ecosystem in your yard. Practitioners of companion planting theorize that specific plants interact favorably with one another. A plant guild is a similar construct, in which the grower groups plants that have a positive synergistic effect on one another.

Exactly which plants grow well together is an ongoing field of study. This is why you will discover wildly differing opinions in books, on the Internet, and in conversations. While these studies continue, we have three pieces of advice: to simplify your life, group plants with the same temperature, soil, light, and water needs together; maximize species diversity by choosing unrelated plants to grow near each other; choose plants that occupy different strata of the root zone. For example, a cherry tree's roots extend 4 to 5 feet below the surface, while the roots of most perennials occupy a much shallower zone of the soil.

Polycultures provide distinct advantages. Their inherent species diversity provides excellent habitat for beneficial organisms that outcompete destructive pathogens. Pestiferous insects have more difficulty finding your fruit, and it's tough for diseases to jump from plant to plant.

A grower in Albuquerque, New Mexico, found an "accidental" guild around his young peach tree. Grain amaranth and sweet corn planted themselves next to the peach, and all three of these completely unrelated plants are thriving.

Polycultures confuse and repel pests, both large and small, and slow the spread of disease. This underplanting of rosemary helps to protect this apple tree from deer, as would other highly aromatic plants like lavender, thyme, and sage. Herbs such as fennel and dill attract beneficial insects to help control insect pests. Flowers like yarrow, cosmos, and rudbeckia also attract beneficial insects.

Include marigolds in the polyculture garden. Their foliage contains strongly scented aromatic compounds, which are effective in suppressing root-knot and other nematodes. African marigolds (*Tagetes erecta*) and French marigolds (*T. patula*) are both effective in suppressing root-knot nematodes, but French marigolds are more effective against a wider variety of nematodes. The soil next to marigolds is not protected, so plant them directly under any specimen you want to protect.

Confuse and repel pests. Insects home in on your fruits and nuts from great distances by smell. Attracted by the scent, the critters fly directly to their hapless prey. If you have several blueberries growing close to one another, insects find them easily. Using a polyculture approach, you would plant the same number of blueberries, but scatter them throughout your yard, surrounding them with other kinds of plants, which masks their scent. As insects approach their target, they switch from olfactory to visual. If the target plants hide behind a wide variety of other kinds of plants, the insects get confused and have difficulty finding the tasty treats they're after. In other words, they have to work harder to damage your fruit. In addition, a mixed bed full of fruits, nuts, flowers, and herbs attracts beneficial organisms that kill and eat the pests.

Inhibit the spread of disease. Diseases caused by bacteria and fungi leap from plant to plant in a variety of ways. Fungi spread by wind or water splash from the ground. Bacteria are carried by insects, windborne rain, or on the gardener's clothing, if plants are wet. Viruses also attack when insects like aphids, leafhoppers, and thrips carry the disease from one plant to another. The closer together plants of the same type are, the easier it is for disease to spread. It's just like people on an airplane. When one person with a bad cold coughs, the entire cabin is exposed to the germs. Many others can get ill. Scattering your plants across your landscape prevents diseases from leapfrogging from one plant to the next.

Container gardening also benefits from the polyculture concept. Plant different kinds of plants in containers in a harmonious combination of color, texture, and form. Then arrange your containers so that unrelated plants sit next to each other. All the plants we discuss in the next section, "Encourage Beneficial Organisms," should be included in a polyculture approach.

ENCOURAGE BENEFICIAL ORGANISMS

Inviting wild creatures into the garden saves you time, money, and effort. Pollinators ensure that you have abundant fruit and nuts to eat. Birds, butterflies, bees, and syrphid flies (aka hoverflies) all provide pollination services. Predatory and parasitic insects make spraying toxic chemicals unnecessary because they hunt and kill the pests you don't like. Wasps, beetles, and beneficial nematodes control harmful pests. Healthy microorganisms such as bacteria and fungi drive pathogens away from your garden. To entice these helpful partners give them healthy habitat, abundant food, nectar, and water.

Birds and spiders are also efficient predators of insects and other pests. A spider's web may be a nuisance if its location is inconvenient for you, but it's better not to kill the spider. She's just doing her job—to catch and eat as many insects as she can. Many birds eat insects exclusively, while some are part-time insect eaters. Other birds relish snails and slugs. Attract birds of all kinds to your garden with water and shelter. They are valuable allies.

Certain plants invite beneficial partners from the wild. Pansies, violas, and other flowers with streaks or dark lines on their petals, called guidelines, that point to the good stuff inside attract bees that will then cruise the garden and pollinate your fruits and nuts.

Queen Anne's lace in the carrot family (Apiaceae) attracts good parasitoid wasps that kill caterpillars. It also attracts lacewings, syrphid and tachinid flies, assassin bugs, and honeybees—all beneficial predators and/or pollinators. Other members of this family valuable for attracting beneficial organisms are dill, coriander (cilantro), parsley, cumin, and fennel. Fennel flowers in particular lure lady beetles (aka ladybugs) into the garden and keep these favorite beneficial insects

Like other members of the daisy family, echinaceas will attract a variety of valuable pollinators to your garden, including bees and butterflies.

Beautiful members of the mint family, agastaches will bring many hummingbirds to your fruit garden along with a plethora of bees.

Cosmos and other daisies attract adult syrphid flies. They pose as bees or wasps but are harmless pollinators that sip nectar and eat pollen. How else do they help? Their babies are voracious predatory maggots that crawl over your plants and eat aphids.

Birds eat huge quantities of insects, and if you provide the right habitat (or specially designed house, as this one, for purple martins) they will nest and feed in your garden.

MAINTAIN A HEALTHY HOME

Weed. Getting rid of weeds is a big help in managing diseases, insect populations, and other pests like slugs and snails. Weeds compete with your plants for water, nutrients, and sunlight. In addition, many weeds harbor plant diseases, harmful insects, and other pests. Some viral and bacterial diseases, for example, are brought into your garden by insects that first feed on infected weeds and then feed on your plants. Weeds also provide hiding places for slugs and snails.

Use a pre-emergent herbicide (aka germination inhibitor) such as corn gluten to prevent all seeds, including weeds, from germinating. It has no effect on established plants; it only suppresses seed germination. It is an organic product that feeds the soil with nitrogen as it degrades. Non-GMO corn gluten is available for those concerned about using genetically modified corn products in gardens. Search for it on the Internet.

Hoe or pull weeds in established gardens where you can work around the plants you want to keep. Some weeds such as horsetails, Canada thistle, and field bindweed regenerate from tiny pieces of root that you leave behind. This can be absolutely maddening, but diligence is rewarded with eventual success.

It is very satisfying to watch those horrible weeds burst into flame and die when you flame them with a weed burner. It goes without saying that you need to be extremely careful not to burn down the neighborhood. Wait for a calm day and do not use it near any area with an extensive fuel load of dead grass, weeds, or brush. This method is illegal in some places, so check local regulations.

Mulch. Mulch is material used to cover the surface of the soil around plants. For container plants mulch (aka top-dressing) is usually more

happy. Both the adults and babies of these familiar beetles devour small, soft-bodied pests, such as aphids, mealybugs, and scale.

Members of the daisy family (Asteraceae) attract many sorts of bees and butterflies, all valuable pollinators, and tiphiid wasps. These solitary black and white wasps parasitize beetle grubs as larvae and pollinate flowers as adults. Plants in this family also lure other helpful parasitoid and predatory wasps, lady beetles, lacewings, syrphid flies, and soldier beetles to your fruit garden. Other valuable daisies: tarragon, chamomile, cosmos, sunflowers, anthemis, echinacea, gaillardia, bachelor's buttons, and yarrow.

Besides attracting pollinators, the aromatic members of the mint family (Lamiaceae) attract beneficial predators like lady beetles and lacewings, which frequent their foliage. Other valuable mints: agastache, catnip, catmint, thyme, rosemary, hyssop, lemon balm, horehound, sage, and pycnanthemum.

decorative than outdoor mulch. Mulching or top-dressing helps prevent weeds, conserve moisture, and control diseases and insect pests that hide in the soil during the day and come out at night to devour your plants. Spreading mulch also prevents water splash. Plant parts close to the ground or growing media are most susceptible to infection from fungal spores, bacteria, and nematodes splashing up from the ground in water.

Many materials can be used for mulch. We do not recommend using compost as mulch. One of the main properties of good mulch is that it is nutrient-poor and helps control weeds. One of the main properties of good compost is that it is nutrient-rich, exactly the opposite of mulch. If you put nutrient-rich compost on the surface of your soil the weeds are going to have a field day. Use biodegradable materials that feed your soil, because they break down over time:

- Sustainably harvested bark mulch. Do not use "Beauty Bark," which may be loaded with herbicides.

- Crushed coconut and other nut husks.

- Pine needles.

- Straw, newspaper, and cardboard. Cardboard should be top-dressed with a more attractive material.

- Fine gravel, decorative stone, or sand. Use as mulch around your fruit garden plants to control root rot fungi. Use as a top-dressing on container plants to control fungus gnats.

- Grass clippings. But be careful. You must be certain the clippings contain no weed seeds and that no weed killer was used on the grass.

Sanitize. This is the term that plant pathologists apply to the act of cleaning out any pest-or disease-ridden plant material. It is the first thing

you should do if you have heavy insect infestations or a rapidly spreading disease infection. During the growing season prune, pick, or break off any part of the plant that is badly affected. Clean tools thoroughly and wash your hands before handling any healthy plants.

If you have diagnosed cedar-apple rust after using the Pome Fruit Problem-Solving Guide, remove all junipers, especially eastern redcedars (*Juniperus virginiana*), from your landscape. They harbor the infection, and it will spread to your apple trees.

In the case of serious fungus infections, you should remove the entire plant, roots, and any soil clinging to the roots. Dispose of infested or infected plant material in such a way that it cannot expose or infect other plants. Burn it, if it is legal and safe to do so, or put it in black plastic garbage bags and send it to the landfill. In general it is not a good idea to compost it. Some people who know how to maintain a hot compost pile (at least 160°F) can add this kind of material to their compost. But if you have any doubt about whether your compost pile is that hot, it is better to just get rid of the plant material.

At the end of each growing season, clean up leftover plant material of all annuals and biennials. If perennials have died to the ground, clean up all the above-ground plant parts. Dispose of this material where it cannot infect other plants. Many pests can live over the winter in the garden if you do not get rid of their cozy habitat. So, don't give them the chance to be around in the spring.

Sterilize tools. Any time you wound a plant with any tool you can inadvertently spread viruses, bacterial diseases, or nematodes. If you prune or cut any plant for any reason, sterilize your tools before you use them on another plant. Be especially vigilant if you suspect a plant is sick but have not yet removed and destroyed it.

One way to sterilize pruning tools is to soak them in a 10-percent solution of household bleach. Add one cup of bleach to nine cups of water and place the pruner blades in this for three minutes. This will corrode your tools over time. Heating the blades with a blowtorch kills 100 percent of pathogens, and will not damage your tools. At a minimum, spray cutting blades with rubbing alcohol. This is the least effective method, but also easiest to do when you are out in the garden.

Pests and diseases can also travel from one location to another on a dirty shovel. After you dig up an infected plant, clean your shovel with a wire brush, and spray it with alcohol.

Move the air. Whether they're on your windowsill, on your deck, or out in the garden, plants crowded together and plants with dense foliage are more susceptible to pests and diseases. Space plants well apart; allow plenty of air-flow between them. In the greenhouse or the house, use a fan on a low setting to keep air moving around foliage and flowers. Prune individual plants to open them up to light and air. In general, prune fruit and nut trees to a scaffold of branches that resembles an inside-out umbrella or a martini glass (open vase style). Keep the center open. These tactics allow the foliage to dry quickly after rain or watering and reduce the number and kind of fungus infections on your plants. These techniques also expose insect pests to predators, allowing the predators to help control the pests.

PRUNE PROPERLY

Pruning is a complex subject, but with guidance and care—and a tall ladder—anyone can do basic maintenance pruning. For starters, always prune a woody plant in this order: dead, damaged, diseased, deranged. After you have removed material in that order, look at your plant to decide if it needs further pruning for shape, size, fruit production, or aesthetic appeal.

Three rules will protect your plants from wanton pruning. One is to always prune just above a node, the place where a leaf joins a stem. The node is where dormant buds are located. These will grow out into new stems. If you prune just below a node or in between two nodes, you leave a stub. Never leave a stub. The section of stem between two nodes, the internode, cannot grow new stems. All it can do is sit there, become infected, and rot. A stub is an open invitation to diseases that can kill your plant.

Another rule is to prune to nodes with buds that face away from the center of the plant, and in the direction you want them to grow. New branches that grow from these buds will grow in the direction the bud is pointing. If you prune properly new growth develops away from the center of the plant, leaving the center open to air and light. This helps to avoid diseases and pests.

Finally, never cut a branch off flush with the trunk or stem. The place where a branch joins the main trunk or larger branch is usually slightly swollen and is called a collar. The collar is special tissue that can quickly grow over and seal the wound when you prune off the branch. Always protect the collar.

Now that you know how to approach the task of pruning, and how to protect plants from pruning mishaps, it's a good idea to learn some basic tips and terminology. Also revisit the plant portrait of your subject plant to make sure you understand its specific growth habit and pruning

First, prune away dead and dying tissue, any branches or twigs that are already dead or clearly dying.

Finally, inspect your plant carefully and prune away deranged branches, those that cross into the middle of the plant or that take off in weird directions.

Next, look for damaged and broken branches and remove them.

Remove diseased branches and stem tissue that has cankers, galls, or any bacterial, fungal, or viral infection, as well as tissue infested by insects or other pests.

Always prune just above a node.

needs. And it bears repeating: if you cut any plant for any reason, sterilize your tools before you use them on another plant.

Tips and terminology for all pruning

Open the center. This allows more air and light to reach the foliage in the interior of the canopy. Better air circulation and rapid drying avoids russeting of the fruit, corky tissue that develops on the surface of the fruit in response to staying too wet too long. It also helps to avoid a large number of fungal and bacterial diseases. Use thinning cuts for this purpose.

Thinning cuts. A thinning cut removes an entire branch at its base where it connects to a larger branch. Thinning cuts in moderation do not stimulate lateral buds into growth so they don't initiate wild growth responses. Too much thinning, however, could overstimulate the tree and result in excessive new growth and water sprouts.

Heading-back cuts. A heading-back cut is one that severs a branch in the middle (but still just above a node) to remove the bud at the tip of a branch. This apical bud makes growth-regulating hormones that suppresses growth of lateral buds further down the branch. Cutting off the apical bud removes these hormones and stimulates lateral buds to begin to grow out into new branches. A moderate amount of heading-back rejuvenates the tree. Too much heading-back overstimulates the tree, resulting in a wild overproduction of new branches and water sprouts.

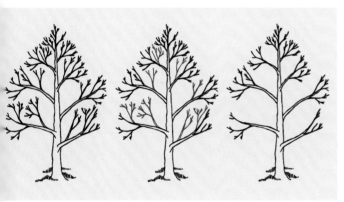

To open the center remove branches crowding the interior of your tree's canopy using thinning cuts. The tree on the left needs to pruned. The middle drawing shows in red all the branches to be removed. The tree on the right has been pruned.

(top) The red bar in this photo shows where a thinning cut should be made.

(bottom) A heading-back cut, where indicated by the red bar, would stimulate the development of side branches.

Tips and terminology for pruning trees

Spurs. Many fruit plants develop spurs, specialized short shoots, along their branches. These natural spurs flower and set fruit every year but they always remain stubby. Spurs live 10 years or more in apples, cherries, and pears and as few as three years in apricots.

Water sprouts. A tree responds to severe pruning by developing fast-growing shoots that grow straight up. These water sprouts, as they are known, are undesirable because they are weak and subject to disease, and bear few fruits. While they are still small grasp them firmly and yank them down and off your tree. Don't just cut them off with your pruners because they will continue to grow new shoots from the base. Tearing them off removes them completely.

Suckers or root sprouts. Nearly all fruit and nut trees are grafted to a rootstock because that is a quick and relatively easy way for growers to propagate them. This means that the above-ground part of the tree and its roots are two different plants. Shoots that develop from the root system never have the kind of fruit or nut you expect. Any time you see shoots growing from below the graft union or directly from the roots, you must remove them. They grow faster and stronger than your above-ground tree, and if you do not get rid of them in a timely manner,

(top) A spur flowers and fruits every year but never grows out into a long branch.

(center) When this poor plum tree was severely pruned a decade ago, it responded with a wild overgrowth of water sprouts, branches that grow very fast and tend to go straight up.

(bottom) All the new shoots growing from the base of this plum tree, some of them root spouts, some of them suckers, are sprouting from below the graft union and will have to be removed.

they may outcompete your tree and even possibly kill it. Look for the graft union at the base of the trunk just above the roots. The graft union is usually slightly swollen or of a slightly different color or texture. New shoots arising below this graft are called suckers. Remove suckers the same way you remove water sprouts. Grasp them firmly and yank them down and off. Do not merely prune them away, because they'll just make lots of new little shoots out of the stubby base that's left behind. Tearing them off your plant will remove them completely. Root sprouts that pop up directly from the root system must be dug up and cut off.

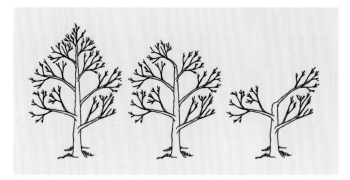

Three pruning styles for fruit and nut trees: central leader on the left, modified central leader in the middle, and open vase on the right.

Central leader. Certain fruit and nut trees, such as apple, avocado, sweet cherry, chestnut, pear, pecan, and walnut, are often pruned to a central leader. In this style the main trunk is allowed to grow tall with multiple major limbs radiating out from it. Smaller, minor limbs are pruned away. Trees pruned in the central leader style can grow quite large, which makes harvesting, pruning, and other necessary management activities more difficult.

Modified central leader. Any of the large trees typically pruned to a central leader can be pruned to a modified central leader to make it easier to manage. This is accomplished by shortening the main trunk while the tree is still young, leaving five to seven side branches in a spiral around the trunk. All other side branches are pruned away. This allows the tree to grow taller than the open vase style, but shorter than the central leader style. This will keep your tree smaller, bushier, and easier to reach.

Open vase. Other fruit and nut trees, such as almond, apricot, pie cherry, guava, hazelnut, loquat, peach, nectarine, and Japanese plum, are usually pruned to an open vase. Apple, sweet cherry, and pear are sometimes pruned in this style as well. Prune off the top of the main trunk early in the life of your tree, leaving three to five branches radiating out from the trunk like the treads of a spiral staircase. Other, lateral branches are also pruned away. The shape of the tree resembles a martini glass because the center is kept open.

Espalier. Many people with limited space choose to espalier a fruit tree by training it to grow flat against a wall or fence. Such a tree might be 12 feet wide and 8 feet tall, but less than 2 feet thick. Develop an espalier over time by starting with a young tree planted against a wooden frame with wire or wooden cross bars at 2-foot intervals of vertical height. Select a pair of side branches as close to the cross bars or wires as possible. Tie one side branch to the wire on the right of the trunk and tie one on the left. These will become the permanent framework of your tree. Use thinning cuts to remove all other branches. You'll use a combination of heading-back and thinning cuts to train your tree to this very narrow shape as the years go by. Fruit trees that naturally develop long-lived spurs, like apples, cherries, and pears, are easy to maintain in an espalier.

Tips and terminology for pruning vines. Fruiting vines like grape, kiwi, and passionfruit are usually planted on a fence, arbor, or trellis structure for support. This affects how you approach pruning.

Grapes. When you prune a grape vine, you encourage it to put its energy into fruit production, so this task is essential if your goal is a healthy crop of yummy grapes. Annual pruning not only makes for better fruit production, it makes the plant itself more manageable. Left to its own devices a grape vine will go crazy, sprawling across the garden, climbing into spaces where it is not wanted, and making small, sour grapes. You've heard the expression, we're sure.

Here's the most important thing you need to know: this year's canes that grow from last year's canes are the only ones that will bear fruit this season. Viticulture resources call this "fruiting on canes from one-year-old wood."

Grapes have two different growth habits. Each requires its own method of pruning. Nearly all American (*Vitis labrusca*) and some French-American hybrid grapes produce very long, floppy canes that dangle and crawl every which way. Prune these vigorous vines using heading-back cuts. Cut the apical bud—the one at the tip of the long cane—off, and allow 10 to 12 lateral buds to remain. Grape growers call this cane pruning. European grapes, derived from *V. vinifera*, are bushy and grow short, erect canes. Almost all require what growers call spur pruning: cut the cane near its base, leaving only two or three buds.

Kiwi. Like grapes, kiwis bear fruit only on canes that sprout from one-year-old wood. In summer the growth of kiwi is rampant so it's a good idea to head-back the canes. Disentangle long twining stems of new growth from each other. In winter head-back the fruiting canes to about 18 inches in length and thin them to about 12 inches apart.

Passionfruit. Every year, after you harvest the fruit, prune vigorous shoots back by a third. Thin out any excess stems by cutting them to the ground.

In case you're wondering, this sprawling, floppy American 'Concord' grape vine has not been pruned in a very long time.

This old kiwi vine has not seen pruning shears in years. It has grown into a huge tangled mass on top of its support structure.

Tips and terminology for pruning shrubs

Blueberry, currant, and gooseberry. The stems of these bushes tend to produce fewer and fewer berries as they age. These shrubs grow new stems every year so you can keep your bushes eternally young and at maximum fruit production by removing branches—cutting older wood to the ground and keeping the younger stems. When a blueberry reaches its sixth year, remove stems that are five years old, and keep all the wood that is one to four years old. Never prune away more than one-third of the stems. Repeat this process every year. For gooseberries and red and white currants remove three-year-old stems every year. For black currants remove all two-year-old wood every year.

Brambles: blackberries and raspberries. All types of bramble fruits have perennial root systems but their stems, or canes, live only two years. Blackberries, boysenberries, loganberries, marionberries, tayberries, and red, purple, and black raspberries are all bramble fruits.

Typical bramble cultivars are summer-bearing. They produce new canes, called primocanes, every year in spring. The primocanes live through the winter. In their second summer these canes are called floricanes because they flower and set fruit. The floricanes die after fruiting. Prune all two-year-old canes to the ground when they are finished fruiting and leave the one-year-old canes for next summer's crop.

Ever-bearing brambles depart from the typical by flowering and fruiting on primocanes in the autumn of their first year as well as on floricanes in the summer of their second year, giving you two crops a year. Prune these by heading-back the top one-third of all canes that flower and fruit in the autumn as soon as that portion of the cane has finished fruiting. Leave the bottom two-thirds of the cane alone. The cane's lower two-thirds will flower and fruit in the summer of its second year after which it will die and can be pruned to the ground.

Many people enjoy obtaining two crops from their berries every year. Some people find the pruning to be a hassle so they simply mow the ever-bearing types to the ground every winter. They get only one crop of berries a year, in the autumn, but pruning is greatly simplified. Obviously you can't do this to summer-bearing types because you'd never get any fruit.

The oldest stems of this red currant are far less fruitful than its younger stems. Removing the oldest stems and keeping younger ones keeps the bush rejuvenated.

The flowers on this marionberry are borne on canes in their second summer. Such floricanes, as they are called, will die after their fruit ripens.

Solve Pest Problems

Most creatures that enter our fruit gardens from the wild are beneficial. Even if destructive, they're just looking to share nature's bounty. Frequently we're better off sharing—it's less work, and costs less time and money; and one could argue that our fellow creatures deserve tasty treats too. Sometimes, though, we want to save the fruits and nuts for ourselves. In our town, for instance, folks tend to share with the deer, but, personally we've kind of had it with our furry friends. When the deer eat all our strawberries—leaves and fruit—in one night, just when we planned to harvest the next day, all bets are off. It's time to do something about the problem and search for options to exclude these beautiful troublemakers.

The same goes for smaller creatures who find their way into the garden in search of food. When they do, we like to take a breath and figure out if the interloper is friend or foe. After all, it's best to get to know wildlife—this approach makes life so much more enjoyable, and simplifies the task of creating the healthy habitat that makes the garden work. Besides, if you do have a pest in the fruit garden, 80 percent of the time an insect is the menace. Here's a little more about their various groups.

Beetles, weevils, and curculios. All are members of the order Coleoptera ("sheath wing"). In this group, the two forewings (aka wing covers) are hard, colorful, shiny, and conceal the entire abdomen. These insects have complete metamorphosis. They are clumsy fliers compared to numerous other insects, and have mouthparts adapted for chewing. The lady beetle is a familiar and beneficial representative, but many destructive pests are also members of this group.

(top) Beetle eggs hatch into larvae that are distinctly different in appearance from the adult insect. Some are white grubs with brown heads and three pairs of jointed legs. They live in the soil and feed on plant roots.

(bottom) Adult Japanese beetles illustrate the main identifying features of beetles. Notice that the head is blunt and rounded, not elongated into a snout, and that the forewings shield the whole abdomen.

Weevil larvae have brown heads and are whitish, like beetle grubs, but unlike beetle grubs weevil and curculio grubs have no legs.

Adult curculios and weevils have a distinctive long snout, a feature that beetles lack, making them fairly easy to identify.

Flies. Flies are members of the order Diptera ("two wings"). This group includes many beneficial insects such as syrphid and tachinid flies, both of which are predators of destructive insect pests. Members of this order have complete metamorphosis. Flies are extremely adept at aerial navigation. Syrphid flies, for example, are as nimble as hummingbirds in their airborne maneuvers. Flies cannot chew. Their mouthparts are adapted for sucking up food. The larval form of flies is a maggot, a worm-like animal with no obvious head and no legs. Maggots are often whitish or yellowish, small, and slimy. An adult fly's wings are often held out at an angle, away from the body, as opposed to lying flat along its back. The wing position frequently provides rapid identification of this group. Destructive flies are legion, from fruit flies to apple maggots. Nuisance pests in this order include mosquitoes.

True bugs. All insects and many other small animals are often called "bugs" colloquially, but true bugs are found only in the order Hemiptera ("half wing"). The forewings of true bugs are hard and sometimes colorful, as in the beetles, but they

Destructive true bugs, both nymphs and adults, stick their needle-like mouthparts into plant cells and suck out the contents.

only partially cover the abdomen. Members of this order have incomplete metamorphosis. Larvae are nymphs which resemble miniature adults without wings. All members have piercing/sucking mouthparts. Beneficial bugs include assassin bugs, big-eyed bugs, and minute pirate bugs. Destructive bugs include squash bugs, stink bugs, and tarnished plant bugs. Nuisance bugs include bedbugs.

Bees, wasps, and ants. All these insects belong to the order Hymenoptera ("membrane wing"). They have four membranous, transparent, and durable wings. All hymenopterans have complete metamorphosis. Hymenopteran larvae resemble maggots except that they have an obvious head. Adults have mouthparts enabling them both to chew and to suck up liquids. Adult bees and wasps have permanent wings. They are excellent fliers. Ants develop wings only briefly, and only in the young queens and males, when they prepare for their mating flight. Many hymenopterans are social insects, living in large colonies founded by a fertile queen. For many bees and wasps, the larvae live in individual cells constructed of wax, paper, mud, or wood. They pupate inside the cell and emerge only as adults. Many hymenopterans protect themselves by stinging when threatened.

Beneficial hymenopterans include honeybees, of course, and many minute wasps which are parasitoids of destructive insects like caterpillars. Many larger wasps feed on caterpillars or spiders. Black and white tiphiid wasps lay their eggs inside beetle grubs and kill them. The order includes several species of ants that are "dairy farmers," who cultivate and care for their "cows"—aphids, scale, and mealybugs—to "milk" for honeydew. Destructive insects in this order include sawflies and carpenter ants. Nuisance hymenopterans include yellowjackets and wasps that are attracted to sweet fruit.

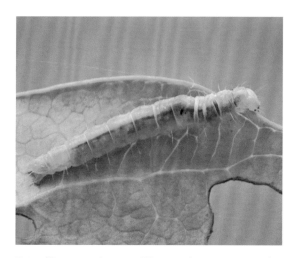

Caterpillars come in many different colors, textures, and sizes, ranging from very furry to quite smooth, and from brightly colored to quite drab. Some are especially good at camouflage and match their background so perfectly they are very difficult to find.

Butterflies and moths. All these insects belong to the order Lepidoptera ("scale wing"). Their wings are covered with minute, often colorful, scales. Most butterflies are active in the daytime and most moths are nocturnal. All lepidopterans have complete metamorphosis. Adults have four large wings and straw-like mouthparts for sucking up nectar. They are much appreciated for their grace, beauty, and beneficial pollination services. Their larvae, on the other hand, are very destructive worm-like caterpillars with chewing mouthparts. They pupate in a chrysalis, cocoon, or in the soil and include such pests as cutworms and leafrollers.

Grasshoppers and earwigs. These insects belong to the order Orthoptera ("straight wing"), which includes katydids and crickets. Adults of some species have four large, membranous wings while other species have very small wings, or no wings at all. Orthopterans have incomplete metamorphosis. Their young are nymphs that look like miniature adults without wings. Nymphs and adults have chewing mouthparts and eat the same food. Praying mantids are perhaps the most beneficial members, locusts the most destructive. Nuisance members include cockroaches.

Thrips. Thrips are in the order Thysanoptera ("fringe wing"). Their four slender wings are fringed with tiny hair-like projections. Thrips are extremely small insects, long and slender, very hard to see with the naked eye. They have incomplete metamorphosis. The nymphs resemble the adults but have no wings. They have rasping, sucking mouthparts, and both nymphs and adults are often found feeding together on their host plants. Thrips nymphs, like the adults, rasp away the surface tissue of plants leaving telltale patches of silvery dead cells behind. Adult thrips can fly, but are not strong fliers. If you suspect a thrips infestation, hold a piece of paper under the questionable plant and tap its stem or foliage. If thrips are present they will fall onto the paper.

Aphids, leafhoppers, psyllids, whitefly, scale, and adelgids. All belong to the order Homoptera ("whole wing"). They have four membranous wings. All are plant eaters, and many are quite destructive. Most are readily identifiable as insects, but scale and adelgids look more like bumps or cotton wads than insects. They have incomplete metamorphosis. The nymphs in some species resemble miniature adults without wings. In other species the nymphs (aka crawlers) are quite different in appearance. All have piercing/sucking mouthparts. Many are sedentary as adults, sitting in one spot with their beaks inserted into a plant's vein while they suck out the life-giving sap. They often occur in colonies. Winged aphid adults appear late in the season to mate and lay eggs for the next generation the following year.

EXCLUSION AND PREVENTION

Row covers. Grow plants under a lightweight, white fabric that lets light, water, and air in, but keeps insects out. Spun-bonded polyester row covers work quite well. Fiberglass window screening, mosquito netting, or sheer fabrics also work, but may be heavier and less flexible. Pay attention to the size of the weave because a coarse weave will permit small insects to get through, and a very tight weave restricts air flow. Keep in mind that insects already present in the soil as eggs, larvae, or overwintering adults will be protected from predators inside this canopy. Also, you'll have to remove the cover when plants begin to flower, so that pollinators can access them.

Cutworm collars. A simple 2-inch-tall cardboard cylinder made from toilet paper or paper towel tubes protects stems. Paper cups or tuna fish cans with the bottoms removed also work. Place these around the base of young seedlings and push the collars down into the ground so that they stand upright. Cutworms won't climb over these barriers.

Cutworm collar.

Wire mesh. Gophers, voles, or other burrowing rodents are stopped in their tracks by lining planting holes with ¼-inch wire mesh hardware cloth. Essentially, you construct a wire basket, place it in the ground, and plant inside it. Make this basket as big as you like.

Floating row covers. Drape a lightweight material over plants, leaving enough slack so that they have room to grow. Place rocks, bricks, or boards along the edges so that the fabric does not blow away.

Rigid row covers. Use the same fabric as you would for floating row covers—lightweight and breathable—but attach it to a rigid framework of wood, PVC pipe, or other like material.

Metal collars. If you enclose tree trunks and vertical branches in slick sheet metal, climbing pests like rats and raccoons can't get a grip. They fail to climb the tree to eat your fruit. This solution is less effective against squirrels, because they are extremely adept at leaping from tree to tree. They'll bypass the collar if a neighboring tree is close enough. Take several 2-foot-long pieces of smooth sheet metal, wrap them around vertical sections of the trunk or branches, and nail them in place. Cover the rough bark completely, and keep the slick surface as close to vertical as you can. Because metal collars don't expand, you'll have to replace them as your tree's trunk and branches get thicker with age.

Trunk guards. There are several styles: a flat spiral-shaped strip of plastic that expands as plants grow; a plastic net that also expands; or a wrapping of chicken wire or hardware cloth that does not expand as the plant grows. Anything you wrap around your tree that does not expand will "girdle" the plant, essentially strangling and killing it. Some people remove the guards in the spring and then put them back in the autumn; other people leave them on all the time. If you decide to leave them on, be sure to loosen them every spring. Trunk guards are especially valuable in the winter when deer, rodents, and rabbits have very little to eat. Be sure that the trunk guard stands above any anticipated snowfall. If the snowpack is deeper than the trunk guard, rodents gain free access to your plants. Whichever style you choose, make sure you push it 2 inches into the ground to prevent voles from gaining access to roots. Once your tree is old enough to have thick, furrowed bark the critters will leave it alone.

Fence. Deer have different food preferences from one region to another, even from one neighborhood to the next. In fact, we've discovered in conversations with gardeners around the country that as the deer population has exploded, the cloven-footed ones have added many items to the menu that they formerly would not have touched. So choosing which plants to enclose behind a fence is a decision you must make through trial and error. Deer are high-flying jumpers and can be quite powerful, so a stout, 8-foot-tall fence is a good investment. Alternatively, add extensions to a shorter fence, and run wire or some other visible material between the extensions. Two shorter fences, each 4 feet tall and 4 feet apart may also work; most deer won't jump into such a narrow space. We do mean most: we have a small population of deer nearby that leap comfortably into the space between, and then on into the garden. Some sources recommend electric fences, but we prefer to keep things simple and low-tech in the fruit garden. If you opt for an electric fence, choose photovoltaic cells to charge it.

Sometimes rabbits eat the bark from fruit trees and shrubs, especially in winter, when other

A fence is a fence is a fence. Unless it's a deer fence. Deer are excellent jumpers and your fence needs to be 8 feet tall, well anchored, and sturdy.

food is scarce. Rabbits are neither high jumpers nor powerful. A 2-foot-high fence of 1-inch chicken wire will keep them out. Be sure to peg the chicken wire to the ground with long, metal U-shaped pins that you can buy at most garden centers. If crafty rabbits learn where the gaps are between the pins and begin to dig under the fence, then bury the chicken wire about 1 foot deep.

Nets. Usually made from plastic, nets rarely exclude rodents but are extremely valuable as protection against birds, deer, and other small mammals eager to "harvest" your sweet fruit and nuts. Netting of various weights and dimension is available.

Bags. Enclose young fruit in paper bags and staple the bags shut. Use small, brown paper lunch sacks, or purchase inexpensive cloth bags made especially for this purpose. Do not use plastic bags; they get too hot and they do not breathe. The bags keep codling moth larvae and other caterpillars, and apple maggots from damaging your fruit. If you have large trees this may not be possible because it's too hard to reach all the fruit. But dwarf, semi-dwarf, and espaliered trees are usually reachable.

Kaolin spray. Since kaolin is a clay coating that repels insects, but does not kill them, use this before pests show up. The product is readily available under various trade names. Purchase it as a dry powder and mix with water, following the directions on the label. Apply when the foliage is dry, and keep in mind that rain will wash it away. This product leaves a white coating on plants, but is safe to use up until one day before you harvest.

Hand-pick pests. Picking up insects or larvae with their hands makes some people squeamish but it's a good way to deal with some pests. Use your bare hands, wear rubber or nitrile gloves, or use a tool to pick them up. Simply removing

Netting protects the upcoming cherry harvest.

Paper bags cover the fruitlets of an apple tree in this small urban farm in Portland, Oregon.

insects from plants helps enormously, reducing the pest population and preventing damage.

Sneak up on Japanese beetles and hold a wide-mouthed jar of soapy water under them; knock the beetles into the jar. This works on any insect that lets you get close enough. Use kitchen tongs to pick up large larvae such as caterpillars. Rub or scrape scale insects off plants with your thumbnail. For plants that have boring insects inside, slit open the stems with a sharp knife, then remove the pests. Alternatively, insert a thin, flexible wire into a borer's hole to hook the pest and drag it out. After you've caught offending insects, drop them into a jar of soapy water. They'll drown almost instantly.

Copper tape. Remove slugs and snails from plants and the ground around them. Don't forget to search nooks and crannies and their other favorite hiding places. After removal, place copper tape along the border of the garden, around a container, or along the edge of a raised bed. Slugs and snails will not crawl across copper.

Blast with hose. Ridding the fruit garden of eggs, larvae, and nymphs contributes to insect pest control. A strong blast from the hose washes them off plants; the crushing force of the water sometimes kills them, but, if not, the impact of hitting the ground will. Adults will often fly away before you can get them, but destroying the next generation is the next best thing. Wash away aphids, mealybugs, thrips, and others about once a week to keep their populations from building up. You may recall that elsewhere we counsel you to keep the foliage of your plants dry, which is still a good idea. Therefore, wash plants on a clear day in the morning so that the leaves and stems have a chance to dry out.

Vacuum. For whitefly indoors, use a household or wet-dry vacuum cleaner to scoop these weak flyers out of the air. Shake the foliage first so that the insects take flight. That way you can keep the vacuum hose away from the leaves.

Fright tactics. Scaring critters away is sometimes your best strategy to keep your fruits and nuts for yourself. A barking dog outside will scare away deer, raccoons, rodents, and birds. Motion-activated sprinklers deter deer and small mammals, but you will need to move it from time to time or the animals learn to tiptoe around them. These will also scare raccoons for awhile, but sometimes these clever pests learn to dismantle them. The recorded sounds of birds of prey that go off at random intervals scare away birds and some rodents. Garden centers and hardware stores sell gizmos that produce ultrasonic sounds, beyond the range of human hearing, that frighten animals. Each unit can be adjusted to different frequencies, and can be set to affect raccoons, squirrels, rabbits, or deer.

Traps
Earwig traps. Earwigs emerge from dark, moist hiding places at night to eat tender, young plant tissue. They also eat more serious pests and are beneficial garden partners, so don't do anything about them unless they are clearly damaging your plants. The simplest method we know of to remove and kill earwigs is a moist, rolled-up newspaper. Roll it fairly loosely and secure it with a rubber band. Moisten it slightly and lay it on the ground in the evening. The earwigs hide in there overnight. Retrieve it in the morning, close up the ends, and roll it tightly so that earwigs cannot escape. Seal the paper, along with its hidden earwigs, in a plastic bag and put that in the garbage. Alternatively you can shake the earwigs into a jar of soapy water.

Sticky bands. These work like old-fashioned flypaper. Paint commercially prepared sticky goo made to mire insects onto pliable plastic, card-stock paper, or metal strips. Wrap the strips around the stems or trunks of plants; the insects get stuck as they climb to reach the yummy foliage. You can also lay these strips along flat edges of a raised bed and see what you catch. Once the goo is littered with insect carcasses, replace the bands with freshly painted traps.

Sticky cards. These work the same way sticky bands work, except that they catch flying insects. Kits are available, but you can also make your own from the same commercially prepared, insect-trapping goo that's available for sticky bands. Ready-made cards are always yellow on one side, because this color attracts insects. If you make your own, paint one side of a 4- by 5-inch piece of plywood or masonite yellow. Paint the yellow side of the card with the goo. Hang the freshly painted cards from tree branches, or attach the unpainted side to a stick, and drive it into the ground next to the troubled plant. Remember to scrape the goop off and paint on fresh goo, when the sticky side gets covered in carcasses.

Rodent traps. There are a few things you can do to discourage rodent populations. The best solution is a cat that enjoys hunting outdoors. If that's not possible, your local humane society frequently loans or rents Havahart traps. Set them up according to the instructions. When the animal is captured, take the pest to its appropriate habitat and release it. Lethal mammal traps are not targeted, which means they will kill animals that you did not intend to.

Slug and snail traps. Capture slugs and snails by placing upside-down pots or boards in strategic locations around the garden. Prop them up on pebbles, so that the critters will seek hiding places beneath them. Then you can easily find and destroy them, or move them far, far away.

In our experience the legendary beer trap does not work, but we know people who swear by it. Place a saucer filled with beer in the garden. Supposedly the slug or snail can't resist and will crawl in and drown. We prefer to use our method, then kick back on the garden bench and drink the beer ourselves.

Apple maggot traps. Trap apple maggot or husk fly adults by hanging an apple-sized red or walnut-sized green sphere coated with sticky material in trees early in the season. When the flies are ready to lay eggs they search for round, apple- or walnut-like objects. They home in on the trap, believing it to be an apple or a walnut, and become mired in the goo. The flies get stuck and die before they have a chance to lay eggs. Ready-made apple maggot traps constructed of red plastic are available to purchase. Husk fly traps are not. You can make your own of either kind. Choose a round object such as a plastic, rubber, or wooden ball of the appropriate size. Paint it red or green, and apply the commercially prepared, insect-trapping goo. Attach a screw eye to one end and hang it in your tree. You're good to go. Scrape off trapped insects and reapply fresh sticky material every two weeks or so.

Jug traps. A friend and fellow gardener in New Mexico shared this innovative, effective technique to protect your fruit trees from beetles. Cut a hole in each side of an empty one-gallon milk jug. The holes should be in the top one-third of the jug, and measure about 1.5 inches across. In two of the holes, cut all four sides. In the other two holes, cut the sides and top of each hole, leaving the bottom to create a flap that is still connected to the jug. Bend the flap outward to make a landing platform for the beetles. Some beetles need the landing platform and some do not. Mix one tablespoon of liquid soap or detergent with one cup of apple juice, and pour this

A homemade pest control device, and great recycling program. To beetles this plastic milk jug seems like a safe haven offering free food within. But it's not. The beetles enter and drown in the soapy-juice mixture at the bottom.

Chickens and ducks are charming and effective predators, but there are also plenty of predatory or parasitic insects and mites that kill and eat garden pests. Most arrive as eggs, but a few are adults. Always release any of these beneficial organisms in the evening, or they may fly away to find food at your neighbor's house. Also, spread them around the garden; many will turn to cannibalism if they can't find enough prey to eat.

Lady beetles. These are among our best fruit garden friends. With the right habitat these popular little red beetles with black spots will find their way to you, but if their numbers are insufficient, buying them is the way to go. Their nymphs will eat many times their weight in aphids, mealybugs, and scale.

Green lacewings. These arrive as tiny eggs mixed with brown rice hulls, moth eggs, and other material. Wash active aphid and other pest populations off your plants, and then sprinkle the lacewing mixture over plants throughout the garden. When the eggs hatch, the lacewing larvae, called aphid lions, crawl across plants and consume up to 1,000 aphids a day. You won't see them, but you should notice a decrease in harmful soft-bodied pests. As well as aphids, green lacewing larvae eat mealybugs, scale, spider mites, caterpillars, whitefly larvae, and a wide variety of moth eggs. The adult green lacewing eats pollen and nectar, not insects.

mixture into the jug. Hang it in the fruit tree. The sweet fragrance of apple juice attracts beetles, which enter through the holes and are unable to get back out. They fall into the soap and die. Take the jugs down periodically; clean the dead insects out; and pour in fresh soapy-juice mixture. This should work well for Japanese beetles, ten-lined and green June beetles, and figeater beetles. Experiment with different juices to see which pests you can attract.

Beneficial predators

The best remedy for any pest problem is to harness the power of beneficial predators. This means that in addition to creating healthy habitat for beneficial organisms (page 260), you may want to purchase some for your property. Not only is this a completely non-toxic solution, it also encourages your healthy garden ecosystem to flourish.

Praying mantids. These insects are really special. Kathryn's sister used to keep one as a pet and its fascinating behavior provided hours of entertainment. They eat beetles, caterpillars, grubs, aphids, grasshoppers, crickets, and almost anything else that crawls by. Purchase an egg case, and place or hang it in a shrub at least 2 feet off the ground. The egg case holds about 200 eggs, and when they hatch the baby praying

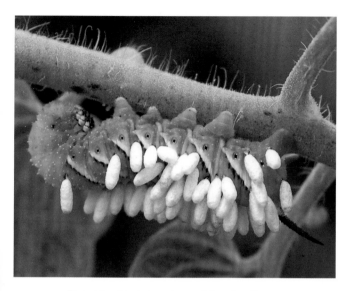

The white objects hanging on this caterpillar carcass are the cocoons of a parasitoid wasp. A new generation of adult wasps will emerge from these cocoons and fly away to kill more caterpillars for you.

Ants tending their aphids, prior to the arrival of mealybug destroyers.

mantids venture out into the garden. If they are happy, praying mantids will overwinter, reproduce, and persist in the garden year after year.

Parasitoid wasps. Several kinds of parasitoid wasps are available for purchase. Braconid wasps kill caterpillars of all kinds by laying their eggs inside the creatures. When the eggs hatch, the larvae eat the pest. The wasp babies then make cocoons which are attached to the caterpillar carcass. The wasps emerge from the cocoons and the cycle begins again. Trichogramma wasps parasitize moths. Purchase containers with cards that hold about 4,000 moth eggs, inside of which the wasps are developing. Uncap the container and place it in the fork of the tree, or carefully remove the card and hang it on a branch with a string or tape. Protect the eggs from ants, and place the container or the card where it will be protected from rain. Other parasitoid wasps attack and kill Japanese beetles.

Delphastus. These are small, shiny black beetles, about a quarter the size of a lady beetle. They eat whitefly eggs and larvae, but if whiteflies are not present they will also feed on spider mites. Both the adult beetle and its larvae are predators. Wash plants to knock pests off, and then sprinkle the tiny beetles in different locations around the garden. These beetles prefer to spend their time in the upper portion of your plants.

Mealybug destroyers. These are small black beetles with orange heads and tails. As their name implies, they love mealybugs, but they also eat aphids, immature scale, and immature whitefly. Since ants are attracted to the honeydew secreted by aphids, mealybugs, and scale, ants will kill mealybug destroyers. Place sticky bands around plant stems to control ants before you buy and release these beetles. Carefully shake the beetles directly onto infested plants on the same day you receive them.

Encarsia formosa. This tiny wasp, about the size of a pencil point, parasitizes the eggs of whitefly. The product you buy is a card filled with wasp eggs. On a day when it is sunny and warm, remove cards from the container, separate along perforations, and hang them on branches of plants where whiteflies are present.

Predatory mites. These seek out and kill pest mites, particularly spider mites. Purchase adult mites in a medium, such as corn grit or vermiculite. The mixture will come in a bottle. Shake them out of the bottle on the day you receive them. Spread them out on leaves where they are likely to find pest mites.

Chickens and ducks. Both absolutely love insects, slugs, and snails, but they will eat practically anything they can get their beaks around. Chickens scratch in the soil and find grubs as well. Fair warning: both birds also eat foliage, roots, fruits, and nuts, so they must be supervised while in the garden. Wild chickens are fairly common in Hawaii. One lived in the courtyard of our condo complex where it kept mango and breadfruit trees free of insect pests. Every night it climbed high into a mango tree to roost.

Beneficial nematodes. These microscopic round worms kill adults and larvae of more than 200 species of pests that live on or in the soil during some part of their life cycle, as when maggots drop to the soil to pupate. Since the product you buy contains the larvae of living nematodes, the package must be handled carefully. Keep them refrigerated until you are ready to use. The nematode larvae are available in a suspension of moist media, typically gel, vermiculite, or peat moss that you mix with water to spray on the soil. Nematodes survive in your garden for about five years if they have enough to eat, so this is a very cost-effective remedy.

Eagle-eyed chickens devour plum curculios and many other pests in this well-managed orchard.

REPELLENTS, BIOLOGICAL CONTROLS, AND CHEMICAL REMEDIES

Garlic spray. Garlic is easy to use, relatively non-toxic, and, best of all, it works. It repels a number of garden pests from insects to black bears, and allegedly, vampires. Make your own garlic spray or purchase one made for garden use, but know that it can kill beneficial insects as well as harmful ones, so be careful. You'll not want to use it routinely as a general preventive spray; instead, use it only when you know that pests are present. No safety label required.

There are lots of recipes for making your own garlic spray. Most use several cloves of garlic in one quart of water whirled in a blender and strained. Put the resulting liquid in a spray bottle and squirt it on your plants. If you add liquid soap as a spreader-sticker take note that the soap will make the product even more effective at killing all insects, including your beneficial ones.

Pepper spray. Hot chili peppers contain capsaicin, a compound which gives them their fiery flavor. We humans love that taste in Thai food or Mexican dishes, but deer and other garden pests find it offensive. Pepper spray, like garlic spray, is easy to make at home, but you can buy a commercial product, if you'd prefer. It is not toxic and, like garlic, it works as a repellent. You can even combine them: hot chili peppers and garlic. Pepper spray is non-targeted, so it kills beneficial organisms as well as pests. No safety label required.

Deer repellent spray. Commercial deer repellents usually contain a mixture of putrescent egg solids—yes, we mean rotten eggs—capsaicin (hot pepper oil), and garlic. Apparently this mixture tastes as foul to deer and other mammals as it might to us. Rain washes it away, so that when the offending mammal returns there may be nothing nasty left. Be prepared to reapply. This may not deter a starving critter, but maybe, if they are that hungry, they need the sustenance more than you do. No safety label required.

Nosema spore. Makers of this biological insecticide mix bran with a protozoan parasite, *Nosema locustae*, to make bait. Grasshoppers and crickets like to eat it, causing them to sicken and die. If they lay eggs after they get infected, but before they die, they pass the infection on to their offspring. Thus, the disease persists from one generation to the next and the garden is protected for years. It is a very effective control for these long-legged, jumping pests. Nosema is highly targeted and safe to use. It affects only grasshoppers and crickets. It does not affect other animals like honeybees, butterflies, dogs, cats, birds, or children. Since adult grasshoppers can and do fly into your garden from the surrounding neighborhood, nosema is extremely effective when you persuade all your neighbors to use it. Try getting together and sharing. No safety label required.

BTI. *Bacillus thuringiensis* is a bacterium from which three different varieties have been developed for use as biological pesticides. The "israelensis" (var. *israelensis*) formulation of this bacterial spray kills fly larvae when they ingest it. Mosquito dunks are made from this product. Research shows that it is also effective as a soil drench against fungus gnats. Safety label: CAUTION.

BTK. *Bacillus thuringiensis* var. *kurstaki* is a bacterial parasite that is suspended in water to make a spray. The "kurstaki" formulation of this bacterial spray kills all caterpillars—and only caterpillars—no matter what we call them. Cutworms, leafrollers, fruitworms—all are caterpillars, the larvae of butterflies or moths. Here's what happens: you spray stems and foliage; the caterpillar chews them, ingesting the bacteria; then the caterpillar dies. Death takes several days to arrive, but the pest usually stops eating almost immediately. The BTK solution works best when you use it about once a week. Apply on dry but cloudy days. Rain washes BTK away, and it becomes less effective in intense sunlight and high heat. Reapply as needed. This product is available in ready-to-use spray bottles, although you can sometimes find it as a liquid concentrate or dust. Read and follow label directions. Safety label: CAUTION.

BTSD. *Bacillus thuringiensis* var. *San Diego* is a bacterial parasite suspended in water to make a spray that you use on stems and foliage. The "San Diego" formulation of this bacterial spray kills all sorts of beetles—June beetles, sap beetles, figeater beetles, Japanese beetles—among other pests. Like BTI and BTK it is highly targeted and must be ingested by the pest as it eats your plants. Therefore, though this variety kills beetles, it does not kill beetles that are beneficial predators, such as lady beetles; it kills only plant eaters. When the pest chews on your plant, it ingests the bacterial solution and dies in several days, but it usually stops eating almost immediately. Apply on dry but cloudy days. Rain washes BTSD away, and it becomes less effective in intense sunlight and high heat. Reapply as needed. It works best when you use it about once a week. You can find it in ready-to-use spray bottles, or sometimes as a liquid concentrate or dust, at garden centers or online. Read and follow label directions. Safety label: CAUTION.

Paecilomyces lilacinus. This product contains spores of a selected strain (251) of a naturally occurring filamentous fungus that lives in healthy, biologically active soils worldwide. The fungus infects and kills eggs and juveniles of pesky nematodes that destroy your plants. It is not a poison, and it is not hazardous to honeybees or other beneficial organisms, including beneficial nematodes. Mix the dispersible granules with water, following label directions. Apply it as a soil drench when you plant, or through drip irrigation systems. You can also spray it on the soil under your plants, but only on the soil. Do not use it on leaves or any other above-ground plant part, and do not spray it on water. There are no adverse health effects to humans because this strain cannot survive at temperatures as high as the human body. Safety label: CAUTION.

Milky spore. This product causes a lethal bacterial infection in Japanese beetle larvae and their relatives. The bacteria are cultivated in laboratories, and then turned into dust or granules. Spread milky spore on the ground beneath plants infested with Japanese beetles. Since this product does not kill adult beetles, they can still fly in from your neighbors' yards, and damage plants. This is why other sources say it doesn't work. It does, but your neighbors must also use it, and you must reapply it every year. The product is available as dust or granules. Read and follow label directions. Safety label: CAUTION.

Granulosis virus. This naturally occurring virus infects and kills only the larvae of the codling moth, *Cydia pomonella*. These caterpillars are a serious problem on apples, pears, and walnut trees. The virus is not a poison, and cannot infect people, pets, beneficial insects, fish and wildlife, or plants. When codling moth caterpillars eat treated fruit, the virus activates and replicates in the insect's gut and "goes viral," infecting other tissue so that the caterpillar soon dies. Then the virus particles are released by dead caterpillars to infect new caterpillars. Mix the product with non-chlorinated water, following label directions. Spray the foliage and fruit of your trees just to the point of runoff. Apply it in late spring, after the first generation of codling moths have laid their eggs, and just before the caterpillars are about to hatch. There are no adverse health effects to humans from the active ingredient, but inactive ingredients may cause moderate eye irritation. Safety label: CAUTION.

Beauveria bassiana. When they land on certain insects' bodies, these fungal spores germinate. Once in place, the spores grow through the insect's cuticle layer (skin) and produce lethal toxins. A pest takes several days to die, and once dead, the fungus grows over its body, creating a white mold. This mold produces spores that infect other insects. Note that if you have used any sort of fungicide, including baking soda spray, within the previous 24 hours, this product will not work. The fungal spores are suspended in a liquid that you spray on the pest and the plant. The best time of day to spray is early morning or early evening. The garden should be cool and moist, so water first if it is dry. Typically you will need to spray several times, with five to seven days between applications, but as long as the solution is fresh when the pest crawls across it, the critter ought to become infected. Make an effort to spray only when you are certain that insects are actively damaging your plants, because this product kills many beneficial insects, including bees; and we all know they're in enough trouble without anyone making it worse. Do not use it on or near water, because it may be toxic to fish. Read and follow label directions. Safety label: CAUTION.

Insecticidal soap. The technical term for soap is potassium salts of fatty acids, and it kills all insects and mites by penetrating their cuticle layer (skin) and causing cell collapse. Wow, that's some bath! Soap is not a poison; it kills only when it's wet; and you must spray it directly on the insect or mite. Therefore, spray only insects or mites that you know are damaging your plants. Do not spray it on benign insects because the soap will kill them. To make your own soap spray, mix a tablespoon of liquid soap with a quart of water, and pour it into a spray bottle. Do not use a detergent because it may damage your plants. If you buy a ready-made product, read and follow label directions. No safety label is required.

Iron phosphate. Makers of this slug and snail killer combine two natural elements found in soil: iron and phosphorus. Slugs and snails find it tasty—who knows why—so they eat it and die. It usually comes as tiny, pale pellets to scatter on the ground. An added benefit: when these elements combine with oxygen, you get fertilizer; as this product dissolves, it feeds the soil. Research shows that it may affect aquatic animals; slugs and snails are mollusks, like clams, oysters, octopus, and squid. Do not use it or dispose of it in water, or any place where water may drain to rivers, lakes, or bays. Always wash up thoroughly after handling this product, because iron phosphate causes eye irritation. Read and follow label directions. Safety label: CAUTION.

Diatomaceous earth. When insects, slugs, and snails encounter this white, powdery grit, it is, for them, like crawling across shards of broken glass. In fact, it kills any small creature that crawls across it. The product is made from diatoms, ancient microscopic plants that have skeletons of glass (aka silicon dioxide). Scatter the dust-like grit on the ground in any area where you have a ground-crawling pest problem. Cover the powder with a board or flower pot that is slightly raised on small pebbles, because if the dust gets wet it is ineffective. Look for the product that is labeled an insecticide—not the one for swimming pool filters. Wear a respirator mask and goggles, because this powder can irritate eyes and cause lung damage. Also wear gloves, a long-sleeved shirt, and pants, because it irritates skin. Safety label: CAUTION.

Spinosad. This product kills both beneficial and destructive insects, so use it only if you know you have a serious pest problem. It is available as a ready-made liquid spray, in which bacteria are suspended, or as a powder that you mix with water. Simply spray it on your plants, and when the insect eats the leaves or stems, it ingests the bacterial toxins. Spinosad remains effective on foliage up to a week. Tests suggest it may be toxic to fish, so don't spray it on water. It's best to use this product in the early morning or late afternoon. You may need to reapply it weekly until the pest population is reduced to acceptable levels. Often Spinosad is pre-mixed with iron phosphate. Read and follow label directions. Safety label: CAUTION.

Neem. This oil is extracted from the poisonous seeds of the neem tree (*Azadirachta indica*), which is native to India. Neem oil works as a pesticide in a variety of unusual and mysterious ways. It repels some insects, sending out a signal that says, "Go away." In others it keeps them from molting, so they cannot mature. And in still others, it stops them from laying eggs. Studies on safety and environmental impacts are ongoing. Therefore, it is best to use neem only when bees and other beneficial insects are not active in the fruit garden. And do not use it on, or near, water. Buy a commercial preparation that has been prepared with a surfactant, such as soap, so that the oil will mix with water. Mix the preparation with water, and spray it on your plants. The effect on insects takes time, so be patient and watchful. You may need to repeat applications every seven

to 14 days, depending on what you see. Read and follow label directions. Safety label: CAUTION.

Horticultural oil. Safe, vegetable-based horticultural oils coat and smother insects, mites, and their eggs and larvae. The oil kills all insects and mites, including beneficials, so do not use this product unless you know you have a serious pest problem. Because horticultural oil has been marketed under various names, including dormant oil and superior oil, purchasing the right product presents a challenge. Accurate product descriptions are difficult to ferret out, too. Some formulations are made from petroleum products, and though a few of these are allowed on organically grown plants, we recommend using only those products made from vegetable oils, even if they are hard to find. If the label does not say that the product is made with vegetable oil, do not use it in your fruit garden.

Horticultural oil has several potential side effects. Do not swallow it or allow it to come in contact with your skin, because it can cause an allergic reaction in some people. It can also cause eye irritation and difficulty breathing. Wear protective clothing, goggles, and a respirator mask; and keep children and pets away while spraying. In addition to protecting yourself, you also need to protect some plants from horticultural oil. Test-spray a small area or a single plant to see how it reacts before using it on the entire plant or throughout the garden. Do not use this product if the temperature is higher than 85°F or below freezing. Always water plants and make sure they are well hydrated before using horticultural oil. Spray plants thoroughly, because this product works only when the pest comes in direct contact with it. To make your own spray, add a tablespoon of liquid soap (not detergent) to one cup of vegetable oil to make a concentrate. Mix a tablespoon of this concentrate into a gallon of water. Alternatively, purchase horticultural oil in ready-to-use spray bottles. Read and follow label directions. Safety label: CAUTION.

Sulfur. Sulfur is a yellow mineral mined from the earth. It kills insects, including beneficial ones, by disrupting their metabolism. Sulfur is another product that you should use only if your pest problem is serious and other, less toxic, techniques have failed. Sulfur poses potential health hazards, particularly for people with allergies. Wear protective clothing, goggles, and a respirator mask. Keep children and pets away when spraying. Since sulfur kills your wild and purchased beneficial insect partners, use it while temperatures are cool and insects are less active. Keep it away from ponds, streams, and lakes, because it kills fish. It can also harm plants under two conditions—when it is above 80°F, and if you have sprayed with horticultural oil within the last month. Finally, if you use sulfur fairly regularly it builds up in the soil, making it more acidic. Spray all above-ground plant parts thoroughly. To kill insect eggs, you need to spray before eggs hatch; and you may need to reapply every seven to 14 days because the product washes off in the rain. Observe your plants for symptoms, and for signs of insect damage. Do not use it more often than you have to. Sulfur is available as a ready-to-use spray or as a concentrate or dust that you mix with water. Read and follow label directions. Safety label: CAUTION.

Pyrethrin. This product is a naturally occurring insecticide/miticide made from a relative of our old friend, the garden mum. The dried flowers are ground into a powder that is mixed with water by the manufacturer. When you spray your plants, the product paralyzes and kills most insects and mites on contact. All the pest has to do is walk over the sprayed area and it's a goner.

This product remains potent for several days and will kill your beneficial partners too. Don't use it unless you have a severe pest problem. Find ready-to-use sprays or concentrates that you mix with water, and spray plants thoroughly. Don't forget the undersides of leaves. Some manufacturers add a synergist to increase the product's toxicity. Wear protective clothing, goggles, and a respirator mask. Keep children and pets away when spraying. Read and follow label directions. Safety label: CAUTION.

Solve Disease Problems

Plants experience stress if they have too much or too little light; too much or too little water; temperatures that are either too hot or too cold; or poor soil. Just like stressed-out people, a stressed plant is vulnerable to attack by fungal, bacterial, or viral infections. Despite your best efforts, you may find that your plant has a disease. A fungal infection is most likely. Bacterial infections, though less common, can be more serious and are often lethal. Avoid plant stress.

Fungal spores and bacteria are everywhere, even in the air you breathe while reading this. There is no avoiding them. In fact, we really wouldn't want to, because fungi and bacteria are also beneficial partners in the fruit garden. Mycorrhizal fungi and nitrogen-fixing bacteria, for example, are extremely important to plant health. A healthy soil ecosystem teems with friendly fungi and bacteria, members of the decomposer community that breaks down dead plant material and releases nutrients. But certain fungi and bacteria are pathogens, which harm or even kill plants. As plant caretakers, we need to keep these diseases in check.

Before using any remedy, please review "Safety First" (page 246). Revisit "Change the Growing Conditions" (page 247) and the portrait for the plant that's in trouble. Did you miss anything that would make the plants in your fruit garden stronger and healthier? Changing the growing conditions is truly your first, most important, most effective solution. Create an environment unfavorable to pathogens, and enhance plant growth, at the same time.

The four most important preventive measures to take before reaching for a remedy:

1. Make sure you have healthy, biologically active soil (page 12).

2. Plant polycultures (page 258).

3. Water soil, not foliage (page 255). Most fungi and all bacteria need a thin layer of moisture on the foliage to gain access and infect your plants.

4. Sanitize (page 263). Cut away and remove all diseased plant parts, and clean up all infected or pest-infested debris. Get it all out of the garden.

BIOLOGICAL CONTROLS AND CHEMICAL REMEDIES

Bacillus amyloliquefaciens. This spore-forming bacterium is a naturally occurring, soil-dwelling organism common in healthy, biologically active soil. Strain D747, a specific form of the species, is a preventive broad-spectrum bio-fungicide; it controls or suppresses both fungal and bacterial plant diseases. It is effective against powdery and downy mildew, sclerotinia white mold, alternaria, bacterial leaf spot, bacterial spot and speck, brown rot, citrus blast, botrytis, and fire blight. The product is mixed with water and sprayed on your plants and/or the soil under your plants, every seven to 10 days as long as environmental conditions favor the disease in question. Following application, the spores germinate to form colonies on the above-ground plant parts as well as on the roots. You can use this product right up to the day of harvest. It is non-toxic to people, pets, fish and wildlife, and plants, but there is always the risk of an allergic reaction, so protect yourself with appropriate safety gear. Read and follow label directions. Safety label: CAUTION.

Bacillus pumilus. This naturally occurring spore-forming bacterium is found in healthy soils worldwide. Selected strains are QST2808 and GB34. It is used to control scab, rust, powdery and downy mildews, primarily as a preventive product. Studies show it may also arrest active disease. This bacterium activates your plant's natural immune system; creates a zone of inhibition that prevents pathogens from becoming established on your plant; and produces an antifungal compound that disrupts cell metabolism and destroys the cell walls of pathogenic fungi. Mix it with water and apply as a foliar spray following the directions on the label. Thorough coverage of the plant is essential for success. This bacterium is non-toxic to people, pets, fish and wildlife, and plants. There is a potential for allergic reaction, so be certain to wear safety gear that protects your skin, eyes, and lungs. Do not allow drift to contaminate streams, lakes, or other bodies of water. Safety label: CAUTION.

Bacillus subtilis. This naturally occurring spore-forming bacterium is found in healthy, biologically active soils all over the world. In addition to competing with fungi for nutrients and space on plant surfaces, a particular strain (QST713) of the bacterium kills fungal pathogens that land on your plants by attaching itself to their cell walls, eventually killing them. While this remedy cannot cure an existing infection, it can prevent new ones. This bacterium is non-toxic to humans, birds, fish, and other aquatic organisms. However, some people have allergic

reactions to this product, so wear protective gear, including a respirator mask, goggles, long sleeves, and pants. The bacteria come in ready-to-use spray bottles, suspended in a liquid that you spray on all plant parts. You may need to reapply it about every two weeks or whenever rain or sprinkler water has washed it away. Read and follow label directions. Safety label: CAUTION.

Pseudomonas fluorescens. This spore-forming bacterial epiphyte is found naturally on leaves, stems, flowers, and fruit. Once it has formed colonies, this beneficial bacterium prevents pathogenic bacteria from gaining access to your plants. A selected strain (A506) protects plants against various diseases, including citrus blast, fire blight, and botrytis bunch rot of grapes. This bacterium is non-toxic to people, pets, fish and wildlife, and plants. There is a potential for allergic reaction, so be sure to wear safety gear that protects your skin, eyes, and lungs. The product comes as a dry powder that you mix with water and apply as a spray following the directions on the label. Thorough coverage of the plant is essential for success. Do not allow drift to contaminate streams, lakes, or other bodies of water. Do not mix it with copper-containing fungicides, because the copper will kill the beneficial bacteria. Safety label: CAUTION.

Reynoutria sachalinensis. The active ingredient of this plant-based extract is derived from *Reynoutria sachalinensis* (giant knotweed). When you spray the product on your plants, it boosts their own internal defense mechanisms against certain pathogens. Mixed with water and applied as a foliar spray, it controls a wide array of fungal and bacterial diseases. People have consumed this plant as food and for its medicinal values for a very long time with no reported adverse effects. It is, however, moderately irritating to eyes and skin. Be certain to wear safety gear to protect your skin, eyes, and lungs, as there is always a potential for allergic reaction. Do not allow drift to contaminate streams, lakes, or other bodies of water. Read and follow label directions. Safety label: CAUTION.

Streptomyces lydicus. Strain WYEC108 of this beneficial microorganism is effective against both bacterial and fungal diseases. It combats powdery and downy mildew, gray mold, black spot, leaf spots, fire blight, and rust. It also controls soilborne fungal diseases such as root rot and fusarium or verticillium wilts. *Streptomyces* species grow naturally on your plant's roots and foliage in a symbiotic relationship. They feed on exudates—substances that plants naturally exude—and in return they attack and kill harmful pathogens. Some species are the original source of the antibiotic streptomycin. This product is non-toxic and is not harmful to people, pets, wildlife, or plants. It is sold as a dry powder. Mix the powder with water according to label directions, and either spray it on above-ground plant parts or apply it as a soil drench. There is a slight risk of allergic reactions, so be sure to protect yourself with appropriate safety gear. Do not allow drift or runoff to contaminate streams, lakes, or other bodies of water. Safety label: CAUTION.

Trichoderma harzianum. Do not use on lemon or apple, but proceed with it as a recommended solution for problems on all other citrus and pome fruits. This naturally occurring fungus is found in healthy, biologically active soils worldwide. It colonizes the root systems of plants in a symbiotic relationship. Your plant feeds its natural excretions to *T. harzianum* and it, in turn, promotes root growth and protects your plants from pathogenic root rot and wilt fungi. This is a preventive product. It will not cure an existing infection. It is available as a powder that you mix with water, which you then use as a soil drench. Soak root systems in it before you plant. The fungus in the powder is alive, so use it right away. Soil temperature should be above 50°F for best results. Do not use this product as a foliar spray on above-ground parts of your food plants. This product won't harm people, pets, wildlife, or plants, but it does cause mild eye irritation. Avoid getting it on your skin or breathing the dust. Wear safety gear to protect your eyes, skin, and lungs, and do not allow runoff to contaminate streams, lakes, or other bodies of water. Read and follow label directions. Safety label: CAUTION.

Baking soda. An oldie but goodie, baking soda causes the cell walls of fungi to collapse and has been used for more than a century to inhibit fungal spores from germinating. This is a preventive measure, not a cure. While it has no known side effects, and it is non-toxic to mammals, insects, and fish, baking soda can burn the leaves of some plants. Spray a few leaves and wait for a day or two to see what happens. If you see no adverse reactions, spray your plants thoroughly, covering all sides of the leaves, stems, and fruits. Repeat every two weeks as needed. Rain and sprinkler water will wash it off. You can make your own mix by adding a tablespoon of baking soda, 2½ tablespoons of vegetable oil, and a teaspoon of liquid soap (not detergent) to a gallon of water, or you can buy ready-to-use spray bottles. Read and follow label directions. Safety label: CAUTION.

Neem. This oil is extracted from the poisonous seeds of the neem tree of India, *Azadirachta indica*. As well as being an insecticide, neem oil prevents fungal spores from germinating. Thus, it is effective as a preventive fungicide. It is not a cure. Studies on safety and environmental impacts are ongoing. Therefore, it is best to use neem only when bees and other beneficial insects are not active in the fruit garden. And do not use it on, or near, water. Buy a commercial preparation that has been prepared with a surfactant, such as soap, so that the oil will mix with water. Mix the preparation with water, and spray plants thoroughly every seven to 14 days. Read and follow label directions. Safety label: CAUTION.

Sulfur. Besides being an insecticide, sulfur prevents fungal spores from germinating. This yellow mineral, mined from the earth, has been used to control fungal diseases of plants since the days of the ancient Romans. Research has shown that it is as effective as synthetic fungicides as a preventive measure. It is not a cure. Sulfur is somewhat toxic to mammals, and can cause breathing problems for anyone with asthma or other allergies. Since it kills beneficial insects and fish, we suggest you use sulfur only if your plants have a serious fungus infection. Sulfur can also harm plants under two conditions—when it is above 80°F, and if you have sprayed with horticultural oil within the last month. Lastly, sulfur can build up in the soil if you use it regularly. Not a good thing. Spray your plants thoroughly. To keep fungal spores from spreading you may need to reapply every seven to 14 days because the product washes off in the rain. Sulfur is available as a ready-to-use spray or as a concentrate or dust that you mix with water. Read and follow label directions. Safety label: CAUTION.

Copper. This natural mineral element has been used as a fungicide and bactericide for 200 years. A preventive measure, not a cure, copper prevents fungal spores from germinating and kills bacteria. It is somewhat toxic to humans, and highly toxic to aquatic invertebrates, fish, and amphibians. Do not use it near water. Wear all your protective gear—you know the drill—goggles, respirator mask, gloves, long-sleeved shirt, pants. If your plants remain wet for too long after you use copper, they can be damaged. Standards set for certified organic food production allow copper to be used up to one day before harvest. Copper is available as ready-to-use liquid sprays, as powder, or as dust. To use the powder you will also have to buy a spreader-sticker, and then mix both products with water. Some liquid sprays require a spreader-sticker as well. To use the dust, you will need to purchase a specially made duster. Spray or dust plants on a dry morning. Make sure your children and pets are indoors when you apply copper. Read and follow all label directions. Safety label: CAUTION.

Resources

For Information on Regulations for Organically Grown Food

USDA, Alternative Farming Systems Information Center, Publications
nal.usda.gov/afsic/pubs/ofp/ofp.shtml

Organic Materials Review Institute
omri.org

For Organic and Biological Remedies

Applied Bio-nomics
appliedbio-nomics.com

Arbico Organics
arbico-organics.com

Beneficial Insectary
insectary.com

Biofac Crop Care
biofac.com

W. Atlee Burpee & Co.
burpee.com

Henry Field's Seed & Nursery Co.
henryfields.com

Foothill Agricultural Research
far-inc.com

Gardens Alive!
gardensalive.com

Grower Central / Evergro Canada
growercentral.com

Harmony Farm Supply
harmonyfarm.com

Hydro-Gardens
hydro-gardens.com

Nature's Control
naturescontrol.com

Orcon
organiccontrol.com

Peaceful Valley Farm Supply
groworganic.com

Rincon-Vitova Insectaries
rinconvitova.com

For Seeds and Plants of Disease- and Pest-Resistant Cultivars

Adams County Nursery
acnursery.com

Ames' Orchard and Nursery
on Facebook

W. Atlee Burpee & Co.
burpee.com

C & O Nursery
c-onursery.com

Farmer Seed and Nursery Co.
farmerseed.com

Freedom Tree Farms
freedomtreefarms.com

Fruit Tree Farm
fruittreefarm.com

Gurney's Seed & Nursery Co.
gurneys.com

Harris Seeds
harrisseeds.com

Henry Field's Seed & Nursery Co.
henryfields.com

Johnny's Selected Seeds
johnnyseeds.com

J. W. Jung Seed Co.
jungseed.com

Kelly Nurseries
kellynurseries.com

Miller Nurseries
millernurseries.com

Nichols Garden Nursery
nicholsgardennursery.com

One Green World
onegreenworld.com

Park Seed Co.
parkseed.com

Pinetree Garden Seeds
superseeds.com

Plants of the Southwest
plantsofthesouthwest.com

Raintree Nursery
raintreenursery.com

Renee's Garden
reneesgarden.com

Southern Exposure Seed Exchange
southernexposure.com

Southmeadow Fruit Gardens
southmeadowfruitgardens.com

Stark Bro's Nurseries & Orchards Co.
starkbros.com

Stokes Seeds
stokeseeds.com

Territorial Seed Co.
territorialseed.com

Thompson & Morgan
tmseeds.com

Victory Seeds
victoryseeds.com

For Fertilizer, Irrigators, and Other Gardening Equipment

Gardener's Supply Co.
gardeners.com

Gardens Alive!
gardensalive.com

Harmony Farm Supply
harmonyfarm.com

The Kinsman Co.
kinsmangarden.com

A. M. Leonard
amleo.com

Mantis Garden Tools
mantis.com

The Natural Gardening Co.
naturalgardening.com

Ohio Earth Food
ohioearthfood.com

Peaceful Valley Farm Supply
groworganic.com

Smith & Hawken
smithandhawken.com

The Urban Farmer Store
urbanfarmerstore.com

Recommended Reading

The following books were particularly helpful to us and our garden. Those marked with an asterisk (*) focus solely on organic gardening techniques.

Agrios, George N. 2005. *Plant Pathology.* 5th ed. Elsevier Academic Press.

Bradley, Fern Marshall, et al. 2009. *Rodale's Ultimate Encyclopedia of Organic Gardening.* Rodale Books.

Brenzel, Kathleen Norris, ed. 2007. *Sunset Western Garden Book.* 8th ed. Sunset Publishing Corp.

* Coleman, Eliot. 1995. *The New Organic Grower.* Rev. ed. Chelsea Green.

* Deardorff, David, and Kathryn Wadsworth. 2009. *What's Wrong With My Plant? (And How Do I Fix It?).* Timber Press.

* ——. 2011. *What's Wrong With My Vegetable Garden?* Timber Press.

* Ellis, Barbara W., and Fern Marshall Bradley, eds. 1996. *The Organic Gardener's Handbook of Natural Insect and Disease Control.* Rev. ed. Rodale Press.

Gillman, Jeff. 2008. *The Truth About Garden Remedies.* Timber Press.

* ——. 2008. *The Truth About Organic Gardening.* Timber Press.

Gillman, Jeff, and Meleah Maynard. 2012. *Decoding Gardening Advice.* Timber Press.

Grissell, Eric. 2001. *Insects and Gardens.* Timber Press.

Lowenfels, Jeff, and Wayne Lewis. 2010. *Teaming with Microbes.* Rev. ed. Timber Press.

Mollison, Bill, and Reny Mia Slay. 1997. *Introduction to Permaculture.* Rev. ed. Tagari Publications.

* Reich, Lee. 2012. *Grow Fruit Naturally.* Taunton Press.

Soler, Ivette. 2011. *The Edible Front Yard.* Timber Press.

Tallamy, Douglas W. 2009. *Bringing Nature Home.* Rev. ed. Timber Press.

USDA Hardiness Zones

To find your specific USDA Hardiness Zone, visit the following website and enter your zip code. The site will tell you your zone: planthardiness. ars.usda.gov/PHZMWeb/

Zone	Average winter low temperatures
1	Colder than -50°F
2a	-45°F to -50°F
2b	-40°F to -45°F
3a	-35°F to -40°F
3b	-30°F to -35°F
4a	-25°F to -30°F
4b	-20°F to -25°F
5a	-15°F to -20°F
5b	-10°F to -15°F
6a	-5°F to -10°F
6b	0°F to -5°F
7a	5°F to 0°F
7b	10°F to 5°F
8a	15°F to 10°F
8b	20°F to 15°F
9a	25°F to 20°F
9b	30°F to 25°F
10a	35°F to 30°F
10b	40°F to 35°F
11a and above	Warmer than 40°F

Useful Conversions

Inches	Centimeters
¼	0.6
½	1.25
¾	1.9
1	2.5
1¼	3.1
1½	3.8
1¾	4.4
2	5.0
3	7.5
4	10
5	12.5
6	15
7	18
8	20
9	23
10	25
12	30
15	38
18	45
20	50
24	60
30	75
32	80
36	90

Feet	Meters
1	0.3
1½	0.5
2	0.6
2½	0.8
3	0.9
4	1.2
5	1.5
6	1.8
7	2.1
8	2.4
9	2.7
10	3.0
12	3.6
15	4.5
18	5.4
20	6.0
25	7.5

Acknowledgments

HEARTFELT THANKS to Regina Ryan who continues to illuminate our path with her amazing knowledge and insight. We are enormously grateful to everyone at Timber Press, especially Tom Fischer. Your professionalism, dedication, and exceptional expertise take our manuscript pages and turn them into beautiful and informative books. Our colleagues at Kona Ink, Rebecca Cantrell (aka Bekka Black), Judith Heath, and Karen Hollinger, have once again selflessly given us their editorial skills, support, and relentless dedication to excellence. We could not have done it without you. You remain the paramount critique group of the world. Our photo safaris have taken us across the country and back again; the kindness and generosity of family and friends have helped us at every step. We owe much to Ruth Murphy, Barbara Ansley-Vensas, Jake and Annod Bickley, Steve and Louise Carroll, Barbara Smith and Randy Deardorff, Brian and Jeannie Glasspell, Judy and Roger Heath, Debra Sharp-Hartmann, Merrily Pierson, Denise Fort, Oksana Fort, Lauren Wadsworth, Sarah Wadsworth, Dawn Swanson, Jeanne Leighton, and Paul Miller.

Photo Credits

Kiwis, page 2, courtesy iStockphoto/ Kadir Barcin.

Black bear, page 226, courtesy iStockphoto/ Pierre Chouinard.

Grapes, page 8, courtesy iStockphoto/ Silke Dietze.

Lemons, page 100, courtesy iStockphoto/ Michalowski Dominik.

Peaches, page 30, courtesy iStockphoto/ Elena Elisseeva.

Orange, page 30, courtesy iStockphoto/ Jean Gill.

Apple blossoms, page 4; lime blossom, page 5; plums, page 244, courtesy Katherine Jones.

Plums, page 6, courtesy iStockphoto/ Anna Karwowska.

Watermelon, page 30, courtesy iStockphoto/ Murat Giray Kaya.

Pomegranates, page 2, courtesy iStockphoto/ Jivko Kazakov.

Watermelon slices, page 244, courtesy iStockphoto/krungchingpixs

Peach blossoms, page 6, courtesy Laura Lovett.

Olives, page 80, courtesy iStockphoto/ Zvonimir Luketina

Almonds, page 32, courtesy iStockphoto/ Olga Lyubkina.

Young raccoons, pages 118 and 207, courtesy Cheryl Merrill.

Strawberries, page 6, courtesy iStockphoto / Tamara Murray.

Pears, page 100, courtesy iStockphoto/ Howard Oates.

Blueberries, page 8, courtesy iStockphoto/Kyu Oh.

Apples, page 100, courtesy iStockphoto/ Smileus.

Blackberries, page 244, courtesy iStockphoto/ tadija

Almonds, page 2, courtesy iStockphoto/ Tioloco.

Avocados, page 244, courtesy iStockphoto/ Carla VanWagoner.

Raspberries, page 244, courtesy iStockphoto/ Sally Wallis.

All other photos are by the authors.

Index

About the Authors

Photos by John W. Bickley

David Deardorff and **Kathryn Wadsworth** are freelance writers and photographers who travel across the country holding popular workshops and lectures. Deardorff's PhD in botany and years of experience as a plant pathologist informs their shared expertise; and Wadsworth's skill as a naturalist and author illuminates the connection between gardens and the natural world. Together they have nurtured fruit gardens in the Desert Southwest, the Pacific Northwest, and Hawaii. They have appeared on numerous U.S. radio shows, including *Martha Stewart Living*, Joe Lamp'l's *Growing a Greener World*, Ken Druse's *Real Dirt*, and Ciscoe Morris's *Gardening with Ciscoe*, and are the authors of the award-winning *What's Wrong With My Plant? (And How Do I Fix It?)* and *What's Wrong With My Vegetable Garden?*, the companion to this volume. They can be found creating bountiful polyculture gardens in Port Townsend, Washington, and online at DDandKW.com.